Great House Rules

First published in Jamaica, 2004 by
Ian Randle Publishers
11 Cunningham Avenue
Box 686, Kingston 6
www.ianrandlepublishers.com

National Library of Jamaica Cataloguing in Publication Data

Beckles, Hilary
   Great house rules : landless freedom and workers' protest in Barbados, 1838-1938
/ Hilary McD Beckles

     p. ;   cm

     Includes bibliographical references

     ISBN 976-637-085-0 (paperback)

1.   Barbados – History
I.   Title

972.981   dc 21

First Published in the United Kingdom, 2004 by
James Currey Publishers
73 Botley Road
Oxford OX2 0BS
www.jamescurrey.co.uk

ISBN 0-85255-493-1 (paperback)

British Library Cataloguing in Publication Data
A cataloguing in publication record is available on request from the British Library

Cover painting "Great House Rules" by Jonna Twigg
Book and Cover design by Shelly-Gail Cooper
Printed in the United States of America

Great House Rules
Landless Emancipation
and Workers' Protest in Barbados, 1838-1938

Hilary McD Beckles

Ian Randle Publishers
Kingston • Miami

James Currey Publishers
Oxford

To the freedom and democracy martyrs of General Bussa's War [1816],
General Green's Rebellion [1876], and
Clement Payne's Revolution [1937].

For Sarah Ann Gill who stood against evil in high places.

Table of Contents

Preface and Acknowledgements /ix

Introduction
The Hundred Year War, 1838-1938 / **xi**

Chapter 1
Free Blacks Before Emancipation / **1**

Chapter 2
A Landless Freedom: The Emancipation Process, 1838–1863 / **29**

Chapter 3
Emancipation Betrayed:
Struggle For Freedom Begins, 1838–1897 / **85**

Chapter 4
The War of General Green: 1876
Rebellion Against Post-Emancipation Slavery / **135**

Chapter 5
Democracy From Below:
The New Grassroots Politics: 1897-1937 / **158**

Bibliography / **194**

Index / **205**

Preface and Acknowledgements

This book was conceived within the context of my participation in the public discourse on political democracy and economic injustice in Barbados during the late 1980s and 1990s. The cause of popular economic enfranchisement in the country invoked the need for historical readings of the economic environment. This political circumstance, and the academic challenge, were principal motivational sources.

Much of what is written here, then, first came into being as dozens of public lectures delivered in Barbados, the wider Caribbean and beyond. I have sought to maintain the discursive spirit of these encounters, and have employed devices such as extensive quotations from unpublished manuscripts in order to convey the texture of historical moments, while keeping references to a minimum. It is of great importance to me that audiences who heard these words should recognise them, and bear witness.

I wish to thank all my friends, family and colleagues who supported this project, especially those who insisted that the text be presented as an accessible document for public consumption, rather than a dense academic production.

Dr Alana Johnson and Dr David Browne, as graduate students, served as research assistants in 1995-97, and I wish to thank them for excavating the dozens of nineteenth and early twentieth century documents that have informed much of the narrative. Dr Henderson Carter and Dr David Browne, at a later date, generously shared with me important archival material that shaped the tone and texture of my arguments. The three of them have offered persistent encouragement and support, and I wish to thank them sincerely.

I have benefited from years of discussion and interaction with the work of experts on nineteenth century Barbados. Woodville Marshall,

Kortright Davis, Cecelia Karch, Bonham Richardson, George Belle, John Gilmore, Noel Titus, Anthony Phillips, Karl Watson, Velma Newton, Janice Mayers, Pedro Welch, Trevor Marshall, Robert Morris and Bentley Gibbs have deepened my understanding of post-slavery reconstruction and the black struggle for a genuine emancipation.

Hilbourne Watson, Farley Brathwaite, Glenford Howe, Don Marshall, Wilber Will, and Alexander Hoyos, especially, have enabled me to see more clearly historical continuities that inform the 1960s discourse on nationhood.

Finally, I would like to express gratitude to Mrs Grace Jutan, my supportive secretary, for working gracefully with unreasonable deadlines on various drafts of this manuscript.

Introduction
The Hundred Year War, 1838-1938

'that period [slavery] is still spoken of by the Negroes as "Barbarity Times" '.[1]

'there still exists a strong feeling in favour of slavery amongst the planters...and there is still a strong disposition to grudge the Negroes their civil, educational, and religious privileges.'[2]

ALL HISTORIANS have a mandate. In newly independent, post-colonial societies this mandate is more clearly defined and urgent than in many other places. It is a discourse that begins with the search of the self for clarity on issues of identity and ends with the politics of everyday life.

Being a historian whose subject is the modern journey to hell and back of African people has determined my sense of that mandate in very special ways. To begin with, the African worldview invests the historian with an almost sacred duty to recall, record and relate the story of the journey of the tribe, and to identify and signify the lessons learnt along the way. The reinvention of 'tribe' by Africans in the Caribbean as insular identities is another aspect of the narrative, but suffice it to note here that communities throughout the archipelago have produced many historians who have delivered on the mandate. They have kept alive, as a part of the discussion in which my generation participated, the idea that the role of historian is one that attracts pain but demands honour.

Shortly after securing membership in the Caribbean community of academic historians I decided that my first contribution would be to research and publish a trilogy on the journey of the sub-tribe of Africans in Barbados. This was a subject that I thought required comprehensive treatment, and whose time had come. My relationship to the project assumed disturbingly strange spiritual dimensions. It was a kind of haunting that suggested ancestral intervention. Maybe they had risen from their enchained graves to demand that their story, and that of their progeny, who continued to wrestle with the legacy of the enchainment, had to be told fairly but forcefully.

It would be a trilogy that speaks to the journey of these tortured souls in the struggle for liberty, justice and redemption. The terrorism and holocaust of chattel enslavement would be investigated and presented in order to demonstrate the survival power of the sub-tribe as it conceived and developed strategies of resistance. Fighting for survival in the face of almost certain violent death that accompanied discovery and failure called for the ownership of a mind that was rare and therefore special. But a larger number, who did not breathe this uncommon wind, found themselves standing in opposition, turning their faces to the world slaveholders had made, and like sentinels, stood erect and refused.

In 1985 the first volume was published under the title *Black Rebellion in Barbados: the Struggle Against Slavery, 1627-1838*. For many people it was a narrative of mythology because it was widely propagated, first by slave owners and then their apologists, and more recently by academics, some of them historians who should know better, that the African in Barbados had made less than a strong contribution to the political tradition which embodies the Caribbean revolutionary search for freedom. For others it was a work with striking archaeological dimensions in that it excavated and rescued this history and situated the enslaved African in Barbados within the mainstream of the radical tradition.

Three years later I revisited this theme on account of a realisation that my gender gaze had not focused adequately on the specific aspects of women's struggles and their unique contributions to the antislavery movement that had become endemic to the slavery world. The results were the publication of an auto critique of the text which appeared in 1987 in the form of an extended essay entitled 'Afro-Caribbean Women and Resistance to Slavery in Barbados', and in 1989 a comprehensive study, 'Natural Rebels: A Social History of Enslaved Black Women in Barbados'.[3]

Since then, the images of the second and third volumes that would begin with the discourse of Abolition and Emancipation and the struggles for human and civil rights deep into the nineteenth century, and the push to nationhood in the 1960s, swirled about my soul like restless spirits desiring rest and recognition. I could see fragments of each volume scattered in the consciousness like fabric in a tailor's shop, set aside, shelved, earmarked, but not ready to be assembled and stitched into the coat originally imagined. Guilt also inhabited this space. Often it seemed hopelessly evident that I would be unable to catch the fire of the original conception.

In 1998 I decided that the way back to the source was to take the journey in 'small' steps. I would not take research leave to return with finished manuscripts. I would nibble away at the project, one chapter at a time, allowing the distance between each to be determined by the ebb and flow of other literary commitments. To my salvation, each bite grew bigger until the juncture was reached where nothing else could compete or distract. The story of the post-Emancipation betrayal by the British of 83,000 Blacks in Barbados would be conceptualised and told as arising from the 'landless freedom' imposed violently upon a community that had reasons to imagine August 1, 1838, as ushering a radical departure from the terms of their everyday lives.

It was the rule of the Great House that subverted the promise of the Emancipation promulgated. Great House rules determined the terms under which the majority of Blacks would seek to reconstruct their lives under the banner of the freedom foisted without liberties. This text would be a narration of Blacks' preparations for persistent resistance and civil war as the only means to effectively break the rule of the Great House and establish preconditions for genuine Emancipation.

Great House Rules, then, as textual narration, sets out the paradigm of the landless emancipation experienced by Blacks and their renewed struggles for rights, respect, and recognition. Daily resistance to planter authority, and the body of hurriedly passed new laws that supported it, served to create a climate of endemic conflict and hostility that shaped social relations for one hundred years. The stitching together of widespread strikes over wages and terms of employment, plantation food raids, urban riots, and counter-attacks on the police, into a movement for structural change and social transformation was the vision and political challenge for the legally emancipated.

The effort to give effect to the desire for a spiritually felt and socially lived emancipation exercised the imagination, thoughts, and courage of successive generations. Grenville Chester, an Englishman who walked among the first and second generations of freed Barbadians, gives us important insights into the circumstances they faced and fought. With respect to the wages they received, he says the following:

> Experience has convinced me that when a Barbadian planter complains of the idleness of the negroes, the real truth is that he himself will not give a fair price for labour. Where this is done labour can always be had, and it is no discredit to a man to refuse to work for starvation prices.

The culture of political resistance fostered by Blacks had its effects in the minds of all Whites who understood the contest in terms of the language and ideology of race. Chester wrote in 1869:

> One predominating characteristic of the white people is their abject fear of the Negroes. Whether on the principle that 'conscience makes cowards of us all', 'this' feeling be only the natural offspring of past tyranny and present scant or unwillingly rendered justice. . . One is continually being told that if the English troops were to be withdrawn. . .that a great massacre of whites would ensue.[4]

The Blacks' search for civil rights, noted Chester, was multi-faceted and carried at the centre a craving for knowledge as an instrument that would fully unlock their potential as a people. He wrote:

> Their thirst for education is certainly great and increasingly so. The rising generations evince a praiseworthy ambition to inform and better themselves and to raise themselves in the world. And many are doing so, inspite of the ungenerous discouragement which they meet with from

the whites, who jeer at progress which is made without their goodwill, and which they would prevent if they could.

The battles over progress were fought on the plantations, in the streets, in the courts, in the Legislative Councils, and wherever Blacks recognised sites to effect change. As was the case during their 'Barbarity Time', they paid a great cost in terms of lives and suffering. There was widespread famine and starvation; persistent denigration and denial of their humanity; and violent deaths from wounds inflicted by guns and bayonets. The barbarity time continued, and so did the struggle against it. Most plantations became venues for at least one rebellion in which the issues of wages, rights, and access to resources were on the agenda. The use of arson as a tool in the battle against the consolidated planter class respected no fences and borders. Again, most plantations, at some moment during the long nineteenth century, became symbols of the dissatisfaction they sowed and harvested.

These events in the chain of organised rebellion were finally linked to produce in 1876, the 'War of General Green'. Defined and named by some as the 'Confederation Riot', this explosion of popular resentment meant that the betrayal of emancipation was now an international political fact. Workers showed how capable they were of creating allies, real or imagined, in order to discredit the legitimacy of the planter dictatorship.

The governor was roped into the network of propaganda by black leaders in order to build the ideological framework for a movement that had as its objective the overthrow of this dictatorship. By issuing public statements that the governor was on their side, and that he was opposed to the planters' subversion of British parliamentary wish for a just post-emancipation society, black rebels effectively used the state of politics in the colony to their end and advantage. It was not the first time that workers had done this kind of thing in an effort to forge solidarity in their ranks. As was the case in 1816 when the enslaved revolted, the 1876 revolution was violently crushed, more by imperial troops who were garrisoned on the island to deal with such an eventuality, than the planter militia.

In the immediate aftermath of the 1876 revolution the volume of worker emigration from the colony increased. The search for betterment outside the walls of the colony was sufficiently focused and intensive as to constitute a movement. The neighbouring islands as well as Guiana were the targets of this search, indicating that for workers the region constituted a wider survival zone. Those who could emigrate did so. Many returned to strengthen the hand of their community, and therefore to improve its chances in the face of planter opposition.

Those who did not return to the island kept their families away from starvation and further loss of social dignity by posting remittances that assured their survival. Such acts of financial solidarity and responsibility promoted and sponsored the economic viability of the black community. At the same time they laid the foundations for a new kind and level of organised political opposition. One important effect was that the community was able to throw up a cadre of workers and professionals who were independent of white economic structures. This seminal circumstance had the effect of shifting the balance of the struggle away from individual plantations, integrating the towns into the campaign, and creating by 1925 a modern, island-wide political network for liberation.

The grand organisational breakthrough came in 1937 with the flashing, thunderous intervention of Clement Payne. He succeeded in capturing the imagination of workers whose political consciousness had matured during the previous two decades of effective organisation by Charles Duncan O'Neal, Clennell Wickham, Herbert Seale, and others within the Pan-African movement stimulated by Marcus Garvey. Payne promoted a new sense of urgency and responsibility in the workers' struggle, and using the Pan-African cells established by activists such as Israel Lovell and Ulric Grant, he enabled workers to see and feel the importance of acting in their own interests.

These political activities, from the period of Prescod to Payne, when taken together, constitute the 'Hundred Year War' against 'Great House Rules'. Generations of workers, and their allies, centered the importance of justice and liberty within the contest for political power. They were determined to bring Emancipation into effect as a living reality rather than a legislated concept framed within the British parliament and defeated by sugar planters still wishing for enslaved labour.

NOTES

1. Grenville John Chester, *Atlantic Sketches in the West Indies* (London, 1869), 20.
2. Chester, *Atlantic Sketches,* 43.
3. Hilary Beckles, *Afro-Caribbean Women and Resistance to Slavery in Barbados* (London: Karnak House, 1987); *Natural Rebels: A Social History of Enslaved Black Women in Barbados.* (New Jersey: Rutgers University Press, 1989).
4. Chester, *Atlantic Sketches.*

- *One* -

Free Blacks
Before Emancipation

*A*mong the millions of enslaved Blacks in the dozens of Caribbean slave societies, a few thousand were able to gain freedom in Barbados. As escapees from legal bondage they were brought under constant close scrutiny by white enslavers. While it was understood that the enslaved majority constituted the principal threat to the survival of the slave system, there was considerable anxiety and fear among enslavers that anti-slavery revolution could be sparked by the actions and attitudes of the free minority.[1]

Free Blacks in Barbados, then, were perceived as a possible catalyst, and therefore enormously 'dangerous'. The general survival tendency among them, however, was not revolutionary but was to seek out and exploit for themselves niche opportunities for status mobility and wealth accumulation within the system. But in general they found it difficult to escape the contradictory social forces that shaped and guided their lives as free Blacks within a white supremacy social arrangement.[2]

In Barbados, the oldest and most densely populated sugar plantation colony in the Caribbean, free Blacks were never sufficiently numerous, politically organised, or financially influential to determine in any meaningful way the general character and directions of the slave society. Their presence and predicament, however, served to highlight the practical limits of legal freedom imagined by the enslaved majority, and to illuminate the thinking that informed their choice of armed conflict.

Importantly, the enslavement free Blacks escaped and dreaded returning to could not be detached in any meaningful way from the texture and terms of everyday life. While in their heads and hearts they might have broken loose from legal slavery, their hands and feet remained effectively tied and attached.[3]

The kinds of social and economic objectives pursued by free Blacks required the adoption of strategic plans that included slave-holding. The colonial economy was designed by free white persons to ensure that ownership and possession of enslaved people constituted the primary engines of status mobility and wealth accumulation. Free Blacks neither discovered nor devised any dependable alternative method, and approached slave-owning relationships in ways similar, though more socially complex than their white counterparts. The evidence shows that their slave-owning patterns and manumission rates, for example, indicate the operation of moral economy forces that expressed their general commitment to anti-slavery.[4]

White enslavers took some comfort in the realisation that free Blacks too had agreed that the ownership of enslaved people was the only mechanism that could guarantee the maintenance and promotion of individual freedom. However, they remained uncertain about the possible political effects of their seemingly ambiguous circumstance. At the same time, some considered it a major victory in public governance that the society they built on black enslavement could carry within its bosom a very small minority of free Blacks.

The historians have had a great deal to say about all of this. Barry Higman was correct to draw attention to Jerome Handler's analysis of the so-called 'freedman' category as a conflation of the ethnically differentiated social groups. A distinction should be made, noted Higman, 'between free colored and free Black slave-owners', even if to demonstrate that the latter were 'less conspicuously oriented to White culture'. Critically, Higman has also shown the striking difference between free black, free coloured and white enslavers' attitudes towards the freeing of the enslaved. This is sufficient, he concludes, to reject Handler's general conclusion that all enslavers approached the matter of enslaving Africans with broadly similar intentions and results.[5]

Most free Blacks in Barbados functioned just above subsistence level in Bridgetown and other parts of the urban socioeconomic system. This was not phenomenal. It reflected the ideological and institutional nature of the rural plantation sugar economy that could not emerge nor embrace them in large numbers. Freedom in the rural society, more so than in Bridgetown, constituted the most important social asset an individual could possess, and the extent of its translation into multi-consumer benefits depended upon other criteria governing general institutional arrangements.

Excluded on the basis of race and class from the system of sugar plantation production [hence the dominant economy], and denied honourable access to the rural commercial services demanded by sugar planters, free Blacks had no option but to huddle around the towns and participate in the design and development of a more elastic, pluralist urban culture.[6]

In Barbados, the overwhelming majority of free Blacks lived in Bridgetown and its neighbouring communities in the St Michael parish. Higman has suggested that in general, manumission was more common in towns than rural districts, and that there was a definite bias towards towns. In the period 1817-1820, when only 12 per cent of the enslaved population lived in Bridgetown, 49 per cent of all manumissions occurred there.

There were broadly similar patterns in St Kitts, Dominica and Jamaica. The explanation seems clear when it is realised that those who owned few enslaved persons, as was the case in towns, were twice as likely to grant freedom than rural owners of a large enslaved labour force. The strong negative correlations between mean slave-holding size and manumission rates held across the English colonies, concluded Higman, had several implications for the kinds of Blacks who were likely to be freed.[7]

There were free black individuals, however, of both sexes, few in number and socially conspicuous, who managed to escape the entrapment of market economy forces and secure considerable material advancement. While their levels of wealth accumulation corresponded to those of many urban Whites, they were never accorded comparable civil honours and social respectability on account of the determining power of white supremacy ideology. The principle of race first, on which the slave system was based, and which was so clearly articulated by John Poyer, the leading local pro-slavery ideologue at the end of the eighteenth century, ensured the effectiveness of social rigidity even when economic barriers were breached.[8]

The free black community in Bridgetown especially developed in much the same way as that of most major towns with hinterland economies based on sugar plantations. Bridgetown, however, had a peculiar social feature that problematised free black presence at the outset. It was the relatively large white labouring class with which it competed in the eighteenth century for employment and a share of the small business sector.

Feeling vulnerable and politically targeted, free Blacks as a result tended to follow the trail made by the free Coloureds who had more wealth, confidence and social prestige. By the early nineteenth century, in response to the increasing pressure of English anti-slavery politics, and the successes of the Haitian Revolution, they evolved a distinct separate political identity. Handler noted that during this time the expression 'free black' was a common self-ascription. He stated, furthermore, that the use of the term as distinct from 'free coloured', which suggests mixed racial ancestry, 'indicates that as the years progressed the proportion of black freed men became larger than it had been in earlier years'. By the end of slavery the free black population was just under half of the total free non-white community.[9]

Table 1

Free Black and Free Coloured Population, Barbados 1773-1829[10]

Number			Percentage		
Year	Coloured	Black	Total	Coloured	Black
1773	136	78	214	63.6	36.4
1825	2,066	1,760	3,829	54.0	46.0
1826	2,169	1,905	4,074	53.2	46.0
1827	2,201	1,947	4,148	53.1	46.9
1828	2,259	1,989	4,248	53.2	46.8
1829	2,313	2,027	4,340	53.3	46.7

London Bourne

The case of London Bourne is strikingly illustrative of the economic success and social exclusion of free blacks in Bridgetown. Like his father, William, London began life as an enslaved man. When he was born in 1793 his father had already established a reputation as a successful black businessman who had purchased a number of properties in the less prestigious commercial parts of the town.

In 1818, William secured the freedom of his wife and four sons through a special negotiation with a Jewish, London-based merchant, Moses Barrow Lousada. London Bourne, now free, and critically literate, married a free black woman, Patience Graham, who also owned in her own right a number of urban properties. Together they had seven children who were all born into freedom. By the late 1820s, London was described as a successful sugar broker, merchant and owner of several stores in Bridgetown. He was also categorised as one of the 'wealthiest' entrepreneurs in the town, with a commercial office in London that employed white clerks and agents.

Bourne was, however, a black man operating within an economic environment dominated by white men who considered it necessary and found it possible to exclude black men from all positions of honour, prestige and power. As a result, he was not invited to the formal business meetings of leading merchants in Bridgetown, even though he owned the very building which these merchants used for such gatherings. The town's commercial elite rented the upper part of one of his buildings for the purposes of conducting a Commercial Exchange; London and his family inhabited the lower floor. Bourne would collect the rent but could not enter the Exchange. It was not until 1838, following the abolition of African enslavement in the British-colonised Caribbean, and as a result of the political agitation of the influential Samuel Prescod and the supportive intervention of Governor McGregor, that the doors of the Barbados Chamber of Commerce were opened to the owners of the building – London Bourne and Son.[11]

Gender and Freedom

Females constituted the majority within both the free black and free coloured populations. This was explained by social commentators in terms of the bias towards women in the enslavers' manumission decisions. Since the legal status of children at birth was derived from that of the mother, free black women were well placed to reproduce the free community.

Enslavers, wishing to suppress black access to freedom, tended to manumit (free by law) enslaved adult women after their child-bearing period. The norm, then, was for free black women to experience freedom within the context of their children's enslavement. Also among the free black community in Bridgetown were persons who had escaped enslavement in neighbouring islands, and Africans who were captured from slave ships and landed on the island. This latter category was gradually absorbed into the free urban community that struggled to eke out a living in its intensely competitive economy.

Table 2
Free Blacks in the Barbados Populations[12]

Year	Free Blacks	Whites	Slaves	Free Coloureds
1773	78	18,532	68,546	136
1825	1,760	14,630	78,096	2,066
1827	1,947	14,687	79,383	2,201
1829	2,027	14,959	81,902	2,313

The path of the journey of Blacks from enslavement to freedom by manumission was policed and politicised by enslavers at every stage; signposts along the way expressed in clearest terms the importance whites attached to controlling and limiting any flight from enslavement for blacks. Parliamentary debates and legislative provisions constitute the rich sources of data that illuminate the ideological positions and political arguments of the white elite. Enslaved Blacks understood all too well that the intensive guarding of manumission mechanisms was to ensure that even in freedom, liberty would be severely curtailed and easily compromised.

Whites who participated personally in the effective manumission of enslaved people, however, did not wish to see them made destitute in freedom; neither did they desire a situation in which free Blacks could rise above the white community in terms of wealth accumulation and social status. The vision of manumitters of enslaved peoples, then, was circumscribed by considerations of white supremacy.

The consolidation and social effectiveness of enslavers' dominance required, at least occasionally, public symbolic displays of personal concern for the welfare of some of the enslaved. As a political ideology, paternalism served to sharpen the power instruments available to enslavers by virtue of its tendency to splinter and diffuse anger and opposition among the subordinated. By liberating enslaved persons who were deemed 'loyal', enslavers signalled to the mass of enslaved peoples, a willingness to hear and respond positively to their claim to humanity and freedom.[13]

The concerns of free coloured enslavers who freed their enslaved Blacks were oftentimes quite different from those of whites, though some similarities can also be discerned. It was a common social occurrence for wealthy free coloured persons to buy and then emancipate members of their enslaved family. This trend is particularly evident from the several cases of free coloured women, for example, who secured the freedom of their black mothers. In such instances, the emotional bonds that held together the mulatto and black children of a black woman were strong enough to remove the slave relations that divided them. The politics of this fractured domesticity and kinship, more often than not, differentiated the free black experience along the lines of manumitter ethnicity.[14]

White enslavers, therefore, were not confronted with the kind of decisions that free black enslavers were forced to make with respect to the freedom of enslaved Blacks. The decision which many free Blacks made to purchase their friends and kin and keep them in legal slavery as an act of social and family reconstitution, often entailed the outlay of a lifetime of accumulated money. The emotional intensity of choices were often matched by the complicated arrangements made to finance as cheaply as possible such manumission. In 1818, for example, William Bourne resorted to the imperial option in seeking his sons' manumission. He 'sold' them (they were 'his slaves') to Moses Lousada who resided in London for £200 Barbados currency. Lousada in turn had a manumission deed drawn up for ten shillings by a London lawyer who secured the Lord Mayor's signature, thereby declaring them free.

The cost of a manumission in Barbados was made prohibitively high by legislative provision in 1739. The law provided that a payment of £50 had to be made to the Vestry by the manumitter, out of which an allowance in the form of four pounds annual pension to the freed man or woman would be made. This law remained active until major revisions were made to it in 1801 by which the manumission fee was raised to an astonishing £300 for females and £200 for males; correspondingly, the allowance in the form of an annual pension was raised to £18 for females and £12 for males.[15]

Betty-Burk Poore's case of 1789 typically illustrates the predicament of less financially sound free black enslavers who wished to manumit a family member. Like many free black women, she had succeeded in securing by purchase the legal ownership of her three children – John, Thomas and Sarah. Under the 1739 Law she needed to raise £150 Barbados currency in order to free these children before she died, so as to exclude them from any charge upon her estate. As her property and chattel, these children were attached to her estate and therefore alienable under law. Betty-Burk could find no easy way of freeing her children and chose before death to sell her two sons in order to raise cash to pay for her daughter's manumission. The compelling logic of her decision is that as a free black person Sarah's children would be born free under law, while her sons, both artisans, had a reasonable chance of achieving freedom through self-purchase.[16]

Government officials complained consistently that far too many socially irresponsible and callous enslavers freed their unproductive enslaved worker as a strategy to abandon financial responsibility for them, resulting in their dependence upon the vestry for poor relief. This occurrence explains, in part, Parliament's concern about the rate and terms of private manumissions.

For sure, freedom was expensive and costly to maintain. It was, nonetheless, greatly valued and aggressively pursued. Had this not been the case, there would be considerable evidence of freed Blacks selling themselves back to slavery as a way of attaining subsistence. Also, many would opt for an amelioration of enslaver-enslaved relations, rather than an end to the institution itself.

Fortunate, therefore, were those individuals who received a substantial asset from their manumitter upon which to build a viable future with freedom. Mary Ann, for example, a black woman owned by Sarah Kirton, received on her freedom in 1790, three acres of land. She may have done better in the long term than Margaret, also a black woman, who received from her manumitter in the same year £150 in an interest bearing-account.[17]

Provisions for entry into freedom, therefore, were considered most supportive when productive, out-of-kin slaves, were offered to the manumitted. In 1766, for example, Robert Harrison's will provided for the freedom of his enslaved black females, Betty and Grace. Betty received, in addition, a cash allowance of £150; more importantly, her former owner provided her with 'two mulatto girl slaves, Phillis and Rachel'. Grace's cash advance of £100 was also supplemented by the gift of an enslaved mulatto girl, Mary. Harrison also made arrangements for both women to receive a dwelling house. As owners of enslaved females, both women could reasonably expect over time to benefit financially from their production, and equally as important, their reproduction. No mention is made in the will of any kinship relation between Betty, Grace, and any of these mulatto girls. A fair assumption would be that these enslaved females were highly valued and specifically chosen as substantial compensation in Harrison's emancipation project.[18]

Like many other white enslavers, Harrison could have chosen the option of investing the manumitted Blacks with possession and use of enslaved labourers rather than ownership, in which case his primary consideration would be the future comfort of the beneficiary rather than their independent accumulation of wealth. In 1772, for example, Francis Ford made provisions in his will for the freedom of enslaved Blacks, Murria and her two children. In addition, Murria was to receive a stipend from his estate of £12 half-year for life, possession of the house which she inhabited, and the 'use and services' of an enslaved black girl. These allowances were made for the duration of Murria's life. While Ford did not sponsor Murria's ownership of these assets, he stipulated that her son, Thomas, was to be 'put to school and decently clothed and bound to apprentice a trade'. Altogether, the package was designed to improve the life chances of this family over time, though Ford, like Harrison, would have been keen to ensure the survival and consolidation of the slavery system on which his own accumulation depended.[19]

From the perspective of free Blacks' capacity to own enslaved persons, accumulate wealth, and consolidate family status, importance should be attached to the process and character of Blacks' self-purchase and their capacity for financial accumulation. In the free black community, considerable status was claimed by persons who secured by self-purchase their own freedom. In fact, such persons boasted possession of an independent character which they held up by way of social distinction.

If self-purchase was in any way proof of an affirmative, anti-slavery consciousness, then the subsequent ownership of enslaved persons by such free Blacks would seem all the more paradoxical. This would be so, however, only within the context of anti-slavery ideology that dichotomised individual and collective strategies of liberation. Since in fact the vast majority of day to day acts of anti-slavery were predicated upon individual searches for betterment, from marronage to negotiations for better jobs and nutrition, it should not be considered phenomenal that free Blacks would include slave-owning as a necessary mechanism for personal advancement.

The Barbados evidence suggests that while self-purchase was preferred by most of those enslaved and pursued by many, it was both discouraged and problematised by the white slave-owning elite. In 1803, a Barbadian noted that some enslaved Blacks who were 'prone to industry, desirous of becoming free, and careful of their profits', did occasionally 'amass money with which they purchase themselves.... Purchasing themselves means the depositing in the hands of the master the sum which he values them at'. Such funds were said to have been commonly accumulated by enslaved people who "work out", tradesmen in the towns, estate drivers who received money rewards for good performance, hucksters, prostitutes and mistresses, and persons with special skills such as medicine and mid-wifery.'[20]

Freedom was always much easier to achieve in this way for less productive enslaved workers who were often encouraged to take this step by low market valuations. This was also the case for women engaged in intimate relations with politically empowered, wealthy white men. But equally, it was a common response for white enslavers to receive requests for self-purchase as an act of defiance, insubordination, and outright rebellion.

Language and dialogue were always open to this interpretation since the object of the exercise was the effective termination of the enslaver's property rights and social power. When the enslaved was able to accumulate sufficient capital for self-purchase a posture of subservience and submission was still necessary in order to secure the enslaver's compliance and agreement. Self-purchase, then, would rarely begin within a spirit of radical self-determination.[21]

The majority of free Blacks were female, creole, and worked as domestics while enslaved. Males tended to be artisans, creole and urban-based. Domestics, tradesmen, sellers and hired enslaved labourers, noted Higman, were 'three times more likely to be manumitted than any other occupational group'. He shows, furthermore, that 'in rural St Michael 23 enslaved people were manumitted between 1817-1820, fourteen of them domestics, three tradesmen, two seamstresses, and four listed no occupation'.

Furthermore, the Barbados evidence shows that free Blacks and free coloured enslavers were twice as likely to manumit enslaved Blacks than Whites. Higman concludes that using the period 1817-1820 it seems necessary to reject Handler's conclusion that in Barbados 'freedmen manumitted at a rate that was roughly comparable to, or even somewhat below, that of Whites, and were not disproportionately inclined to manumit their slaves.'[22]

The slave registration data for Barbados, furthermore, show that free Blacks were the most likely manumitters of enslaved Blacks. In Bridgetown, free Blacks freed their enslaved property at a greater rate than free Coloureds or Whites. For the period 1817-1820, some 10.4 per cent of enslaved persons owned by free Blacks were freed, followed by those belonging to free mulatto men (3 per cent), free black women (2.7 per cent), free mulatto women (1.6 per cent), white women (1.5 per cent) and white men (0.6 per cent).

These data suggest that free black men and white men resided at the extremes of the emancipation project, and that the social process of patriarchal family reconstitution operated forcefully within the free black community. Free black men were more likely to own and free their families than free black women, which accounts for the substantial difference in manumission rates between the two groups.[23]

Free Blacks in Bridgetown

The concentration in towns of free black enslavers also speaks to the specific conditions of the urban and rural economies, and the nature of their interaction. The dominant sugar plantation sector effectively marginalised and impoverished all persons without slave-holding and land possession. A feature of the urban economy was a substantial community of landless slave-holders, including mostly free Blacks, free Coloureds and unmarried white women. Free Blacks and the enslaved workers they owned, then, huddled together on the margins of the urban economy, seeking to accumulate capital against the forces of white male colonial domination.

As property owners, however, their engagement in the slave-owning culture was marginal and minimum. In 1817, a total of 174 free Blacks owned 563 enslaved people. At the same time there were 476 'mulatto' enslavers who owned 1,990 enslaved people. The total number of enslaved people in the colony was an estimated 92,580. Free Blacks,

then, owned a mere 0.61 per cent of all enslaved people, while free
mulattos owned 2.14 per cent. The total number of enslavers in
Bridgetown was 2,140, 6.44 per cent of whom were free Blacks who
owned 8.15 per cent of the 5,394 enslaved people in the town. Of these,
50 per cent were classified as domestics, 12 per cent as skilled artisans
and the remaining 38 per cent either had no specific occupation or
were employed in selling, fishing, transport and miscellaneous services.
Among the enslaved there were 168 seamstresses, 124 tailors and 140
shoemakers in Bridgetown, and less than 25 per cent of whom were
owned by free Blacks.[24]

Table 3
Distribution of Free Black Slaveholders, 1817[25]

Parish	Owners	Males Slaves	Owners	Female Slaves
St Michael Bridgetown	42	144	196	296
St Michael: Rural	3	14	3	18
St Philip	6	14	4	20
Christ Church	2	9	1	4
St Thomas	2	5	2	4
St George	2	10	2	6
St James	-	-	-	-
St John	2	4	1	1
St Peter	1	1	5	13
St Andrew	-	-	-	-
St Lucy	-	-	-	-
St Joseph	-	-	-	-
Totals	60	201	214	362

Blacks however, were not enslavers and made a living as workers
alongside the enslaved. For much the reasons that the enslaved aspired to
freedom, free Blacks sought entry to slave-owning status. The worlds of
both groups overlapped as changing legal status could not in one

generation lead to extensive reorganisation of personal and kinship ties. Distinctions were often blurred, as the enslaved who 'worked out' in the towns exercised as much social autonomy as free Blacks, and oftentimes possessed the support of influential owners to endorse their public conduct. Neither was it uncommon for free Blacks without labour skills, and driven to destitution by unemployment and propertylessness, to depend upon the charity of those enslaved people who were more materially secure. Competition for scarce employment did not always go in favor of free Blacks, and their condition in some instances was not dissimilar to that of marginalised 'poor Whites' who were described as generally 'sunk with despair and consequent indolence into a state of profligate and vagrant beggary'.[26]

The condition of skilled free Blacks was altogether more secure despite severe competition from skilled enslaved and white workers. An 1814 report on artisan services in Bridgetown stated that 'Free Negroes carried on all the lighter mechanical trades, such as tailors, shoemakers, jewelers' and that the quality of their work was commendable. A description of the town at the end of slavery states that the free Blacks had cornered the market for skilled labour at the expense of slaves and white artisans because of 'their superior industry'.[27] A visitor to the island about this time noted that 'most of the respectable mechanics in Bridgetown are Negroes who own large establishments and employ only workmen of their own color.' Here it is noted that free Black businesses were committed to employing other free Blacks in addition to hiring and buying enslaved people. Free black women approached their professions, whether as seamstresses, nurses, or hucksters, with a similar sense of social commitment to their group.[28]

Restrictive Legislation

The white community found it necessary and important to ensure that free Black enterprises, whether they employed enslaved people or other free Blacks, existed under a cloud of social suspicion with respect to the legality of their operations. The political tendency to criminalise free Black business by associating and linking them to transactions in illegal goods had the effect of stigmatising their accumulation process. Throughout the eighteenth century, the legislature purposefully made this association and laws designed to regulate illegal commercial activities focused on alleged criminal relations between larceny among enslaved persons and free Black commerce.

Free Blacks were represented in the text of the legislative provisions, as well as in general pro-slavery literature as the covert allies of the enslaved in the conspiracy to appropriate and dispose of properties owned by Whites. In this regard, free black men were publicly represented by Whites as participants in a criminal commercial subculture that paralleled the stereotype of free black women as living off immoral earnings.[29]

Joshua Steele, in the late eighteenth century, an advocate of amelioration policies for enslaved people, made mention in 1788 of free Blacks and enslaved persons in Bridgetown constituting a marketing network in 'all sorts of stolen goods'. Also involved in these arrangements were poor Whites who according to Steele, found it convenient to hide behind free Blacks, who, in the event of prosecution could not give evidence in court in which the accused was white.[30] The campaign against 'Huckster Negroes', both enslaved and free, was carried out in the Legislature against the background of these charges which gained intensity over time. The objective of the white elite – to suppress, control, and where possible to eradicate the commercial culture of Blacks – was intended to secure for the white community monopoly dominance at all levels of the economy.[31]

The resort to a licensing strategy by government came into effect by legislation in 1779. This law required all 'Huckster Negroes' to register annually with the colony's treasurer and receive a licence on the payment of £10 local currency and a service charge of 25 shillings.[32] An important effect of this financial imposition upon free Blacks was to undermine their capacity to purchase or hire enslaved workers to expand their business operations. As a tax upon the black business sector, government's licensing policy was intended also to fracture the growing relations between urban white owners of rented enslaved labourers and black employers. Free black retail operators who normally hired enslaved people to sell their products found the tax prohibitive. Many of them opted to trade illegally, risking severe punishments, such as property confiscation and imprisonment.

Free Blacks in Business

Despite the oppressiveness of legislation within the racialised social environment, some free Blacks succeeded in establishing substantial businesses that utilised large numbers of enslaved Blacks. Without the large-scale ownership or possession of enslaved workers, black entrepreneurs would have been further handicapped with respect to the accumulation process. In these businesses, the enslaved workers were oftentimes the main capital investment, and were used in the normal way as collateral on the money market. A visitor from the United States to the colony in 1814 found it significant that there was a concentration of free black enslavers in the shopkeeping business. He suggested that in Bridgetown free Blacks and free Coloureds managed and owned 'the largest number of shops'.[33] The same was said of Speightstown, the second largest town. Critically, these businesses operated in conjunction with highly organised trading links with enslaved plantation workers, who found outlets for their kitchen garden provisions and livestock.

The discriminatory policy of government significantly limited the scope of the economic relations between black shopkeepers and enslaved agricultural producers. Successful entrepreneurs such as Joseph Rachell, however, were able to emerge as testimony to the commercial acumen of free Blacks. Described as 'a Black merchant in Bridgetown, who had large and extensive concerns', Rachell's business success in the mid-eighteenth century was explained by white contemporaries in terms of his charismatic personality and humanitarian nature. They made reference to his slavery origins, manumission, rise through the dry goods business, and emergence as a leading money lender and philanthropist. That he owned many enslaved Blacks, employed white workers and had good relations with prominent white merchants and planters, was considered significant attributes of an entrepreneurial style. By 1750, success in his principal business, the inter-Caribbean trade, had set him apart within the mercantile community as a respected gentleman.[34] By the end of the century, Rachell's example had found expression in the achievements of other free Blacks such as London Bourne.

Both men achieved a level of economic success to which free black women also aspired. While no black woman was able to attain the kind of economic status Rachell and Bourne achieved, several managed to establish businesses, purchase the freedom of their enslaved kin, and generally own enslaved workers as an expression of personal success. One such woman was Phoebe Forde. Born enslaved, her determination to achieve freedom for herself and family was intense and informed her strategic judgements as a young woman. 'By her industry,' the records tell us, 'she earned and saved a sum of money with which she purchased her freedom from her owner'. The negotiation over her manumission did not deplete her financial resources, and within a short time, she was operating a retail store in Holetown and was known throughout the parish as a reputable business woman of strong character. An inventory of her assets at death in 1823 establishes her as an owner of enslaved people, house owner, and mother of free children whom she had purchased and manumitted.[35]

Free Blacks, then, were committed as a community to two immediate, paradoxical and contradictory agendas. In most cases their personal experiences of slavery and understanding of the social order, enabled them to develop aggressive anti-slavery attitudes with respect to family reconstitution. Records of their decision-making throughout the slavery period indicate commitment to the purchase and manumission of kith and kin as a principal social objective. To this end, however, free blacks found it in their financial interest, in most cases, to own or hire enslaved people. Freedom, therefore, for their free black families came as an end result of their entry into slave-owning. This process and its relations, furthermore, were often blurred because the practical circumstances of economic activity necessitated the effective enslavement of family members as a pre-condition to attaining their freedom. The tendency was, in addition, for free Blacks to adopt attitudes toward work that corresponded with the dominant ideologies of the pro-slavery interest. Governor Parry reported in 1788 that he had observed a mentality among them towards manual labour that was in no way dissimilar to that of Whites. Distance from manual, degrading work was an important part of the meaning of freedom in the Caribbean society, and free blacks, noted the governor, 'are so proud and indolent that many of them will not labour for their own maintenance'. The depth of this resistance, the governor suggested, was such an important feature of free black mentalities that some chose to 'become beggars' and be 'supported by the parish' rather than labour in tasks normally performed by enslaved workers.[36] Steele tells us, however, that the few free Blacks who found themselves in a destitute condition were outnumbered by Whites who 'pester' the colony and are seen begging 'covered with only filthy rags'.[37] In effect, Steele concludes, free Blacks were not a significant element among the poorest of the poor; the market economy had allocated that status to mostly unskilled white workers and 'abandoned, infirm, and diseased' enslaved labourers.

There were no phenotypically black plantation owners during the eighteenth century, though several persons socially defined as 'coloured' entered the landed elite. Persons labelled as 'mulattos' were dominant within this small group, some of whom were described as sufficiently white 'to go unmolested'. The white plantation elite seemed more accommodating to a minority of 'coloureds', but resisted black entry with considerable tenacity. The ideological world of the sugar plantations constituted the effective force within the wider society. The unwillingness of Whites to sell plantation properties to Blacks was endemic and as the evidence shows, survived slavery into the twenty-first century.

The complex social circumstances that surrounded Blacks' ownership of enslaved people, furthermore, could not facilitate their successful operation of large scale sugar plantations. Clearly, the extreme cruelty surrounding slave relations in the plantation sector would have problematised 'Black on Black' slavery in ways that the flexible, open conditions of urban slavery did not. It is possible that Blacks' confinement to the urban context was indicative of their realisation that the social culture of towns represented the practical limits of their effective slave-owning. Essentially, their slave-owning demand was governed by the real need for domestic, artisanal and casual labour, rather than the desire for racial domination, sexual exploitation and cultural superiority.

As an expression of class relation, however, black slave-ownership operated its own distinct ideological agendas, but would have contradicted the full range of ideological practices found within the sugar plantation sector. While it is true, for example, that in the urban sex industry black male and female entrepreneurs were ruthless in the way they degraded and marketed the sexuality of enslaved black women, the vulgar culture of such a trade, it seemed, offered a measure of social liberty and opportunity for personal autonomy to some enslaved women not generally associated with sugar plantation slavery.

Rachel Pringle, the famed Coloured woman who ran a hotel which offered enslaved women as prostitutes to guests, freed six of her enslaved women by terms of her will in 1791. When Dr George Pinckard visited Barbados in the mid-1790s he observed that enslaved females were commonly offered to guests as prostitutes in most Bridgetown taverns and inns. This activity, he concluded, offered enslaved women 'the only hope they have of procuring a sum of money, wherewith to purchase their freedom'.

While many visitors to the colony noted the severe exploitation of enslaved black females in this way and saw it as evidence of the moral corruption of colonial society, the dominant observation was that prostitution was an important route used by enslaved black women to pursue and achieve freedom and financial independence.[38]

By the end of the eighteenth century, free Blacks had become accustomed to their slave-owning and employer status. In this context, they allied with free Coloureds, wrote joint petitions and memoranda, and spoke with one public voice on issues of civil liberties. While their 'Coloured' counterparts were financially more successful, having penetrated both the urban trade sector and rural plantation economy, they no longer had pedigree in the business of slave-owning. It is instructive to note, for example, that the St Michael vestry records as early as the 1670s and 1680s show two families of 'free Negroes' as owners of several enslaved people.[39]

This early start is reflected in Jerome Handler's conclusion that throughout the period of African enslavement there is no evidence that as a group, free Blacks 'had any compunction against owning or employing slaves', and that all the information led to the conclusion that slaves were regarded by them 'as desirable forms of property'. Furthermore, that the 'emphasis on slave-ownership was not restricted to those who had been born free, but also extended to former slaves who, after their manumission, often acquired their own human property'.[40]

It is important, then, to discern two tendencies within the free black slave-owning experience; one which relates to strategies of liberating family reconstitution, and another which was driven purely by the accumulation process. While some overlap occurred between the two, and the extent of this should be carefully assessed, they were effectively discrete social and economic actions. With regard to the latter, however, the dozens of free Blacks who signed the 1803 petition along with over 200 free Coloureds, calling upon Council not to approve legislation to limit their slave-owning and property accumulation rights, may not have spoken for the majority within the group.

In the 1803 petition to Council, free Blacks made reference to their being 'accustomed to the assistance of slaves' without which it would be required of them to 'perform every menial office with [their] own hands'. 'Our children,' the petitioners claimed, 'who are now grown almost to the years of maturity have from their earliest infancy been accustomed to be attended by slaves.' The 'greatest blessing attending upon freedom,' they concluded, 'is the acquirement and enjoyment of property,' and 'surely death would be preferable to such a situation' of slavelessness.[41] While members of Parliament were swayed not to legislate limitation upon their capacity to own other Blacks and other forms of property, they remained generally disturbed by the trend which showed their increasing activity on the property market.

Here again, two discernible trends in free black slave-owning culture are illuminated by the discourse on the relative 'treatment' of the enslaved in which critics and defenders of slavery engaged. While the evidence shows that free black slave-holders manumitted enslaved people at a rate considerably above Whites, and were effectively the greatest emancipators of the enslaved, several observers of slavery noted that free Blacks 'treated' their slaves with less compassion than Whites.

William Dickson, for example, who established a reputation in Barbados and England at the end of the eighteenth century as a knowledgeable critic of Barbadian slavery, paid particular attention to the social relations of free Blacks. Dickson was not an emancipationist, but an ameliorationist, who believed that the terms and conditions of enslavement could be modified to meet the requirements of a liberal conscience. He promoted the civil rights of free Blacks, encouraged Whites to free enslaved skilled artisans in greater numbers, and spoke highly of the quality of the work of free black artisans. But he was at pains to point out that with respect to the treatment of the enslaved, 'free Blacks are generally more severe, being less enlightened owners than White people.'[42]

Dickson provided no evidence to support this belief, and may have been swayed by the view that because of their ethnicity free Blacks should not participate in the promotion of racialised slave relations and the inhumane excesses they imposed upon enslaved Blacks. Such a perspective would carry as an assumption the existence of an ideologically monolithic mentality among Blacks and an endorsement of the belief in the moral plurality of Whites. Denying free Blacks a diverse range of opinions, position and strategic responses on slavery would suggest that black anti-slavery politics was not rooted in a complex, sophisticated cosmology.

The enslaving practices of some Blacks were undoubtedly consistent with Europeans' concept of Enlightenment modernity that articulated ideas about social freedom with the notion of human progress. Also, the commitment of free Blacks to property accumulation and social mobility strategies that required engagement in enslaving other Blacks was matched by their determination to preserve and protect freedom, as conceived by white intellectuals and enslavers. The belief that this ideological world, which defined the nature of the pro-slavery establishment, could be fractured by a race-based master politics of anti-slavery solidarity, contradicts all that is known about gender, class and race divisions within the colonial context. While contradictory, subjective, political circumstances often surrounded free and enslaved Blacks, resolutions were sought in multiple ways, and the collective armed struggle for freedom was but one.

The United States commentator who resided in Bridgetown in 1814 appreciated the meaning of these wider issues and considerably prolematised Dickson's thesis that black enslavers were the most severe of all. His method was to destabilise Dickson's claim with the observation that it was 'a character given by Whites' rather than Blacks, and was open therefore to doubt and disbelief. Furthermore, the United States visitor showed that the negative opinion of free Blacks was propagated by 'Whites who seemed to entertain a hostile feeling against them'. [43]

The ability of pro-slavery advocates to tarnish the relations of free Blacks with the negative slave-owning images, then, was part of a wider campaign to limit the liberation projects of all Blacks, and to suggest to critics of slavery that race was not the critical issue in the slavery debate. Reformers and anti-slavery agents arrived at the same judgement with respect to black slave-owners, because they wished to show the extent of the corrupting nature of the slave system. Their objective, then, was to show that even former enslaved persons were forced to aggressively participate in slavery in order to live above subsistence.

Following the outlawing of the English trade in African captives in 1807, new levels of constraints upon the labour market forced all slave owners to devise rationalisation schemes to consolidate their investments in enslaved labour. By abolishing the trade in Africans, the British government drove the majority of enslavers to resort to 'slave breeding' as the main mechanism of labour reproduction. The scramble to secure an effective share of the internal supply of enslaved labour did not favour black enslavers, though sugar plantation owners seemed satisfied that in general all was well within their sector. While the skilled labour of free Blacks attracted better wages after 1807, their opportunities to purchase or hire enslaved Blacks were diminished in the fierce competition with sugar producers.

The dominant political strategy free Blacks developed during the period after 1807 was to campaign with free Coloureds for an expansion of civil rights, particularly the ability to give evidence in courts against Whites and to hold office in government. Their public politics at no stage involved support for the abolition of slavery. Indeed, they stayed clear of any open association with the locally reported and discussed activities of William Wilberforce in England; and the revolutionary anti-slavery movement was spearheaded by enslaved Blacks. Neither did they promote any oppositional politics around specific issues of concern to those enslaved such as the separation of families, desire for formal education, preventing the corporal punishment of women, and the wish for religious tolerance. In effect, the free black community showed its formal opposition to slavery primarily in its manumission performance and in its own aggressive but fruitless search for civil rights equality with Whites.

The failure of the civil rights movement in the decade after 1806 had effects throughout the entire political culture of the colony. Enslaved Blacks knew by then that white society had no intention of either radically reforming or abolishing slavery. Free Blacks' requests for judicial equality with Whites were dismissed by the Legislature that threatened them with a reduction of civil rights if they persisted with their campaign. They were made to understand that the few rights they enjoyed were gifts to treasure and that they were impertinent to make further demands upon the government. The veiled threat used by their counterparts in Jamaica, Grenada and Saint Domingue, for example, of leading, supporting or encouraging rebellion among those enslaved was not made in Barbados. Enslaved people in Barbados had not attempted a significant revolt on the island since 1692, and the entire eighteenth century was free of armed insurrection. Whites were confident in the public management of those they enslaved and thought they had good reasons to be complacent in their political achievement.

A major revolt of enslaved people finally came on April 14, 1816; two years after the Assembly had enacted the imperial Registry Bill that mandated a count and documentation of the entire enslaved population. The enslaved organised an island-wide conspiracy to overthrow the enslavers and thereby obtain their freedom. The Haitian model of armed insurrection was their inspiration; this much was made clear by the several confessions of black rebels. The leadership of the rebellion was located within the community of enslaved drivers, overseers and artisans, that is, persons most likely to gain freedom by manumission from their owners. There were no enslaved field hands within this leadership group. It was a strike for freedom led by enslaved people who, according to Whites, long enjoyed as many liberties as free Blacks. No mention was made of a supportive role played by free Blacks, though the official report of the Assembly into the rebellion shows that a small group of labouring free coloured men with close kinship and social ties to slaves were co-conspirators.[44]

A large number of free Blacks, however, gave evidence before the Assembly's Investigative Committee. The published testimony of one of them, William Yard, indicates quite clearly his political disassociation from the revolt. In his deposition, Yard, a tailor by profession, stated that the enslaved were anxiously awaiting news of their freedom from England since the passage of the Registry Bill, and that he was questioned by several of them regarding his knowledge of the same. He also stated that 'one of his boys' was questioned at his shop outside of Bridgetown by 'country slaves' 'whether he know anything about their freedom.' His 'boy', Yard said, had 'pretended to read to them from a newspaper that they were to be free', for which he 'rebuked the boy for attempting to impose on the negroes'.[45]

Within three days the revolt was crushed by a joint force of militia regiments and imperial soldiers who were stationed on the island as part of the operation to keep out the French. Some 1,000 enslaved persons, two soldiers and one militiaman lost their lives. No free Blacks, but four free Coloureds, according to the reports, were included among the fatalities. Three years later another 123 slaves held in various prisons were deported to Honduras, and then to Sierra Leone as political prisoners. Many Whites, however, according to one report, died as a result of 'fatigue' caused by the widespread devastation. Some 177 property holders across seven of the 11 parishes submitted claims to the government for compensation from the public relief.[46]

The political leadership of the colony highly commended both free Blacks and free Coloureds for their loyalty to Whites and plantation society during the rebellion. This attachment to the cause of property-holders, said John Beckles, Speaker of the House, was effective in quelling enslaved rebels and in his opinion, deserved a reward. Addressing the Assembly in January 1817, Beckles noted that this 'free' but 'restricted' element of the society has always made their complaints 'in respectful language, and in terms of moderation'. Furthermore, he said, they 'have manifested a determination to do their duty by the country, and a devotion to the interest of the Whites.'[47] Within the year the Assembly passed legislation to reward them with the long sought after right, to give evidence in court under all circumstances in order to protect their freedom and property. Finally in 1831, they secured the final concession from the legislature: full civil equality with Whites.

'Black on Black' slavery, then, reflected a range of peculiar and sometimes contradictory experiences specific to the aspirations of the black population. At the same time it illuminated features of the deepest ends and most remote corners of the enslaving culture that underpinned the political economy of Caribbean and Atlantic colonialism. While enslaving as a brutal and alienating anti-black culture constituted the principal mechanism of wealth generation and status mobility, it also enabled some Blacks to engage in a desperate attempt at family reconstitution, kinship protection, and social inclusion. Adjusted more to the urban context than the sugar plantation sector, 'Black on Black' slavery operated with a set of complex socioeconomic arrangements that promoted the quest for property accumulation, in itself a necessary activity for the long-term attainment and protection of freedom.

As a strategic response for status consolidation free Blacks generally formed political alliances with free Coloureds, whose anti-black attitudes also reflected the depth of 'negrophobia' endemic to white society. Divided by the vein, free Coloureds dealt with their social contradictions and projected a range of attitudes to slavery that were consistent with their multi-ethnic origins. The ultimate objective pursued by all Blacks was flight from enslavement. The door of owning enslaved Africans was one that opened along the journey and free Blacks entered boldly but redefined important aspects of the room they entered and inhabited.

NOTES

1   See N.A.T. Hall, 'The 1816 Freedman Petition in the Danish West Indies: Its Background and consequences', *Boletin de Estudios Latinoamericanos y del Caribe 29* (1980): 55-73; Gad Heuman, 'The Social Structure of Slave Societies in the Caribbean', in Franklin W. Knight (ed.), *General History of the Caribbean:The Slave Societies*, vol. 3 (London: UNESCO, Macmillan, 1997), 3:138-69; Michael Craton, 'Forms of Resistance to Slavery', ibid., 222-71; Arnold Sio, 'Marginality and Free Colored Identity in Caribbean Slave Society', *Slavery and Abolition* 8 (1987): 166-68.

2   Hilary McD Beckles, 'The Literate Few: An Historical Sketch of the Slavery Origins of Black Elites in the English West Indies', *Caribbean Journal of Education* 11 (1984); 'On the Backs of Blacks: The Barbados Free-Coloreds' Pursuit of Civil Rights and the 1816 Rebellion', *Immigrants and Minorities* 3 (1984).

3   See John Garrigus, 'A Struggle for Respect:The Free Coloreds of Pre-Revolutionary Saint-Domingue, 1760-69' (unpublished PhD dissertation, Johns Hopkins University, 1988); M.G. Smith, 'Some Aspects of Social Structure in the British Caribbean about 1820', *Social and Economic Studies* l (1953).

4   See Gwendolyn Midlo Hall, *Social Control in Slave Plantation Societies: A Comparison of St. Domingue and Cuba* (Baton Rouge: Louisiana State University Press, 1996 [1971]), 113-32.

5   See Barry W. Higman, *Slave Populations of the British Caribbean, 1807-1834* (Kingston:The Press, the University of the West Indies, 1995 [1984]), 112; Jerome Handler, *The Unappropriated People: Freedmen in the Slave Society of Barbados* (Baltimore: Johns Hopkins University Press, 1974), 18-25, 150, 187.

6   See Carl Campbell, 'The Rise of the Free Colored Plantocracy in Trinidad, 1783-1813', *Boletin de Estudios Latinoamericanos y del Caribe 29* (1980): 46-47; Barry W. Higman, 'Urban Slavery in the British Caribbean', in E.Thomas-Hope (ed.), *Perspectives on Caribbean Regional Identity* (Liverpool: Centre for Latin American Studies, University of Liverpool, 1984).

7   Higman, *Slave Populations*, 382.

8   [John Poyer], 'A letter addressed to . . . Lord Seaforth by a Barbadian' (Bridgetown, 1801). See also Ronald Hughes, 'Jacob Hinds (?-1832), White Father of a Colored Clan', Seminar Paper 2, Department of History, UWI, Cave Hill, 1982-83.

9   Handler, *The Unappropriated People*, 17.

10 Handler, *The Unappropriated People*, 21.

11 Cecelia Karch, 'London Bourne of Barbados', paper presented at the 15th Annual Conference of Caribbean Historians, Mona, UWI, Jamaica, 1983; Warren Alleyne, 'London Bourne', *The Bajan and Caribbean Magazine*, April 1979; Handler, *The Unappropriated People*, 132-33.

12 Handler, *The Unappropriated People*, 20-21; see also Hilary McD Beckles, *Natural Rebels: A Social History of Enslaved Black Women in Barbados* (New Brunswick, N.J.: Rutgers University Press, 1989), 15-17.

13 See Claudia Goldin, 'The Economics of Emancipation', *Journal of Economic History* 33: 66-85; Gad Heuman, *Between Black and White: Race, Politics and the Free Coloreds in Jamaica, 1792-1865* (Westport, Conn.: Greenwood, 1981).

14 See Edward Cox, *Free Coloreds in the Slave Societies of St. Kitts and Grenada, 1763-1865* (Knoxville: University of Tennessee Press, 1984); Handler, *The Unappropriated People*, 29-82.

15 Karch, 'London Bourne', 2-3; Karl Watson, *The Civilised Island: Barbados: A Social History, 1750-1816* (Bridgetown: The Author, 1979), 101.

16 Will of Betty-Burk, alias Betty-Burk Poore, free Negro, November 6, 1789. RB6/19, Barbados Archives.

17 These cases are set out in the wills of Sarah Kirton and Laurentia Lavine, 1790, RB6/19, Barbados Archives. See also Watson, *The Civilised Island*, 102.

18 See B.M. Shilstone, 'Harrison of Barbados', *Journal of the Barbados Museum and Historical Society* 8 (1941): 30-32.

19 The will of Francis Ford is cited in B.M. Cracknell, ed., *The Barbadian Diary of General Robert Haynes, 1787-1836* (England, 1934), 58-60.

20 Quotation from an anonymous author, *Letter from a Gentleman in Barbados to His Friends in London, on the Subject of Manumission from Slavery, Granted in the Cay of London and in the West Indian Colonies* (London, 1803), 21.

21 Higman, *Slave Populations*, 382.

22 Higman, *Slave Populations*, 384-85.

23 Higman, *Slave Populations*, 385-86.

24 Higman, *Slave Populations*, 436.

25 Higman, *Slave Populations*, 233, 433-46.

26 Cited in Samuel Moore, *The Public Acts in Force, Passed by the Legislature of Barbados from May 11, 1762-April 8, 1800 Inclusive* (London, 1801), 226-28.

27 Cited in [Benjamin Browne], *The Yarn of a Yankee Privateer*, Nathaniel Hawthorne, ed. (New York: Funk & Wagnalls, 1926), 112.

28 See Sylvester Hovey, *Letters from the West Indies* (New York, 1838), 205.

29 As early as October 1694 two bills were debated by the Assembly on the subject. The first was to prohibit 'the sale of goods to Negroes' and second to prohibit 'the employment of Negroes in selling'. Journal of the Assembly of Barbados, October 17, 1694, *Calendar of State Papers, Colonial Series, 1693-1696*, F. 381.

30 See Joshua Steele's reply to questions asked by Governor Parry on the subject in *Parliamentary Papers*, 1789, vol. 26, 31.

31 See Hilary McD Beckles, 'An Economic Life of Their Own: Slaves as Commodity Producers and Distributors in Barbados', *Slavery and Abolition*, vol. 12, no. 1 (1991).

32 Moore, *The Public Acts in Force*, 154-70. See Also Hilary McD Beckles, *Black Rebellion in Barbados: The Struggles Against Slavery, 1627-1838* (Bridgetown: The Antilles Press, 1983), 71-72.

33 Cited in [Browne], *The Yarn of a Yankee Privateer*, 103.

34 See Jerome Handler, 'Joseph Rachell and Rachel Pringle-Polgreen: Petty Entrepreneurs',
    in D. Sweet and G. Nash, eds., *Struggle and Survival in Colonial America* (Berkeley: University
    of California Press, 1981).

35 Phoebe Forde's case is outlined in *Petition of Samuel Gabriel, Catherine Duke and William Forde,
    Colored Persons, Inhabitants of this Island of Barbdos, 8 March 1823*, CO28/92 Series, No. 16.

36 Cited in Handler, *The Unappropriated People*, 138.

37 Steele's assessment is set out in a reply to Governor Parry, 1788, *Parliamentary Papers*, 1789,
    vol. 26, 33. See also Daniel McKinnen, *A Tour Through the British West Indies in the Years 1802
    and 1803* (London, 1804). On pages 15-16, McKinnen states that the filth and crowded
    slums of Bridgetown were the social effects of freed slaves concentrating their lives in one
    place.

38 See Handler, *The Unappropriated People*, 135-37.

39 St Michael Parish Register, Barbados, Vol. 1A, R.L. 1/1, Barbados Archives.

40 Handler, *The Unappropriated People*, 146.

41 'The Humble Petition of the Free Coloured People, Inhabitants of the Island', was submitted
    to the Governor in Council on November 1, 1803. See Minutes of Council, November 1,
    1803.

42 See William Dickson, *Letters on Slavery* (London, 1814), 55.

43 Cited in [Browne], *The Yarn of a Yankee Privateer*, 103.

44 *See Report from A Select Committee of the House of Assembly Appointed to Inquire into the Origins,
    Cause and Progress of the Late Insurrection, April 1816* (Barbados, 1819).

45 Deposition of William Yard.

46 Anonymous, 'An Account of the Late Negro Insurrection which took Place in the Island
    of Barbados on Easter Sunday, April 14, 1816', New York Public Library, Mss. Division;
    Hilary McD Beckles, *Black Rebellion*, 86-120.

47 Minutes of the Assembly, January 7, 1817; Beckles, *Black Rebellion*, 110; Hilary McD
    Beckles, 'On the Backs of Blacks: The Barbados Free-Coloreds; Pursuit of Civil Rights and
    the 1816 Slave Rebellion', *Immigrants and Minorities*, vol. 3, no. 2 (1984): 1-12.

- *Two* -

A Landless Freedom:
The Emancipation Process,
1838–1863

During the 1820s, the opposition of slave owners, white as well as coloured, did not reduce the pressure of black anti-slavery politics, nor the intensity of the imperial campaign for the abolition of slavery. In 1832, when the British Parliament adopted an irreversible abolitionist stance, it was aware that the imposition of emancipation measures would not be an easy task. In order to facilitate the process, however, Parliament brought Barbados and the Windward Islands under a common governor-generalship in 1833, headed by Sir Lionel Smith. The task of the new governor on arrival in Barbados in 1833 was to win the confidence of the slave owners, give assurances to the enslaved and illustrate to both groups that emancipation would not lead to any worsening of economic conditions in the colony. In fact, Smith, in his first address to the Barbados legislature in May 1833, intimated that his intention was to be 'attentive to the interests of the people of both races'.[1]

Smith's campaign did not gain him many friends among planters, who remained, in general, opposed to imperial legislative interventions in their domestic affairs. In May 1833, E.G. Stanley (Lord Derby), Secretary for Colonies, introduced the Emancipation Bill into the House of Commons. By then, Barbadian absentee planters in London, more aware than their colleagues at home of the mechanics of the parliamentary procedure, had accepted the inevitability of emancipation by imperial legislation. Stanley's introduction of the Bill was flavoured by his insistence that only by British legislation could slavery be abolished, as West Indian slave owners, especially the Barbadians, remained recalcitrant on matters of slave amelioration. Parliament, he argued, in fulfilling its commitment to the enslaved population, had no choice but to impose the emancipation process upon the colonies.[2]

The Emancipation Act was clear in its intention. On August 1, 1834, all enslaved persons, black and coloured under the age of six years, would be totally and unconditionally emancipated; furthermore, all enslaved persons over the age of six years were also freed, but under the stipulation that they were to serve their former owners as apprentices for a period of 12 years. The perception of English politicians behind the 12 year period of apprenticeship was that it would allow the enslaved and enslavers time to become adjusted gradually to the state of freedom. Critically, it would give slave owners sufficient time to restructure their economies and adjust their social values and attitudes to the presence of the free black community and their employment as wage labourers. The Act carried further stipulations that wages were not to be paid to apprentices, except for additional work conducted in their free time. Employers were expected to carry on the slavery days tasks of providing material subsistence for apprentices. Recognising that slave owners were likely to intensify the degree of labour exploitation during this transitional period, the Emancipation Act provided for the establishment of a judicial agency to mediate the conflicts that might arise. These special justices, or stipendiary magistrates, were appointed and paid by the Crown. It was hoped that their imperial mission would free their decisions from planter influence.[3]

Finally accepting the fact of the emancipation process, West Indian slave owners prepared to do battle with the Colonial Office over its legislative details. One of their first demands was for compensation for the loss of chattel property which emancipation represented. In July 1833, Parliament was informed by the Barbados Assembly:

> As England is avowedly the author and was for a long time the chief gainer [of slavery] . . . let her bear her share of the penalty of expiation . . . Let a fair and just indemnity be first secured to the owner of the property which is to be put to risk . . . and then the colonists will cooperate in accomplishing a real and effective emancipation of the slaves. All wise and well intentioned emancipationists will hail this alliance, conscious that

without the cooperation and instrumentality of the resident colonists, their object can only be attained through rapine violence and bloodshed, destroying all the elements of civilisation and ending in anarchy. [4]

This policy demand was aggressive. If England, the Assembly added, was repenting 'the parts she has had in establishing and cherishing a system which she now thinks is criminal', then let her pay the cost of the newly found humanitarianism in the form of a cash indemnity to slave owners and not in the form of an adjustment loan.

The slave owners, supported by the London-based West India Committee, won this battle, and Parliament agreed to pay in cash to slave owners in the West Indies £20 million compensation money instead of the previously stated £15 million in loans. This enormous concession to slave owners angered many elements within the humanitarian movement who perceived the £20 million as proof of Parliament's capitulation to immoral slave-owning interest, though the point made by a few members that perhaps the enslaved should also be compensated for past injustices was not pressed very hard. The humanitarians, nonetheless, now demanded from Parliament that the apprenticeship period be reduced from 12 to six years for field workers and to four years for artisans and domestic servants. This demand was also granted.

Table 1
Apprentices' scale of allowances and commutations in Barbados

ALLOWANCES	COMMUTATIONS
30 lb of roots per week or 10 pints of guinea corn to all apprentices above 10 years of age; to all under 10, half the quantity	To all apprentices above 16 years of age, ½ acre of land for raising provisions; to all under 16, ¼ acre of land.
2 lb of fish per week to all apprentices	£1.5s a year or 17 days free of work
1 jacket or penistone 2 shirts or shifts 2 petticoats or trousers 1 cap or kerchief 6 skeins of thread	In money for each full-grown man or woman, 2 dollars 8 bits; for a second size man or woman, 2 dollars; for an apprentice 10-16 years of age, 17½ bits; for apprentices from 10 years of age down, 15 bits.
1 blanket every 2 years	1 dollar

Source: C. Levy. *Emancipation, Sugar and Federalism, p. 60: Barbados and the West Indies, 1833–1876* (Gainsville: University Press of Florida, 1980).

According to Levy, Barbadian slave owners were eager to augment their share of the £20 million voted by Parliament, and were prepared to forego their right to apprenticed labour altogether in return for a larger per capita payment. But the imperial government was unwilling to make any new concessions, because it believed that the island already enjoyed an advantage over the other colonies as a result of its abundant labour supply. This argument suggests that Barbadians, unlike the imperial government, were not fully committed to an apprenticeship period as a prelude to full emancipation. In this regard, they might have entertained the possibility of moving to full freedom for Blacks in 1834, as the Antigua and Bermuda slave owners did. The amount they received by way of compensation for their loss of slave property was £1.75 million.[5]

Table 2

Compensation for Emancipation of Slaves in British West Indies

	Number of slaves	Total compensation (£)	Average compensation per slave (£. s. d.)
Jamaica	311,070	6,149,955	19.15. 1
British Guiana	82,824	4,295,989	51.17. 1
Barbados	83,150	1,719,980	20.13. 8
Trinidad	20,657	1,033,992	51. 1. 1
Grenada	23,638	616,255	26. 1. 4
St. Vincent	22,266	550,777	26.10. 7
Antigua	29,121	425,547	14. 2. 3
St. Lucia	13,291	334,495	25. 3. 2
St. Kitts	19,780	329,393	16.13. 0
Dominica	14,175	275,547	19. 8. 9
Tobago	11,589	233,875	23. 7. 0
Nevis	8,815	151,006	17. 2. 7
Bahamas	10,086	128,296	12.14.4
Montserrat	6,401	103,556	16. 3. 3
British Honduras	1,901	101,399	53. 6. 9
Virgin Islands	5,135	72, 63 8	14.1.10
Bermuda	4,026	50,409	12.10.5

Sources: *Parliamentary Papers, 1837–38, vol. 44:154*; C. Levy, *Emancipation, Sugar and Federalism: Barbados and the West Indies, 1833–1876* Gainesville: Univ. Press of Florida, 1980 p. 55

Refused any further concessions by Parliament in terms of compensation money, Barbadian slave-owners decided to slow down the process of local legislation for black freedom with the intention of frustrating Parliament and asserting the strength of their dominance over local constitutional affairs. As late as September 1833 they had not legislated emancipation, and the following month Governor Smith, showing excessive restraint, politely suggested that is was time for the Legislature to implement Parliament's policy. The Legislature refused to act, and towards the end of the year Governor Smith could only remind it that the compensation money allocated for the colony could only be obtained upon Parliament being convinced that local government had performed its duty satisfactorily. It was in April 1834 that the Legislature passed the bill instituting the Apprenticeship System as from August 1 that year, and therein abolishing slavery.

Many aspects of the Barbados Act did not please Parliament, but it consented to the law in order to facilitate the speedy movement of the emancipation process. Planters retained full control of the police system and Justices of the Peace, two law and order agencies which Governor Smith was convinced would be used indiscriminately against Blacks. While Smith spoke of the 'unbending spirit of the planters', they in turn referred to his hasty and ill-informed attempts to undermine the foundations of the world they had made.

Governor Smith, meanwhile, took every opportunity to inform the Colonial Offce that the planters' refusal to apply the 'spirit of the new order' to their proceedings, and their determination to consolidate political, military and judicial power at the expense of Blacks, were likely to result in social unrest. In full awareness that any violent uprising of labourers would have to be effectively suppressed, Smith took the decision to dispatch several units of imperial soldiers to Bridgetown on August 1, Emancipation Day. He took this precautionary measure as a show of imperial strength, and to impress upon the minds of Blacks that emancipation was not intended to turn the social world upside down. Blacks were then told by Smith that 'the law is strong,' and all those who did not work, 'the law will punish'. He had hoped to mark August 1 as a thanksgiving holiday but the Legislature, still not warming to the emancipation process, rejected his suggestion.[6]

Emancipation Day, then, though not representing true freedom as far as Blacks were concerned, was a peaceful one. In Trinidad, there were riots in Port of Spain, and rumours of disturbances in the countryside as Blacks voiced their protest to the provisional freedom. Threats of disorder were also reported in Essequibo (British Guiana), and some unrest also occurred in St Kitts and Montserrat. Governor Smith, however, had the pleasure of informing the Colonial Office that on Emancipation Day Barbados was 'never more tranquil' though Blacks had verbally expressed their disenchantment with the restrictive conditions imposed upon their freedom.

Part-Free and the 1838 Emancipation Law

A survey of the enslaved population revealed that on August 1, 1834, 83,150 persons were freed from legal slavery – a labour force that would remain in excess of the economic needs of the sugar industry. Of those who became apprentices, 52,193 were categorised as praedials and 14,732 as non-praedials. The remainder were classified as children under six years, who were fully freed, and 'worn out' and infirm persons. This meant that in terms of Blacks per square mile Barbados had a total of 501, compared with Antigua and dependencies, 269, and St Kitts, 290. With this concentration of labourers on the island, most planters knew, inspite of their politically motivated statements to the contrary, that if they could maintain effective socio-political control of Blacks, the labour market would function in the interest of the plantation sector.[7]

The Colonial Office was not satisfied with the provisions found within the Barbados legislation for the functioning of the Apprenticeship System. Planters remained hostile to the idea of the imposed emancipation, and as was the case in the 1824 House of Assembly debate on the Colonial Office's ameliorative policies, made attempts to tighten their grip over the labour market. They implemented a series of measures designed to ensure that the level of conflict between themselves and Blacks over terms and conditions of work would increase rather than decrease. For example, they transferred non-praedials to the fields and so attempted to extend their apprenticeship to 1840 rather than 1838. They also insisted that many skilled workers, such as boilermen and carpenters, should serve as apprentices until 1840.

In addition to these manoeuvres, the food rations offered Blacks remained among the most meagre in the West Indies in spite of the fact that they alone were experiencing expansion of sugar production and general economic buoyancy. Under criticism from Secretary Thomas Spring-Rice, Stanley's replacement at the Colonial Office, the Barbados Legislature amended their Emancipation Act in November, a mere three months after the Apprenticeship System had begun functioning. Their adjustments were significant:

a) stipendiary magistrates could investigate conditions in prisons;
b) watchmen and cattle tenders had their hours of work reduced to the standard 45 hours per week (five days of nine hours, excluding Saturday and Sunday);
c) non-praedials would still be transferred to the fields for insubordination, though they would still be freed in 1838.

By 1835, when Lord Glenelg took over at the Colonial Office, the tone of discussions about the functioning of the Apprenticeship System was undergoing substantial changes. Glenelg, under the guidance of James Stephen, attempted to intimidate Barbadian planters by suggesting that the Apprenticeship System was more about Blacks slowly becoming free men than about slave owners adjusting to a wage labour system. He implied, furthermore, that it should be terminated prematurely as a just concession to workers. Robert Bowcher Clarke, considered the most liberal-minded Assemblyman among the planter elite, sought to defend the Assembly's right to maintain legislative control over the Apprenticeship System. He recognised, nonetheless, that it was a system which by design bred discord between Blacks and planter, and suggested that its survival was not necessarily in the colony's long-term interest.

As Solicitor General for the colony, Clarke was positioned to assert intense pressure upon the Legislature; as a result he sought to show the House that it would do the colony no harm by embracing the perspective of Lord Glenelg.

The reports of Crown-appointed special (stipendiary) magistrates suggest that it was not uncommon for Blacks to be given inadequate food rations, driven to work beyond normal time without proper rest periods, and punished with imprisonment for offences that would have been ignored by many planters during the slavery era. Furthermore, they point towards the deterioration of work relations on estates, and the hardening of judicial attitudes towards workers. Meanwhile, planters complained about the insolence, insubordinate and lawless social manner of Blacks, in addition to their slack attitudes towards work, duties and civic responsibilities. In spite of these attacks upon the character of Blacks, the volume of Barbados sugar exports increased from an estimated 17,234 tons in 1835 to 23,679 tons in 1838.

Blacks, however, not surprisingly, expressed in no uncertain terms the desire to obtain their full freedom by self-purchase before the dates set by law for final emancipation. But few of them were able to achieve this end. The fragmented data show that during the first year of apprenticeship some 907 apprentices were freed – the vast majority of these were cases of employers voluntarily surrendering their legal rights in labourers. The fact that over 70 per cent of these voluntary discharges of apprentices occurred in the Bridgetown area suggests that the sugar planters showed less compassion on the question of black freedom than their urban counterparts. Furthermore, only about forty apprentices, most of whom were from Bridgetown, were able to purchase their freedom during this year, which suggests that the plantation sector proved relatively more rigid in its responses to emancipation. Blacks willing to purchase their freedom were often forced to resort to all manner of trickery so as to obtain a low valuation from Justices – sometimes by faking infirmity, sickness and old age.

Undoubtedly – and this point has been stressed by historians – it was the 14,000 children under the age of six who were fully freed in

1834, who added greatly to the number of social destitutes in the colony. Parents were not keen to offer their children's labour to plantations, and employers responded by abandoning any responsibility for infants within their sphere of influence. Workers struggled to provide for children during the apprenticeship, and since planters took up responsibility only for those they employed, the dependent part of the black family felt the pinch. The result was that the level of infant mortality, on the decrease during the final years of slavery, began once again an upward path. Reverend Thomas Parry took up the campaign against this aspect of the apprenticeship before becoming Bishop of Barbados, but recognised that his efforts bore little fruit.

In the early part of 1836, the questions of child abandonment and rising infant mortality became issues around which criticisms of the Apprenticeship System revolved. Governor Smith went on the offensive and abused planters for not accepting their social responsibility to the defenceless, and for using children as pawns in the bargaining process between themselves and adult workers. In order not to give the imperial government such an excuse to abolish the Apprenticeship System, planters encouraged their Legislature to pass an act which made it unlawful for the plantations to apprentice children, or for parents to offer their children as apprentices. With this issue behind them, planters settled down to making a positive evaluation of the apprenticeship. Their economy had not suffered as a result and they felt assured of a future supply of cheap, reliable, landless labourers to work their estates.

By early 1838, the Colonial Office seemed determined to abolish completely the apprenticeship that year. It was persuasively argued in Parliament that planters were making a mockery of this transition period by preserving some of the worst aspects of their slave management, and were threatening to show the futility of the Emancipation Act of 1833. In Barbados, Governor MacGregor did well to convince the legislature that it should abolish the system, and that it should support the general plan of action outlined by Glenelg. His argument rested on the notions that labour would continue to be plentiful, and that it would assist planters to establish some measure of moral authority over labourers.

Solicitor General Clarke was also quite eloquent in the articulation of these ideas. He was instrumental in persuading the House to recognise that the creation of 'a happy and contented . . . community of free men' depended upon a speedy abolition of the system of apprenticed labour. Also, that a future order of social cohesion and political stability, which such an abolition would enhance, was infinitely more valuable to all Barbadians than the extra units of sugar production which planters sought to extract from the apprentices. Bishop Coleridge added to this campaign, and pleaded with the Legislature to exercise vision on the matter. In May 1838 the Barbados Legislature passed a law for the complete emancipation of all Blacks to take effect on August 1 that year – two years earlier than was provided for in the 1834 law of emancipation. On June 2, Governor MacGregor issued this statement:

BARBADOS. His Excellency Major General Sir Evan John Murray MacGregor, Bart., Companion of the Most Honourable Military Order of the Bath, Knight Commander of the Hanoverian Guelphic Order, Governor and Commander-in-Chief in and over the Islands of Barbados, Saint Vincent, Grenada, Tobago, St. Lucia, and Trinidad, etc, etc, etc.

A PROCLAMATION

Whereas it hath pleased Almighty God, great in Council and mighty in Works, whose eyes are open upon all the Sons of Men, disposing and turning them as seemeth best to his Godly Wisdom, to incline the Legislature of this Colony to terminate altogether, by a Public Act, the System of Apprenticeship, and thus to accomplish, before the period prescribed by Law, the entire Emancipation of a large portion of its Inhabitants:

And whereas it is of the Lord's blessing on human agency that great undertakings are brought to a happy completion; and that therefore it is our bounden duty, on the present eventful occasion, openly to acknowledge in all thankfulness of heart His gracious interposition, and to implore the continuance, over this Land, of His providential guidance and protection:

I do hereby, by and with the advice of Her Majesty's Privy Council, set
apart the First Day of August next, as a day of Solemn Thanksgiving and
Devout Supplication to Almighty God, and do require that it be duly
observed in all Churches, Chapels, and other places of Public Worship
throughout the Land, as becometh a considerate and Christian People.
Given under my Hand and Seal this second day of July, One thousand
eight hundred and thirty eight, and in the second year of Her Majesty's
Reign. GOD SAVE THE QUEEN!
By His Excellency's Command
C.T. CUNNINGHAM, Col. Sec.

Some planters, however, continued to express fears of a labour
shortage arising from a workers' boycott of their enterprises. Many Blacks
believed that the circumstances under which freedom would be attained
– hardships in obtaining land and acceptable wages – would still ensure
their socio-political subordination to employers. In spite of the widespread
recognition that material living standards would fall owing to inadequate
wages, many saw freedom as the opening of considerable possibilities –
such as migration, family constitution and educational development.
Discussions of the possibilities of social unrest were commonplace,
especially within the governor's circle; yet once again, as on August 1,
1834, this did not happen.

Emancipation Day passed quietly and peaceably. No riots or reports
of serious disturbances occurred. Many Blacks attended church services
in the morning and took part in festive activities for the remainder of
the day. The militia and imperial soldiers were out in force to ensure that
Blacks did not heave off their chains with any turbulent behaviour.
Barbados, then, did not begin its history as a constitutionally free society
with an experience of violent conflict. The inequality of power
distribution, however, remained such that Governor MacGregor
considered it necessary to issue a proclamation on August 13 that year
in order to reassure Blacks that it was 'absolutely impossible that any of
them can be compelled to revert to their past condition, either as
apprentices or slaves'.[8]

If emancipation represented a major battle won by Blacks and the British anti-slavery movement, then it would not be outrageous to suggest that in Barbados, slave owners might have benefited from their defeat. During the period after 1816, the year that enslaved Blacks had attempted to free themselves by armed rebellion, the imperial government made some effort to loosen, even if slightly, the firm grip which the white community held over the Black population. On May 16, 1838, the Assembly's Act for the Abolition of the Apprenticeship System meant that slave owners had no choice in removing the traditional legal forms of socio-political control. Neither the Blacks nor the British Government, however, were surprised when they immediately began the task of reconstructing a new machinery of black domination and the formulation of social policies for the social control of the new social order.

These new measures were designed to ensure that the plantations survived by having access to a reliable supply of cheap and subordinate labour. The Apprenticeship system, defined by imperial administrators as a process of transition from slavery to freedom, was understood by the enslaved as a minor modification of the slave system. Others shared this opinion and were unequivocal in the view that it was the beginning of a long-term arrangement to perpetrate a fraud upon Blacks in order to maintain the social and economic dominance of the slave owning elite. According to J. Sturge and T. Harvey, who observed the so-called transition in Barbados:

> The apprenticeship is not Emancipation, but slavery under another name; and though it appears to be in some respects a modified and mitigated slavery, it has also its peculiar disadvantages, which more than counter-balance whatever good it contains. It is not in any sense a state of preparation for slavery. [9]

Two other contemporaries, J. Thome and H. Kimball, described the apprenticeship system as a 'mockery to the hopes of the slaves . . . as it was held out to them as a needful preparatory stage for them to pass through'. [10]

Rise of Samuel Jackman Prescod

Sugar planters were not convinced that they had eliminated the radical leadership of the black community during and immediately after the 1816 Bussa Rebellion. In the 1820s anti-slavery protest continued with Sarah Ann Gill emerging as a popular leader. By the early 1830s, however, Samuel Jackman Prescod, a free coloured man, became associated with anti-slavery opinions that emanated from the slave yards. By 1838, he was the most popular and astute spokesman for the emancipated people and represented a major figure around which criticisms of planter policy were rallied.

Prescod was in many respects an outstanding individual. He was born in 1806, the son of a free coloured woman and a white planter. He had broken socio-politically from the pro-slavery ideological thrust of his free coloured social group. He became editor of the *Liberal*, a radical newspaper which expressed the anti-planter grievances of a range of disadvantaged groups within the free community. Under his editorship, the *Liberal* gave expression and leadership to the black working class. On June 6, 1843, black voters in Bridgetown contributed to his election to the Assembly – the first man of known black ancestry to sit in the House. By the time of his death on September 26, 1871, he had agitated on behalf of the less privileged classes on a wide range of issues. The range of his political arguments suggests that he was undoubtedly the greatest leader of popular opinions in the colony during the post-slavery era.

On Wednesday, August 1, 1838, Prescod wasted no time in congratulating the Blacks on the attainment of full legal freedom. In the editorial of the *Liberal* for that day, he wrote: 'Fellow men and Friends! I have lived to see you declared Freemen, and I hope. . . to live and see you made free . . .' This statement illustrated the perceptions of Prescod on the meaning of the landless emancipation and his intention to agitate on the Blacks' behalf for the gaining of the civil rights which would give acceptable meaning to the term 'freedom'.[11]

Neither did he procrastinate in informing former slave masters that there would be no tolerance of the socio-political disabilities which still shaped the lives of the landless majority. On August 11, 1838, his editorial stated: 'Gentlemen, you cannot require me to inform you, that it is not by declaring people free, that they are made free in reality – but that it is by conferring on them such privileges as put some proportion of the power which you now exclusively enjoy into their hands'. It was the objective of winning some measure of political power for the black people, by strictly constitutional means, that shaped the political activities of Prescod over the next 20 years.[12]

The spirit and objectives of emancipation, as perceived by the British Parliament, was resisted by Barbadian planters in the years after 1838 as tenaciously as in the years before. Blacks and a few within the British abolitionist movement had hoped for an emancipation that would result in 'humane and amicable labour relations'; instead they were confronted with the stubborn determination on the part of planters to retain exclusive control over the labour market in a manner which was reminiscent of slavery. On October 27, 1838, the *Liberal* carried a memorial prepared by Samuel Prescod, on behalf of the Central Negro Emancipation Committee, and which was sent to Lord Glenelg. It set out the nature of these fears, that Whites who had opposed emancipation would use their considerable power to undermine and reduce the freedom Blacks had won. It stated:

> Constituted as society is at the present moment . . . with a large body of the labouring classes who have been long and cruelly oppressed, and who have but just emerged into a state of freedom, on the one hand; and with an influential and powerful body of proprietors or their representatives, full of fears, jealousies, and prejudices, and still retaining to a great extent the power to oppress – on the other hand – the Committee feel that they should not discharge the duties which they are solemnly pledged, did they not exercise the utmost vigilance to detect and use every legitimate and constitutional means to prevent any attempt to reduce the liberated slaves, either legally or practically under a new state of bondage, and thus to deprive them of the blessings of that freedom which has been purchased at a costly sacrifice of the national treasure, and which has been guaranteed to them by the solemn decisions of the British Legislature.[13]

Prescod considered it necessary to set up an oppositional political programme to such reactionary attitudes, and to use his skills as an advocate and journalist to construct a watchdog network in order to protect the benefits of emancipation from White encroachment and resistance.

In addition to a failure to relate fairly to the freed Blacks, sugar planters who still dominated government at all levels, refused to place the kind of importance on pro-worker rehabilitation social policies, such as education, health, poor relief and housing, that the imperial government had wished for. Rather, the planter Legislature concentrated upon the task of strengthening social control over Blacks since it feared that the abolition of the slave laws opened up avenues along which Blacks might wish to travel to the detriment of the White community.

Solicitor-General Clarke summed up this fear of pending freedom in 1838 as follows:

> . . . the good order of the society and the prosperity of the colony would be placed at the mercy of a population, composed of recently emancipated slaves, who although they now are well disposed towards their employers and loyal to Her Majesty might soon cease to be so and become the prey of the disaffected.[14]

The *Barbadian*, the principal newspaper of the White elite community, in its edition of August 10, 1838, expressed the extreme version of Clarke's sentiment and opinion:

> The bad feelings we noticed in our last paper is spreading through those very estates where there is least reason to expect it. Striking work is spreading like wild fire, who would have expected that people accustomed to the kindest, most humane liberal treatment, are refusing to work, absolutely refusing to enter into any contract for wages, which may subject them if they violate it to be taken before a magistrate, and yet claiming to hold possession of their houses and land . . . There is not only passive resistance, but it has come to our knowledge that there is an insolent bearing on the part of some of the labourers – a sort of defiance in their manner – which calls for some prompt and energetic measures on the part of the magistracy of the island.[15]

To the extent that editorials in the *Barbadian* reflected planter class opinions, the former slave owners were calling for a major legal and military offensive against the emancipated community in order to ensure its continued subordination on grounds of race and class. Emancipation for planters was not to produce upward social mobility and a new mentality of liberation among Blacks. All such thoughts and expectations, in their opinion, were to be confronted, crushed, and discredited.

Landless Freedom

The colonial and imperial agenda for emancipation in Barbados was to give effect to a landless freedom for the black community. Landlessness for Blacks was considered the principal modality by which the White community could maintain its monopoly hold on the economy, the political process, and assure white social elitism. At the same time, landlessness would assure black subordination in the market place by creating employment conditions favourable to employers, such as low wages and the binding of workers to estates at subsistence levels. Poverty assurance for Blacks was associated with their landlessness, and this condition was considered necessary to drive Blacks to work at below subsistence wages, and under legal conditions that they knew to be contrary to the spirit of freedom they had desired, imagined, and fought for. Land was considered the basis of social and political power, and economic independence. This was so for all social groups within the colonial world. It gave the right to vote, to maintain economic viability, and win respect and recognition. Blacks wanted land, and they wanted it with an intensity that was equalled to that of their former slave owners.

According to George Belle:

> In 1838 all of the island's agriculturally usable land resources, estimated at 100,000 acres, were fully appropriated; the land owned by the Crown was reported to be nil . . ., less than 1,874 persons with holdings of one acre and over, and constituting only 1.7% of the estimated population of 1838, were in possession of almost all the land resources. . . ; the owners

of the existing 489 plantations, the main sugar units, controlled as much
as 84.3% of the total land area . . ., almost all of the 625 persons in
possession of ten acres of land and over were white. This group's ownership
of the sugar estates was virtually monopolistic in 1838; they owned all
but three of the 489 sugar plantations. In fact, only a small number of non
whites had managed to penetrate the ranks of the land owning class.[16]

The desire of Blacks for land was to give effect to their social freedom
by establishing a bargaining posture with respect to the dominant
economy. With land in hand, they could negotiate with, or reject the
wage offers of the plantations. They could reconstitute their families
broken and scattered by slavery as viable social entities. Land, they knew,
was the key to personal and community development. It could also mean
their political enfranchisement, as the right to vote was property qualified.

Landlessness, then, was a principal source of poverty, destitution,
social marginalisation, disenfranchisement, and status deprivation.
Furthermore, landlessness represented exclusion from the mainstream
of society. The act of emancipation was designed to produce landlessness
among the Blacks and was therefore an exercise in hostility and malice.
Betterment could not be an outcome for the emancipated if landlessness
was to be the primary outcome of the process. Clearly, the essential
agenda within such a construction had to be the continuing subjection
and subordination of Blacks, as well as a desire to see them fixed in the
social station that slavery had guaranteed.

The design of the emancipation project in Barbados, then, was to
produce the outcome of landlessness and its socio-economic
consequences for Blacks and Whites alike. The Bussa Rebellion of 1816,
and subsequent acts of rebellion, did not produce a political scenario
on the island that would result in Whites fleeing, abandoning their lands
in the process. Also, elite Whites in general believed that they could
continue to monopolise power, at all levels. They were certain that as a
social elite they could use the instruments of legal and political coercion
to circumscribe the objectives of emancipation legislation, and fashion a
free order more to their interest, if not liking. While they were shaken,
stirred, and stunned by the aggression with which the imperial government

had pushed through the emancipation process over their heads, down their throats, and against their will, Barbadian slave owners were determined to hold on to their lands, official power, and retrieve as much as possible from the world they had made during 211 years of African enslavement.

To do all this, they had to declare a social, legal, economic, and political war upon the black community, to let it know and feel the continuing effects of white supremacy. Confrontation, conflict, and daily contests resided at the centre of the emancipation procedures and outcomes. All sides clearly understood each other – the formerly enslaved, the imperial government, and the former slave owners.

On the question of landlessness, there was an alliance between former slave owners and the imperial government. The rationale of each group was different, but they agreed that the future assurance of white rule in the colony required landlessness and enforced labour as the reality for Blacks. The imperial government believed that black landlessness was critical to economic development. The fear of black subsistence or commercial farming, as indeed, all forms of independent activities, was very real indeed among the abolitionists in the British Parliament. They considered the idea that Blacks could deprive the planter of labour for the sugar plantation a nightmare.

On this score the abolitionists, and their friends in the British Parliament, fell into the trap set by the pro-slavery lobby. Those who defended slavery considered black independence as the beginning of colonial degeneration. They pointed to Haiti where peasant formation took up an opposition to large scale commercial farming. It was understood that there was a psychological aspect to this reaction. Blacks would not wish to work for their former enslavers unless driven to do so by fear of hunger.

Landlessness, then, was the consensus arrived at by the dominant white factions within the emancipation discourse. A few white voices did rise in support of land reform and the creation of a black peasantry, but these were marginalised. Emancipation, the abolitionists said, should not result in the economic collapse of the plantation sector, as was the case in Haiti, neither should it remove the European community from the centre of social and economic life of the colony. The export orientation of the colony should be sustained, and commerce remained the 'life line' of its inhabitants.

The linking of commerce and economic development with colonial prosperity did not take into consideration that the Blacks, with time, could transform themselves into commercial farmers. The reason was simple. Long distance trade within the Empire was part of a network of ethnic solidarity within a nationalist framework. Merchants, planters, brokers, agents, financiers, politicians, lawyers, all within the ethnic-national complex of the imperial culture, were gathered in celebration of the global power of the European. The liberated African was not invited to participate in this commercial world. Their exclusion was assured by the power of racism as a cultural action, and the chauvinism of ethnicity as an organising principle.

Not invited, then, Blacks were deemed unwilling to attend. It was said that their preference was for crude subsistence, just enough to keep body and soul together day by day, while resisting the employer whose development agenda they wished to see crash to the ground and not built on the soil they refused to till. Rationalisations took this racist twist, and every effort was made to ensure that Blacks remained landless and free to work for Whites. If their response to landlessness was listlessness, then the pangs of the belly, and the dread of the dungeons, would act as an adequate stimulus to industry.

Barbadian planters feared that the truth of the Jamaican case would subvert the reasons offered within their racist rationale. They had seen in Jamaica a large section of the emancipated black community emerge as commercial farmers, supplying the black and the white community with food stuffs, and the merchants of Kingston, Spanish Town, and elsewhere with commodities for export. They marvelled at the commercial culture and financial aggression of Blacks who were determined to build a new life upon the independent economic system they had begun during the slavery period.

The planters in Barbados had opposed the liberation of the enslaved, and continued with this attitude. The Jamaica peasant was considered a symbol of the world turned upside down, and they dreaded such an occurrence in Barbados. The Jamaican peasant made significant headway into the economy as independent producers and commercialists, and also converted their property into a political force, thereby emerging as an enfranchised community very sensitive to its constitutional rights.

According to Belle, Whites in Barbados had no intention of sharing the formal political culture with emancipated Blacks. He noted:

> The whites, by virtue of their extensive control of real property, enjoyed a virtual monopoly of political power. In 1838, almost all of the 625 registered voters whose qualifications were based on land as well as 92.8% of those whose qualifications were based on housing property were white. The white domination of the electoral franchise resulted in their absolute control of the elective institutions, the laws of political power. At the time of emancipation, all vestrymen and assemblymen were white. In fact, the whites controlled the entire governmental apparatus. The Head of the Executive, the Governor, was white as well as all the members of the nominated council and the judicial personnel.[17]

With economic assets and political rights, the Jamaican peasant laid the foundation for a democratic sensibility that resulted in an early claim upon the 'ownership' of the country as a place built upon their sweat and blood, and for which they held the first lien.

Not so in Barbados. The planter there, with the support of colonial officials, crafted the entrapment of Blacks, and devised a network of effective legal methods to this end. The main instrument which was invented, or dusted off and reinvented, was the tenantry system, a kind of local share-cropping relationship. This was in clear opposition to the concept of a peasantry, though the two were often used interchangeably. The tenantry system was about legal alienation from the land. It was a provision whereby planters rented to workers portions of inferior land for their own account cultivation on condition that they provide the plantation, to which these lands belong, and therefore on which they were housed, with dependable and frequent labour as specified by contract.

The tenantry system, then, was a form of debt bondage, a legal system of entrapment. The tenant was always determined to be in some form of debt to the plantation, always owing, never in credit, and therefore easily vulnerable to legal action, and critically, to eviction. The arrangement Blacks faced could be summed up in the term: you work or you walk. At the heart of this relationship, therefore, were the elements of bondage, compulsion, and terror. The worker was victimised into becoming a tenant, and terrorised into accepting the terms and conditions as set out by employers.

Barbados workers could and did walk, but there was no safe place on the island to run. Being able to walk and not run summed up the effectiveness of planters' capacity to determine the greater part of the culture of work and ownership. Some 80 per cent of the 106,000 acres of land that constituted the island was under plantation ownership and cultivation in 1838.

In 1840, very little had changed, and the option of the emancipated was to settle as oppressed tenants on plantation lands, or seek out a near impossible niche within the spaces between. Over 90 per cent of the 508 plantations that occupied 80 per cent of the land space was in the ownership or management hands of Whites. The 83,150 emancipated persons in 1838 were released into this closed and hostile world that offered no real options. They constituted about 80 per cent of the island population, and knew all too well that for most, material conditions would deteriorate with the attainment of freedom.

Trapped within their landlessness, and seeing no negotiable future in any direction, they engaged the process of tenantry slavery in order to be housed and fed. But they did so with all the turbulence and resentment possible. According to Bentley Gibbs:

> The plantation, then, by virtue of its substantial ownership of these assets, was the one institution capable of meeting this demand. It was the plantation, therefore, that the emancipated people were compelled to look, in very large numbers, for the necessities of house and land. There

was to be no turning of backs on the plantations. Each plantation had interests of its own. It wanted to secure an adequate number of labourers who could be compelled to give as regular and constant a service to plantation economic activity as in the pre-1838 era. It was out of this situation that the plantation tenantry system evolved.[18]

The predominance of the tenantry system was the measure of the landlessness of the Barbados Emancipation exercise. It was this new institution that combined the slavery of the past with the bondage of the future.

Terror of the Tenantry

The tenantry system as a mechanism to maintain slave-like control over the black population was carefully conceived and firmly implemented by plantation owners who knew precisely their labour requirements. While the Emancipation Bill was being discussed, some slave owners were looking to the future and conceiving systems by which they could maintain rigid control over labourers. One of the largest slave owners in the island, George Carrington, giving evidence before the 1848 Select Committee on Sugar and Coffee Planting, stated that long before emancipation had come into effect, he thought the only chance . . . of securing labour was to encourage a system of tenantry.[19]

Carrington had no intention of abandoning his three estates, or taking them out of sugar production. He would remain in Barbados, survive emancipation, and join his planting colleagues in devising a system to dominate and regulate labour. This meant keeping workers landless and surviving below the subsistence threshold. Since workers would not be allowed to own the land in order to establish their class independence, the choice was either to rent small portions to them in conjunction with their offering labour, or keep them away from any form of land possession and feed them from plantation stores. The idea of offering Blacks a wage with which they would be entirely responsible for their own subsistence was not considered an acceptable general model for two main reasons. First, it would not guarantee the planter effective control over labour, that is, to command it legally in the exclusive fashion desired. Second, it would not assure employers effective control over the level of wages and the terms of employment.

The tenantry system offered these objectives to plantation employers. They could confine the worker to the estate by contractual sanction, and at the same time guarantee exclusive access to the labourer located on the plantation. There were two variables within the relationship which tied the labourer to the estate. One was the workers' use of a plantation dwelling and the other, their use of a small parcel of land for garden cultivation. The house and land were formally free of rent as long as labour was supplied to the plantation on terms set out by the planter.

Access to accommodation and subsistence farming was predicated upon workers being tied exclusively and reliably to the plantation of domicile. The payment of a wage for labour performed was adjusted downwards to account for the worker's access to house and land. That is, a form of rent was built into the wage negotiation, even though it was not formally described as such. This aspect of the industrial relation was critical, and became overt when workers breached or rejected the terms of employment as set out by employers.

At Emancipation most Blacks did not own the huts in which they lived. These were the properties of the estates on which they were enslaved. Freedom began, then, with fear of homelessness, and the certainty of landlessness. Blacks were therefore expected by landlords to begin the process of seeking permission to dwell in houses they had made their homes, and to which they had no right of ownership. Freedom led to the legal stripping of the workers of customary facilities such as houses, access to marginal estate lands, social services such as health care, and critically, the provision of foodstuff.

The 83,150 freed workers in Barbados therefore began their emancipation without right to a home or the security of food supplies. That the estates needed cheap labour was their salvation. In effect, they could be starved and driven to destitution for non-compliance with planters. And many did starve and die from nutritional failure. The estates took prime labourers under tenantry agreements, and threw the others off onto the streets. The old, indigent, and infirmed; the sick and mentally ill were driven out as estates made structured adjustments to accommodate only the able bodied and dedicated.

Barbados emerged the prime example of emancipation working as a structural adjustment that enabled plantations to improve their efficiency. The slave plantation was notorious, at least in economic terms, for its structural rigidities, inefficiencies and inelasticity. The slave owner was bound by law and custom to house and feed the sick, old and infirm enslaved persons.

These unproductive hands constituted a measurable charge upon the estate; their presence was described as adversely affecting productivity levels. The typical Barbados plantation of 100 acres, which carried 60 slaves, could count on no more than 30 of them being prime workers. The remainder were unemployable casualties of the system, many of whom were cut loose at Emancipation. Insufficient poor law provisions to accommodate paupers and vagrants meant that estates were legally obligated to absorb significant numbers of such dependent persons. Slavery and unemployment, then, did not rest well together in neither economic theory nor management practice.

Emancipation enabled a reconciliation of such industrial relations contradictions within the economics of slavery. It enabled the plantation owner to retrench a significant part of the labour force, and rely upon a core unit. The evidence from Barbados shows that it was the only Caribbean colony to substantially increase production in the decade after Emancipation, and it did so with 25 per cent less labour than during the last decade of slavery. This was a significant productivity achievement by the sugar planters. All around them in the sub-region their colleagues experienced falling production, in large measure caused by labour shortages and unreliability. Barbados sugar producers effectively exploited their advantages within the emancipation process, and emerged as successful entrepreneurs.

The early 1830s saw the intensification of the depressed economic conditions of the 1820s. Though legal trade was allowed with the United States in 1830, a development hailed by the Barbadians, the evidence of pending emancipation led to a reduction in confidence by metropolitan moneylenders, and planters experienced a reduction in credit levels that year. 'The Great Hurricane' of 1831 added to the dismal conditions by taking the lives of some 1,590 enslaved persons and destroying an estimated £1,603,880 worth of property. The British Government made a donation of £50,000, and as a mark of goodwill temporarily lifted the customary and controversial 4½ per cent custom duty.

In spite of the 1831 catastrophe, the colony experienced bumper harvests in 1832 and 1833, and talk of economic recovery was not uncommon. Sugar production levels continued to rise through the 1830s, but planters were aware, nonetheless, that as their returns on capital increased, the traditional structures of their economy were being torn down. In 1832 the colony exported 13,325 tons of sugar, and its total export values were £408,363, while in 1838 it exported 23,679 tons of sugar, and had total export values of £960,368. Though a rapidly increasing import bill during the 1830s reduced the value of benefits derived from rising exports, planters in Barbados, unlike most of their colleagues in the colonies, were satisfied that emancipation had not adversely affected their sugar economy, and if anything, it had brought a measure of prosperity. After 1838, sugar producers prepared to strengthen their economic position, and contemporary observers, far from suggesting the ruin of this class, made reference to its socio-economic revitalisation.

There was nothing paradoxical about this experience. The explanation resides in the circumstances peculiar to the colony. Barbados was the site where the old world of slavery was most effectively retained and consolidated. Sugar planters tightened their grip, dug in, and successfully maintained their control of labour, lands, and access to liberty. They were challenged by the workers who resisted and established a renewed level of opposition and rebellion. But their successes were less than spectacular, even though their legal freedom was won in the teeth of deep, unrelenting opposition from their former enslavers.

The institution that facilitated the achievements of the sugar planting elite was the tenantry. It concretised the worker into a tenant-landlord relation that reflected the ancient world of serfdom and debt-peonage. It contradicted the modern order that emancipation had anticipated, that the worker would be a free wage agent in equal and equitable negotiation with employers in respect of the terms and conditions of work and social living. The worker became an entrapped tenant rather than a free wage earner. It was a modification of the master-slave relations rather than its abolition. In this way the Barbados worker was placed on the margins of a new form of slavery, and not distanced from its servility and sensibility.

Table 3
Volume changes in sugar production in the British West Indies 1831-1834, 1835-38

Percentage of increase or Percentage Colony decrease	
Barbados +24	Jamaica -15
British Guiana +9	Grenada -20
St. Vincent -5	Dominica -33
Trinidad -7	Tobago -36
St. Lucia -12	Nevis - 40
St. Kitts -13	Montserrat -50

Source: C. Levy, *Emancipation, Sugar and Federalism: Barbados and the West Indies, 1833-1876* Gainesville: Univ. Press of Florida p. 59

The estate tenant as a fixed or located worker received between seven and thirteen pence per day, across the island, during the post-slavery decade. Workers who were not fixed or entrapped upon an estate, and therefore not in occupation of a hut or cultivating a plot of land, received about 50 per cent more in wages. This suggests that house and land were subject to significant rent deductions to the value of 50 per cent of gross wages. It was a highly exploitative system that bred further resentment and resistance by workers.

Barbados planters established a notorious reputation as employers for the sanguine nature with which they implemented the terms of the tenantry system. In 1838, for example, William Sharpe informed the rural police that if his tenants were unreliable in their provision of labour that he wasted no time in having them evicted from the plantation. The law stipulated that employers were required to give workers one month's notice before effecting an eviction. Also, in the event that the worker refused to accept the eviction and sought a legal hearing of the case the employer was required to secure the services of the law in the form of police, a magistrate or justice of the peace, who were required to supervise all evictions.[20]

Police Magistrates provided a steady flow of accurate information on the daily workings of the tenantry system. Their records were submitted monthly to colonial officials and constituted the basis of the governor's monthly reports to the London Colonial Office. Many of them lamented the aggressiveness of the system, and found it difficult to implement it because of its injustices. They were called upon to physically remove workers from their homes and garden plots, and abandon them in the streets as vagrants and destitutes. Thereafter, they were expected to legally frustrate workers' claims upon the law for justice and redress.

In 1841 the Police Magistrate of the St Philip parish, the core of hostile worker resistance, accurately described the working of the tenantry system in his jurisdiction:

> The conditions of tenancy, as they exist at present, are, I conceive, inconsistent, in a great measure, with the free agency of the labourer; his action is circumscribed. The labourer receives a house from his employer, of which he is to be tenant without rent as long as he gives his continuous service to the employer; but if he is absent without reasonable cause from his work, a rent is charged for that day, and in most cases an exorbitant rent, so as to compel his constant service.[21]

But this was not all; the colonial government provided in June 1838, that all contracts should be in writing, and that their signature should be read as indicating an agreement for a full year. Stretching the length of servitude was as important to planters as extending the daily hours of work. The workers rebelled, and during the month of February 1840, a quarter of all the island's estates were affected by strikes. Many workers walked off the estates vowing never to return; there was widespread arson, and industrial relations collapsed under the weight of rising insincerity.

The workers, it seemed, could walk, but they could not run. Fences were built all around to contain their movements and survival initiatives. Some walked from estate to estate seeking just wages and working conditions while rejecting places that were known for anti-worker attitudes and policies. There wasn't much room to negotiate. Some planters were more liberal than others, and a few did try to show a humane face to their overwhelming power. But in general, they used the House of Assembly to formulate laws that circumscribed freedom and to punish workers who resisted the logic of the legalised industrial relations system.

In order to suppress the ability of workers to move between estates, seeking an advantage and undermining employer solidarity, the Assembly enacted a law that made it possible for located workers to be legally fined for moving off their domicile estates in search of alternative or additional employment. A located labourer could be fined five or ten pence for each transgression. This provision became known as the notorious rent-fine law, and was the centre of a major opposition campaign by workers. But it was the final touch to the legal architecture of a system whose core objective was to maintain the slavery vision of Whites towards the emancipated black community.

By 1848 less than one per cent of the agricultural land in Barbados was owned by Blacks, and 90 per cent of those working were employed in agriculture. The plantation, and its tenantry arrangement, had fossilised their landlessness and entrenched their social subordination. Black workers, the white community determined, were free to work on the estates or starve in the streets of towns. The Blacks fought back with all means available, including flight to the towns where they etched out a precarious living in the margins of the growing commercial culture.

The power of the planter, and hence the socioeconomic domination of the white elite community, was undoubtedly based upon the ownership and control of economic resources and the administrative structures of government. The sugar interest remained predominant and therefore the Legislature was mobilised into action in order to protect the rule of the Great House. The first and major consideration was the question of retaining an adequate supply of disciplined labour; around this objective all other matters revolved. Indeed, it was the determination of the Legislature to defend the sugar interests that defined the limits and nature of government policies in the years after emancipation, rather than considerations of restructuring the new order along lines of reasonable representation for all sections of the society. Not surprisingly, historians have made much of the fact that two months after the abolition of the Apprenticeship the Legislature sent for approval at the Colonial Office, Acts designed to:

(a) authorise the appointment of rural constables;
(b) prevent the increase of vagrancy; and
(c) prevent the occurrence of tumults and riotous Assemblies.

Solicitor General Clarke, who had shown noteworthy liberalism in his judgements during the Apprenticeship, became a principal defender of the planters' vision of the role of workers in the new order. In his portfolio as a law and order man, he was respected by whites for his allegedly skilful judicial mind. In commenting on the abovementioned pieces of legislation, Clarke spoke of the need for 'preserving peace in the Negro villages', and checking 'the spirit of litigation with which the Negro character is strongly imbued'. Indeed, he was instrumental in giving legislative form to the repressive attitudes and opinions of Whites, and therefore was a leading architect in the abortion of the hopes which emancipation offered for substantive change.[22]

Myth of Freedom

In August 1838, then, some 83,150 Blacks, 12,000 Coloureds and 15,000 Whites, embarked on a social course which the white ruling elite hoped to chart. Sugar planters remained in a monopolistic position as far as the economy was concerned and assumed that their political authority should not be weakened. In that year only three of the 297 sugar plantations were owned by non Whites: Ellis Castle, Ruby, and Graeme Hall — 480, 418, and 244 acres respectively. In Bridgetown, the capital, Whites owned 75 per cent of properties of an annual value of £30, or over; of the remaining 25 per cent, Coloureds held an overwhelming share.

Whites did not intend to undergo any reduction in their wealth or power, and considered it necessary to intensify the use of the ideology of racism in order to further distance themselves from Coloureds and Blacks. Neither did they intend to loosen their grip upon decision-making within public institutions. In 1838, Codrington College and Harrisons, two leading educational institutions, were still refusing Coloureds and Blacks, and the Anglican clergy showed no serious signs of desegregating churches.

All signs along the road to emancipation in Barbados led to the Great House as the centre of power in the new dispensation. The Great House would rule, and scattered as they were along the landscape, they formed a network of monuments to terror and military might. Freedom was not designed to weaken the walls of the Great House, but to ensure its long term viability within minimally adjusted circumstances. The rules of the Great House, furthermore, would continue to run along minimally modified lines, it was hoped, even though it was understood that in some ways the Emancipation Act was not dissimilar from the opening of the proverbial barn door.

In the shadow of the few hundred Great Houses were thousands of chattel houses in which the legally liberated Blacks would be socially imprisoned. The chattel house, the hovel in which Blacks reconstituted their domestic worlds after the holocaust of slavery, was an institution that expressed the landlessness of the emancipation received. A concerned

Barbadian from the Great House elite had this much to say about the Chattel House world:

> ... many of us, who live close to our Negro yards, would stand aghast if we knew what was being perpetrated and enacted within a stone's throw of our habitation. The melancholy circumstance is, that we do not know, and that many of us, alas! Take no pains to know.
>
> Furthermore who has ever entered one of those wretched hovels, those almost loathsome scenes of human existence, without being shocked at the misery and extreme degradation in every corner of the dwelling? In a wooden hut, not twenty feet by ten, with the bare, unleveled earth for a flooring, you not uncommonly find families of eight, ten, twelve in number, of every age and sex, crowded and herding together more like the beasts that perish than members of a Christian household.[23]

The limitations which planter government imposed upon reforms in education for freed Blacks, were illustrative of those found in other sectors. First, planters did not accept the imperial ruling that basic secular education for Blacks should be a prerequisite for freedom. Rather, they held to the traditional concept that education would create among Blacks certain unrealistic expectations and therefore reduce their willingness to be productive workers. Second, they argued that educational instruction would make it more difficult for Blacks to accept their subordinate social status. That some of the leaders of the 1816 rebellion were described as literate, hardened this view among the enslavers.

Emancipation, nonetheless, opened up possibilities for Blacks to pursue educational development. There developed a 'cult' of education among the older generation who insisted upon their children's acquisition of formal schooling. The 1838 report of an Education Commission stated that 'on the part of the labourers themselves there appears to be generally a greater wish to secure for their children the blessings of education'. But as Blacks' demand for education was expanding, the financial base for educational provision was contracting owing to weak imperial policy and planter-government indifference. Church of England financial contributions diminished considerably in the 1840s, and the imperial education grant issued in 1842 was terminated in 1845.

Samuel Prescod called upon planters to vote money for educational development, but the Assembly failed to respond enthusiastically. The £750 voted for the schooling of the 'poor' in 1846 for three years was considered an insult to educational interest. Religious instruction for Blacks had priority as part of the planters' renewed campaign to improve the morality and character of Blacks. When Governor Grey suggested in 1845 that the education of Blacks should be of a secular nature he immediately incurred the wrath of the Assembly, as well as that of prominent Anglican clergymen. Black children, they insisted, should be taught how to labour honestly and 'fear God', while schools for white children were maintained from vestry funds, in addition to receiving money votes from the Assembly.

This state of affairs remained largely unaltered when Bishop Mitchinson submitted his report on education in 1875. His opposition to the status quo led to the perhaps misguided opinion that he was anti-planter in terms of his social visions and attitudes. This report, nonetheless, led to the 1878 Education Act which represented the basis of a modernising approach to working class education. It provided for the removal of responsibility for education from vestries to central government, established the basis for compulsory elementary education, removed financial aid for schools that were exclusively white, and established a Board of Education to manage and develop educational facilities and instruments. It took government, therefore, some 40 years after emancipation to accept legislative responsibility for the education of the black working class within the framework of a comprehensive, structured policy.[24]

The development of government policy on social welfare was also hampered by the effectiveness of planter opposition and an application of racist attitudes towards Blacks. The official committee on Poor Relief reported in 1844 that poverty among a major section of the black population was increasing and manifested in rising infant mortality rates. The report illustrated that vestry poor relief facilities were woefully inadequate for the new era, as plantations had relinquished their responsibility for their sick, infirm and aged persons; only a central government policy could cope with the care of these and other such socially disadvantaged persons. Since the vestries had no legal obligation to provide poor relief, and were managed by planters, many persons were refused assistance on the basis of their having a labour record which was considered unexemplary.

The Legislature moved slowly and reluctantly, in the piecemeal establishment of public welfare facilities. In 1844 it provided £4,079 for the construction of a lunatic asylum for the mentally ill, but still holding to the opinion that the poverty of the unemployed poor was self-imposed, continued to pay less attention to poor relief. In addition, the matter of public health facilities was also not given governmental priority. The expansion of slums around Bridgetown after 1838 and the unplanned growth of plantation-based villages contributed greatly to already known unsanitary conditions about the island. Minor epidemics of dysentery, yellow fever, whooping cough, small pox and measles during the 1840s did not jerk the Legislature into action, even though the mortality rate was recorded as high – especially among black youths. There had been a Board of Health operative since the legislation of 1833, but it was assigned the task of using the quarantine technique to prevent the spread of contagious disease; preventive medicine, increasingly popular in England, did not figure prominently in government policy.

It was fear of cholera, already widespread in some parts of the Caribbean, notably Jamaica, which during the mid-century forced the government to look more closely at a public health policy. This disease, noted for striking down the rich and poor alike, was perhaps the catalytic force. The Public Health Act of 1851 addressed matters of sanitation, and gave health commissioners extensive powers to search and investigate communities throughout the island. The Act was amended in 1853, extending the powers of commissioners in their preventative measures, but in 1854, the disease struck, killing more than 20,000 people. Because of high urban mortality levels, Bridgetown was reported to be the most unsanitary town in the West Indies – its water supply polluted, open cesspools and canals being used to remove sewage from households, gutters clogged and stinking, and filth lying about even major thoroughfares.

After the epidemic, Governor Colebrooke dismissed the Board of Health and appointed a new Board. This action was followed by the 1856 Public Health Act which illustrates, clearly for the first time, the government's recognition that a centralised public health machinery was necessary and vital. Bridgetown was divided into seven districts for health purposes with two medical officers appointed to each; the General Hospital came under greater administrative control by the central government, and for the first time, the basics of health studies placed in school curricula.

While social welfare measures were developed too late by the central government, law and order provisions in contrast were hastily put in place. Indeed, the Legislature was at its most productive during the decade after emancipation as civic order bills dominated the proceedings of the Assembly. The abolition of the slave codes, and the removal of planters' personal policing powers, meant that the government became the central law enforcing agency. In 1834, a constabulary was legislatively constituted, and the island was divided into seven districts for police administration; the Bridgetown district, as well as the six rural districts, each had its own police force, in addition to a prison. Between 1838 and 1850, law and order expenditures represented between 50 and 60 per cent of all government expenditures, while education, health and poor relief accounted for less than ten per cent.

In addition, Police Magistrates were given extensive powers over the black population, which they generally exercised in favour of the white community. Vagrancy laws were worded so as to give police the right to arrest Blacks in transit at any time and confine them to prisons. Laws against 'riotous assemblies' were used by legal officers to break up even civic or ceremonial gatherings by Blacks. These provisions constituted a successful frontal legislative assault upon the rights which Blacks had gained in 1838. Though Governor Smith recognised that the Legislature would never act 'except for themselves', he did little to prevent the erosion of black civil rights. It was left to the Blacks, and their coloured allies, to mount effective protest against this development.

Bishop Coleridge showed himself to be out of touch with the state of consciousness within the black community. Maybe, also, his commitment to the cause of the 'Great House' clouded his spiritual connection to the mentality of chattel house residents. For him, the novelty of freedom among the blacks would soon evaporate leaving behind the uplifting condition of their being 'sensible of the obligations which they are under to labour for their masters'. Furthermore, he added:

> They may not yet fully understand their position in the social scale; . . . they may think that a state of freedom admits of more liberties than are consistent, as they will soon learn, with the various and continual demands of West Indian agriculture. But in a few months all the misapprehensions, unreasonable expectations, and even improprieties of conduct, assignable to the novelty of their situation . . . will have passed away.[25]

This was not an accurate assessment of the situation. The level of awareness of the formerly enslaved had reached maturity deep within the trenches of the struggle against legal slavery. Many of those who celebrate emancipation as an event were martyrs and survivors of the War of General Bussa in 1816. The workers knew what they wanted, and what was feasible within the restricted circumstance. The novelty would not wear, it would be entrenched with a renewed effort at civil rights liberation.

Anatomy of a Racist Society

The English founders of Barbados as a slave society were principal players in the construction of the colonial system. They used slaves in order to develop plantations as engines of growth in the globalising economy. They rebuilt the island society upon the concept of white supremacy within the context of a multi-racial social order. The idea of race was used as the main instrument by which to separate and manage all ethnic groups.

Racism became the most effective social idea that determined ownership and access to economic resources, social status, and cultural legitimacy. Over the 211 years during which Africans were legally enslaved, socially brutalised and psychologically terrorised because of their black identity, the values and practices of racism, the idea that people can be kept subordinate, and deemed inferior because of their cultural and physical differences, was legally concretised as the norm and benchmark.

Slavery constituted a reign of terror unleashed upon the African community. In other Caribbean societies it took the form of a genocidal holocaust because the black population could not reproduce itself naturally, and suffered long term, persistent decline. The culture of anti-black racism kept the white community in a state of material and social dominance and privilege. White Barbadian intellectuals joined with enslavers, politicians, lawyers, colonial and imperial administrators in an effort to give legitimacy to the social order. A major intellectual project was launched with the objective of illustrating that slavery and the racism it required were 'natural', 'rational' and 'desirable'. Conversely, that freedom for Blacks was unnatural, irrational, and undesirable.

The leading white intellectual of Barbados during the era of emancipation was John Poyer, the local historian and political activist. He wrote at a time when the anti-slavery discourse was gaining powerful allies for an emancipation agenda. He was therefore a writer whose time was associated with the decline of the slave system, and was an advocate of its defence. It was Poyer who set out clearest how the Barbadian white community, of which he was a distinguished member, saw the importance of racism as the most important organising principle of society. In a letter addressed to Governor Seaforth, he explained the structure of Barbados society as follows:

> In every well constituted society, a state of subordination necessarily arises from the nature of civil government. Without this no political union can long subsist. To maintain this fundamental principle, it becomes absolutely necessary to preserve the distinction which naturally exists or are accidentally introduced into the community. With us, two grand distinctions

exist resulting from the nature of our society. First, between the white inhabitants and free people of colour, and secondly, between masters and slaves. Nature has strongly defined the differences not only in complexion, but in the mental intellectual, and corporal faculties of the different species. Our colonial code has acknowledged and adopted the distinction . . .[26]

In order to give effect to this vision of social organisation the white community found it necessary to develop modes of social living that violently suppressed Blacks in pursuit of their freedom. It was necessary for the white community to cultivate such modes of living within the fabric of households and domestic relations. Furthermore, they had to be sustained, passed on through generations, until the practices of racism had become common sense knowledge for each white child.

Poyer's vision, then, served the challenge of managing enslaved people on a day to day basis. When John Waller visited Barbados on the eve of emancipation he reported that Poyer's world had become the home of white children who were socialised with the values of white supremacy. He wrote:

> Accustomed from their childhood to command, these people have no notion of doing anything for themselves, and of course they grow up in habits of indolence. All who can afford it, send a coloured child with their own children to school, where it is accustomed to be kicked and pinched by its young master or mistress, just as caprice may dictate. It is usual here to make over to the child, almost at its birth, a slave of the same sex and age; which circumstance the former soon gets to learn; and though there frequently exists a kind of mutual sympathetic affection, yet a constant tyranny is exercised by the young Creole, who is hereby brought up with lofty notions of superiority over the coloured race.[27]

Critical to the implementation of the racist ideology was the notion that black life, despite the rising cost of enslaved labour, was socially cheap and readily dispensable. Whites had to be socialised into placing a similar social value upon black life as they did upon animals who were listed alongside humans as chattel and real estate in property inventories. It was as late as 1803 that legislation was passed to criminalise the casual killing of Blacks. It was resisted by a significant section of the white community who argued that the effect would be for Blacks to place a value upon their life that was not consistent with their status as chattel.

When Thome and Kimball visited Barbados during the Emancipation decade, they reported an incident that communicates clearly how Whites used the pretence of rebellion in order to murder Blacks as a form of social entertainment. They wrote:

> White men made a regular sport of shooting Negroes . . . ; one . . . young man had sworn that he would kill ten Negroes before a certain time. When he had shot nine he went to take breakfast with a neighbour, and carried his gun along. The first slave he met on the estate, he accused of being concerned in the rebellion. The Negro protested that he was innocent, and begged mercy. The man told him to be gone, and as he turned to go away, he shot him dead.[28]

But skin colour was not a reliable guide with respect to the implementation of a racist social policy. Many families that were 'mixed race' were 'whitened' through the process of inter-racial reproduction. The society therefore was required to rely as much on hearsay and memory as research in order to guard the entrances to 'whiteness'. Once a person was 'known' to be racially mixed, despite their phenotypical white skin marker, white society sought their exclusion and subordination.

This was the reality that George Sewell found among the immediate post emancipation generation of Whites. He wrote in 1862: 'The distinctions of caste are more strictly observed in Barbados than in any other British West Indian colony. No person, male or female, with the slightest taint of African blood, is admitted to white society.'[29] There was nothing scientific about it, and many mixed race persons slipped through the cracks of the system into the category of 'white'. The purpose of determining identification in the racist society was to set out a method of allocations with respect to access to institutions and public facilities. The objective was to support the principle of white privilege in all spheres of social living.

In effect, elite Whites tried to create two distinct worlds in the formal, official space, the worlds of day work and night leisure. An example of this was recorded in 1879 when members of the Royal Family of England visited the colony. The Royal Party remarked that they had seen many Blacks on their morning island tour and few Whites. Yet, at the governor's ball in the evening all was reversed: 'Tonight there was not one black face in all the rooms, and we wondered where all the English came from. Black men and women everywhere all day, white men and women only to be seen at night.' [30]

The established Anglican Church was an important site to witness the application of these attitudes and social markers. At the height of slavery, towards the end of the eighteenth century, the Rev John Brathwaite, rector at the St John Parish Church, was arguably among the five largest slave owners on the island. The Church was corrupted by the culture of slavery, and was one of its most important advocates. Each parish church kept up a colour system of seating, with the concept of 'blacks at the back' guiding all arrangements. The St Michael's Cathedral was the benchmark for this system. People of colour, whether free or slave, on the eve of emancipation, were told by the Bishop to 'remember their situation'. Rev Austin had no time for Blacks. In his opinion their only interest was 'to hear of anything that would bring them higher wages, or what they prefer to higher wages, simply food with wages, plenty to eat and sleep without work'.

Sturge and Harvey, who witnessed the emancipation experience in Barbados, noted that St Mary's church in Bridgetown reflected equally the tensions between slavery and freedom. According to them: 'Though the Rector is free from prejudice himself, distinctions of colour are still kept up in his congregation. Formerly, black and coloured persons were confined to the gallery; now they are allowed to occupy the pews in the lower half of the church.' [31]

The *Times* of Barbados editorialised that Bishop Parry 'Hates a dark skin with venom' and was an advocate for the racism that coloured the emancipation project. [32] What was true of the church as an important social institution was also the case with respect to the local vestries over which they exercised considerable influence. C.J. Latrobe, in his 1838 Report to Lord Glenelg on the state of education for Blacks, noted that the Christ Church vestry had capacity within one of its schools to admit children of 'a darker class'. But this was not done because it would lead to major political problems among white elite parishioners. He wrote:

> The vestry, it is understood, is not disinclined to open it for the admittance of those of the coloured classes; but such is the peculiar state of feeling in the island, that there is reason to believe that such a measure would not be productive of the good designed, or perhaps be acceptable to the very class which it is intended to benefit . . . .[33]

Governor Smith in 1835 indicated that the Abolition Act of 1833 did not confront the psychological aspect of white supremacy. In reference to the white elite, who sat in his Legislative Council, he confessed that the 'influence of their old prejudices' still determined their social reflections. With respect to the Blacks, the governor stated, the planters 'still cling to the love of power over them, and have yielded nothing . . .' Total power, the governor noted, had been their desire with respect to Blacks on their plantation. They enjoyed and loved the sensation, and were not prepared to give it up.

But the Blacks had never accepted that Whites should have such power over them, and had responded with patterns of resistance that were as complex as the power system they encountered. After emancipation, they merely intensified their resistance with the result, accordingly to Solicitor-General Boucher Clarke, that something new had to be tried in the interest of 'preserving peace in the Negro villages'.

The ideology of racism, then, on which Barbados as a colonial society was founded, had become the basis for a way of life for white inhabitants. All institutions were designed upon the idea, and the entire legal and judicial machinery of public administration reflected its values. Racism was endemic, but was embraced within the white community as part of a natural order — rather than a social construction.

For these reasons the processes of abolition and emancipation struck at the core of the world the enslavers had made. They resisted freedom aggressively, and were only overpowered by their own sense of inferiority and dependence with respect to the imperial power system. While August 1, 1838 was celebrated as liberation day by Blacks with a special service of thanksgiving, Whites had enormous misgivings about the event that they viewed as a calamity. Not surprisingly, then, an observer of race relations in 1851 summed up the situation in Barbados by noting that Emancipation Day 'is ignored except by the Negroes themselves, who constantly are injured by feeling that they have a cause of joy in which their superiors do not sympathise'.[34]

Conflict on the Labour Market

The imperial government assisted in perpetrating the tendency among planters to perceive workers as servile persons. It offered to supply them after emancipation with juvenile labour from English prisons or Africans from captured slave vessels. Solicitor-General Clarke, replying to the imperial offer on the Assembly's behalf, stated that colonists would not wish to be accused, once again, of enslaving Whites, nor would they wish to have African 'savages' in their midst, especially after they had removed the dependency of their economy on the slave trade. The offer, even if a gesture, was reflective of the imperial government's determination to ensure that emancipation did not undermine the plantation system and white supremacy by placing its labour supply in jeopardy.

In 1838, workers and their employers were unaccustomed to the culture of free collective bargaining over the terms and conditions of employment. Workers wanted what they considered to be a fair wage for their labour, and unslave-like conditions of work. Employers believed that Blacks tended to over-value the worth of their labour and that some measure of coercion was necessary in order to maintain a reliable supply. Conflict of interest was therefore inevitable, and both groups showed signs of digging in their heels for a struggle over the labour market.

Furthermore, it was clear to all parties to the Emancipation process that industrial relations would be influenced by forces other than the market, as employers found difficulty in coming to terms with the fact that they were required to negotiate with persons they had enslaved.

The Barbados Legislature declared planters' intentions towards Blacks in 1838 in the passing of the Masters and Servant Act, which became known as the notorious Contract Law. Other colonies also resorted to contract laws in order to maintain legal control over workers. The Barbados law was worded from the Antiguan Provision of 1834. According to the Barbados legislation, any worker who provided five days of continuous labour to a planter was deemed as hired for one year. Such a worker could reside on the plantation, and occupy cottages provided by the planter.

The Barbados Act provided for the legal dissolution of the arrangement by either party once one month's notice was given. It was the consequences of contracts breaking which showed the extent to which workers were placed at a substantial disadvantage. If a worker terminated his contract he was required to remove himself and belongings from the plantation premises. If he was dismissed by the planter, then he was entitled only to the value of crops planted by himself on plantation lands allotted him for use – the value of which was determined by a Justice of the Peace from the parish in which the estate was located.

The 1838 law also provided for the socio-political control of the hired worker during working hours. It is here that the legislation transcended mere labour supply considerations and touched upon issues of public order. If workers behaved in a manner considered by the planter as insubordinate they could be evicted from cottages, and the plantation, without wage compensation, and furthermore, imprisoned. In addition, workers could be jailed for foul language, gambling, or forming illegal combinations to improve wage levels. These provisions, in a very real way, returned to the planter some rights of social control which the government had fully assumed responsibility for under the emancipation laws. Planters implemented this last provision under a clause within the

Contract Law which gave them the right to employ private policemen on their estates.

Governor MacGregor was not satisfied with the Contract Law; he considered it unfair to workers, and believed that it was implemented within the spirit of the old slave codes. That five days continuous labour should be considered the basis of a year's hiring was, in his opinion, grossly unreasonable to workers, and the hiring of special policemen no more than an attempt to bully and intimidate them into submission. He succeeded in persuading the Colonial Office to disallow the law, as well as the one concerning vagrancy, which planters were already using rather indiscriminately. On the other hand, he supported the planters' call for the removal of special (stipendiary) magistrates from the colony on the grounds that they rarely knew enough of local circumstances in order to adjudicate fairly in master-worker conflicts.

The intensification of conflicts over wage levels and terms of labour, however, created the context for the passing of a mildly modified Contract Law in 1840. Workers believed that the 10 d per day offered by estates for field-work was too low and planters were unwilling to negotiate. In nearby Trinidad, and in Guiana, wages fluctuated between 20–25 pence per day and knowledge of this condition confirmed the impression among workers that their employers were determined to pay 'slave' wages. In response, many workers were prepared to work no more than a few days a week so as to undermine the Contract Law, even in cases where employers were prepared to offer higher wages for a week's work.

Under pressure from employers, and unaware that the imperial government had disallowed the law, Governor MacGregor informed workers that five days of continuous labour constituted a verbal contract for one year, and that only a month's notice was required to terminate the agreement. Once again workers would forfeit their right to estate housing and use of its lands if they did not contract on the estate on which they lived. Correspondence reached the governor in October 1838 that the law had been rejected, and estate life was once again brought to crisis levels. MacGregor accepted the imperial ruling, and suggested to workers that they should meanwhile make verbal but unofficial agreements with employers and continue to negotiate for better conditions. This call had some positive results and by November, most estates were reported to be in a productive and satisfactory state.

The modified Contract Law of 1840 provided for contracts of one month instead of one year. In addition, workers were now required to pay employers rent for plantation buildings and land they used which amounted to one-sixth of their wages. Of course, if the workers were not tenants on the plantation for which they worked no deductions were made from their wages. For most of 1840, wage levels for resident field hands fluctuated between nine and eleven pence per day, and for non-residents one shilling. Tenants were required to provide labour exclusively for the estate on which they resided, and in return, employers reduced the rent on cottages and ground provisions. Irregular labour could lead to the tenant's eviction with one month's notice from the estate manager.

Workers seeking to make the best of these limited conditions, would attempt to move from estate to estate in search of lighter work and better wages, but even this strategy encountered opposition from planters, government and imperial officials. When the 1840 law was finally accepted by Parliament, there was no doubt that it allowed planters to coerce Blacks into a labour market that already favoured the plantation. But Parliament, perhaps idealistically, believed that within it resided positive elements for the future establishment of mutually acceptable labour relations.

Workers had little room in which to manoeuvre; they were given the choice of starving, working under unsatisfactory conditions, or migrating. Increasing population growth over the century increased labour supply to the estates. In spite of this level of coercion, production hours did not diminish since, as Governor Colebrooke stated, there 'exists little diversity of employment' for labourers. Rural unemployment was a structural feature of the economy, and the already severe competition for limited tenantries increased rather than decreased. The located labourers system, and rent exactions for absented days, continued until circumstances following the 1937 revolution led to their legislative removal.

Spirit of Litigation

On November 26, 1839, Governor MacGregor submitted a dispatch to Lord John Russell at the Colonial Office under the title 'Affairs of Barbados'. It contained a number of documents, mostly dealing with the recommendations of a committee established to look into the idea of setting up a Court of Reconciliation to hear and settle disputes between workers in town and country. In his dispatch the governor made reference to the 'Litigious spirit that exists among' the workers. This spirit, he concluded, was finding expression not only in respect of hostility and resistance to employers, but as an explosion of contestations between the Blacks themselves who were not provided with any reliable and trustworthy legal machinery to settle their difference, and to give effect to community development within the free society.

Case of Phil, A Labourer

The evidence before the governor seemed clear enough. Blacks distrusted their employers, resented their confinement to the sugar plantations and were hostile to the working arrangements imposed upon them by the Contract Law that sought to retain the culture of slavery within freedom. The case of a labourer, named Phil, was highlighted to illustrate the attitude and ideological posture of workers with respect to the 'subject of labour and wages generally'. Phil had indicated his 'objections' to the labour arrangements determined by his employer within the context of the Contract Law. According to the Governor, Phil 'showed by his manner that there was a lurking suspicion in his mind, that the consequences (of work arrangements) would be prejudicial to his liberty'. He refused to agree to a nine-hour work day, and being bound to the estate. Another worker, Henry Buck, did not share Phil's philosophy and asked the question: 'who can make me a slave again?' Phil's position was that the terms of work as set out under the oppressive Contract Law did not put him 'on a level' with the estate manager, and in his judgement freedom was meant to place worker and employer on equal terms.

Despite the assertion by Henry Buck that the nine-hour day could not lead, or did not represent his re-enslavement, Phil, like most Barbadian workers, refused to submit to employers' demand for a nine-hour day. For them, freedom meant a work regime in which they would provide eight hours per day and four days per week. This was a reaction to the labour conditions of slavery, and freedom for them also meant time to reconstitute family life, social culture, and devise means to establish independent economic strategies to subsist and survive. In the February 5, 1840 edition of the *Liberal*, Prescod clearly argued this position for the emancipated community:

> The nine hours day's labour deprives them of that portion of time which, otherwise, they had (in the afternoon) to attend to the weeding, etc., of their garden grounds. That Saturday being a market day, they were unable to devote the whole of it to the cultivation or dressing of their lands... That besides (there is) the short period which it afforded nursing mothers to attend to their infants, and toilworn fathers to digest their hasty meals and recover their exhausted strength.[35]

Governor MacGregor was told by the workers at two plantations, Salters and Haynesfield, that they would 'die rather than yield' to employers' insistence of slave-like working conditions. The police were called in by the managers of these estates, and those who refused to accept the terms, including their spokespersons, were not only evicted from the plantations but were imprisoned.

Eviction and imprisonment were the devices used to intimidate the workers in their search for justice and freedom. The state of labour relations indicated the extent to which the meaning of freedom was hotly contested by Blacks and Whites. The debate was not confined to the plantations. The principal site for the ventilation of oppositional opinions, the planter newspaper, the *Barbadian*, carried a series of editorials in 1839, the first year of freedom, that best reflected white opinion on the island. On February 6, readers were informed: 'These people are so insufferably proud of their new state of freedom that it is with the greatest difficulty any of them can be persuaded to perform any menial offices – any drudgery work of a house. Pride, indolence and insolence characterize the greater part of them . . . Their character is not improved – rather it is worse.'[36]

In general, the discourse of freedom for Blacks within the empowered white community proceeded along lines that led to judgments about the character of the 'black'. The determination to give effect to their freedom by resisting the culture of slavery was interpreted as insolence and indolence. Opposition to the attempts of employers to extract the essence of freedom from the meaning of emancipation was considered insubordination. Whites were settled in their minds that freedom for Blacks merely meant freedom to serve, be subordination, and to accept servility.

But the workers had other ideas. Solicitor-General Clarke, recognising the spirit of resistance within the black community, informed the governor on October 29, 1839, that the 'many errors and irregularities in the character and conduct of the labourers' should be considered 'the effects of their past condition than a part of their natural disposition'. Whatever the cause, the spirit, the Solicitor General noted, had to be checked. The mechanisms he suggested were more police and constables, and a strengthening of the legal and judicial machinery, including the establishment of a Court of Reconciliation to deal with minor offences.

The organised political responses of workers took place at two levels. Many were keen supporters and activists in formal groups such as Prescod's organisation, 'The Colonial Union of Coloured Classes' which was established in 1840. The objectives of the Union, according to the *Liberal*, September 12, 1840, were:

> To effect for our race – that is, for the Negroes and mulattoes . . . A perfect practical equality with the white race, forming with us the communities of these colonies: to put the two races upon a complete footing of equality, that so the black man and the mulatto man may . . . occupy the same position in civil society with the white man.[37]

Then, there were plantation-based cells that spoke on behalf of contracted workers on a daily basis, defining and determining the nature of freedom in the workplace. These groups, activists on the ground, so to speak, constituted the hard political interface with police, magistrates and estate managers. These were the leaders who, according to Governor MacGregor, were spreading a spirit of litigation and rebellion throughout the island, representing their freedom as a state of opposition to white authority and society. They determined the proliferation of strike action on the estates, and constituted the ancestral leaders of the proto-trade union movement of the country.

Surrounding these actions was the frequent burning of plantation canes as an act of rebellion and negotiation. Arson was a popular instrument of resistance during slavery, and persisted into the free society, at times with greater frequency and comprehensiveness. Arson attacks on the estates and period strikes led by plantation workers within the context of the slave-like Contract Laws were the most visible, universal expressions of opposition to what Prescod called the 'management system' of plantation colonialism and its racist value system.

Throughout 1839 and 1840, Governor MacGregor informed the imperial government that the Blacks were burning canes with increasing frequency in order to let it be known that employers' attempts to restore their enslavement would be resisted. The print media, likewise, reported daily the incidents of arson, and the social outrage of workers.

The governor understood this aspect of industrial relations all too well, and on February 8, 1840, informed Lord Russell at the Colonial Office in London that the commonplace arson attacks were 'indiscriminate' and 'resorted to by the peasantry for the gratification of resentment either against the employers or fellow labourers'. His strategic response was for more police to patrol the countryside, and the publication of a reward system to encourage informers. He offered a reward of £300 to persons who provided the police with information leading to the conviction of arsonists.

The attack on estates continued, particularly in the parish of St Philip which was identified as the heartland of organised rebellion. When Sunbury estate was fired in January 1840, a labourer by the name of Jack Will was accused. The workers on the estate refused to comment on the matter and frustrated the investigation. The governor notified the Police Magistrate that he had increased the reward for information that could convict Will, but received no support and the case was eventually abandoned. This was the general pattern. Workers sought to establish solidarity in the face of employer treachery. In general, they were successful, but the oppressiveness of the Contract Law remained.[38]

Flight from the Land

During the 'Barbarity Times' Barbados was a main base from which the English colonisation and settlement of Trinidad, Guiana and the Windward Islands was launched. Blacks, both enslaved and free, were part of this process. In this way the enslaved community was able to develop a considerable knowledge about regional affairs. Barbados runaways regularly fled to these neighbouring colonies, and together with those Blacks who worked on the schooners that plied between the colonies, they contributed to the store of information available to plantation workers about economic conditions in the region. This information represented the basis on which Blacks built their emigration movement after 1838.

News received by Barbadian workers suggested that wages in Trinidad and Guiana were much higher than at home, and that in those colonies there was relatively unrestricted access to farming land, and at lower prices.

Such factors alone were sufficient to entice Barbadians to migrate to these colonies once the tenantry system had taken shape as a new form of slavery. During the Apprenticeship, Guianese planters had expressed an interest in attracting Barbadian workers; from this time they had also incurred the disapproval of Barbadian governors and sugar planters who feared that able-bodied migrants would abandon their families and other dependents who would add to the list of poor law recipients. Planters feared a drain upon their prime labour stock, and increases in wage levels. Not surprisingly, the Legislature passed a law to prevent persons enticing inhabitants to 'desert their homes and families and helpless infants'. This law provided that potential migrants had to first obtain a ticket of leave from the vestry of the parish in which they resided. The vestry was empowered to refuse the issue of such a pass if it believed that the applicant would leave destitute any dependents.

Table 4
West Indian Wages for First Class Labourers, 1840-1850

Year	Barbados	St Lucia	Trinidad	Guiana
1840	10d	15.3d	-	15.5d
1842	1.5.3d	15.10d	25.1d	25.0d
1844	15.1 d	15.8d	25.1 d	25.0d
1846	15.0d	15.8d	25.1 d	25.0d
1848	7d	15.3d	25.1d	15.8d
1850	8d	15.4d	25.1 d	15.6d

Source: E. Riviere, *'Labour shortage in the British West Indies after Emancipation', Journal of Caribbean History, Vol. 4, 1972*; Governor Walker of Barbados to Lord Newcastle, 15 July, 1863, co 28/196

But Guianese planters saw in the Barbadian worker a seasoned productive colonist who was prepared to tackle frontier conditions. As such, in 1838, they voted £400,000 for the sponsoring of an immigration programme to attract Barbadian and other West Indian workers. Barbadian planters went on the offensive and launched a propaganda campaign to the effect that the Dutch and English planters in Guiana were preparing to re-enslave Blacks, and that the majority of migrants would die of yellow fever, malaria or cholera within one year. In addition, the Bridgetown Legislature provided that a fine of £50 would be imposed upon any person who attempted to encourage workers into emigration.

Workers responded by accusing the Legislature of tampering with their rights as free persons to travel and work where they so desired. Governor MacGregor denied that this was the intention, and set about to ensure that emigration schemes were bona fide and that facilities on ships were adequate. But the Council had already declared its opposition to the workers' right to emigrate from the colony in search of better opportunities. Even before agents had arrived in Barbados to formally organise for workers to exercise their freedom to emigrate, Council's position was that any attempt to encourage workers:

> to emigrate must be viewed by the Proprietary body with a very jealous eye. If therefore, agents from British Guiana, or elsewhere, be sent to Barbados to tamper with the agricultural labourers, the Legislature will feel themselves called upon to adopt measures of retaliation and at any cost. [39]

By 1840, hundreds of predominantly male workers had departed for Trinidad and Guiana. In that year, the Barbados Legislature, defending the interest of the plantation sector, passed a law which made it illegal for emigration agents to function in Barbados, which was allowed by the Colonial Office, though pro-emigration lobbies in Barbados argued that it infringed upon workers' rights to free movement. By January 1841, however, over 2,500 workers had departed for Guiana, and by 1870 at least 16,000 had emigrated to other colonies.

Not all migrants, however, turned their backs totally upon the land of their 'nativity'. For most, migration was one way of socioeconomic betterment and not an anti-Barbados action. The evidence relevant to the Guiana migration shows, for example, that Barbadians rarely committed themselves to any estate for a length of time, but attempted to use the variation in seasons between the two colonies to their advantage. The Guiana immigration report for 1883 stated:

> They seldom labour for more than limited periods on sugar estates. A large proportion of them arrive in the colony after the end of June when work becomes scarce in Barbados, and return to the island to spend

Christmas and croptime, while large numbers of them remain in Georgetown to swell the ranks of the unemployed.[40]

This pattern of seasonal migration, then, reflected both workers' regional perception of the labour market as well as an attachment to their homeland. Though some workers went as far as Cuba, Curacao and Brazil, migration was not an attractive option for most, and the 110,000 Blacks recorded as resident in the 1871 census data attest to this. Most workers prepared to make the best of the limited opportunities offered in the colony, and this assisted in ensuring that the plantation system survived as the predominant socioeconomic unit.

Peasant Movement

The ability of workers to cement their freedom with the ownership of land was limited by four major factors. First, the plantation sector's monopoly over land ownership and land-use patterns: 441 of the 508 estates in 1842 engrossed 81 per cent of the 106,000 acres of land which comprised the colony. Second, the refusal of the planters to provide land for sale to workers as policy; there were no crown lands, as in

Table 5
Land Values in the West Indies in the late 1840s

Average Price Range	
Colony	per Acre (£)
Dominica	1-3
Trinidad	1-13
Guiana	1 -30
Jamaica	4-20
Antigua	40-80
Barbados	60-200

Jamaica, which could be squatted on by workers. Third, the price of arable land was prohibitively high, which meant that the accumulated wages of workers could hardly allow them to enter the land market.

Fourth, Governments, both local and imperial, were committed to a policy of creating from the Black population a landless proletariat rather than a peasantry.

The plantation sector in Barbados was clearly victorious in confining peasant activity and formation to levels tolerable to sugar production and the white community's conception of the role of Blacks within the economy. In 1845, 30,000 people provided regular labour to the estates. These workers who were offered the lowest wage in the region by a major sugar economy, could not be expected to make cash down payments on land. Some did manage, however, to obtain freehold ownership of small amounts of land, and functioned socioeconomically as peasants. They were few in number, and posed no problem, political or economic, for the planter class. In 1842, the Police Magistrate of the St Michael parish gave the following account on the factors limiting peasant development:

> Little progress has been made by the labourers in establishing themselves as freeholders, not from any disinclination on their part to become so, but circumstanced as our island is, there is little probability of any great number being able to obtain freeholds. The reason is obvious; there is not in the whole island a spot of waste land fit for cultivation; and as the land is principally divided into plantations, the proprietors are not likely to sell off small plots for that purpose; and there being no public lands available it is plain that freeholders to any extent cannot be established in this country.[41]

The tenantry system did allow Blacks some access to land, and plantation owners were, in general, keen to allocate marginal lands for their use in return for a reliable, resident labour supply. But the insecurity of land use under this arrangement, plus the fact that land was rented in return for regular labour, meant that Blacks could hardly have perceived this form of access to plantation land an effective way of entrenching their socioeconomic freedom. At best, the tenantry system was an extension of what had gone before during slavery – when planters, in order to reduce their food bills, allowed the enslaved to cultivate small plots around their homes. The tenantry system did allow some Blacks to become, over time, lease hold users of land without offering their labour to estates, but this development should be distinguished from the socioeconomic implications of owning land by freehold. In 1897, nonetheless, it had been estimated that about 8,500 of these small proprietors had legally acquired about 10,000 acres of land while another 4,580 acres were rented by labourers from plantations.

Occasional acts of planter philanthropy, however, allowed some Blacks to obtain freehold ownership of land. For example, the death of Reynold Alleyne Elcock in 1821, owner of Mount Wilton Plantation in the St Thomas parish, afforded his enslaved workers the opportunity of buying land through his bequest. In 1841-42, part of the estate was subdivided and Blacks managed to purchase by instalments 'small allotments of land in no case exceeding two acres, and in many cases much less'. As a result, the village of Rock Hall was established by labourers who were undoubtedly proud of the fact that they were owners of land rather than leasers, or plantation tenants. Similar circumstances surrounded the formation of Workman's village in the St George parish. In this case, Peter Chapman, owner of Enterprise Estate, in 1856-57, divided up 102 acres of the Estate in 1-2 acre lots which labourers purchased by instalments.

Blacks who were artisans, or in possession of well remunerated skills, who could accumulate savings, constituted the majority of those who held freeholds on land. In 1860 the number of freeholders was officially stated at 2,674 and in 1878, 4,982. Some of these freeholders were poor Whites, Coloureds and Blacks, who were probably not enslaved in 1838. Most, however, used their access to land in order to accumulate cash by producing and marketing foodstuff; this meant the consolidation of the traditional occupation of huckstering which was the main way in which slaves had participated in the economy as autonomous agents. Some planted sugar cane which was milled by plantation factories and received annually moderate sums of capital. In such cases, their dependency upon the plantation sector meant that they could not organise opinions considered hostile to the white community. In general, then, some Blacks were able to use land ownership as an instrument to strengthen their position within the plantation dominated order. But very few were able to emerge as substantial landowners with social and political influence.

NOTES

1   Smith to Goderich, May 7,1833, 'An Address of the Governor to the Council and Assembly of Barbados', co 31/51.
2   See Hansard, 1833, vol. 17, pp. 1190-1262. Also, Stanley to Smith, July 13, 1833, co 29/22.
3   Journal of the Barbados General Assembly, July 30, 1833, co. 31/51.
4   A Petition from the Council and Assembly of Barbados to the House of Commons, co 31/51, Jul 6, 1833.
5   C. Levy, *Emanicpation, Sugar and Federalism: Barbados and the West Indies* 1833-1876 p. 35. See also Journal of the Barbados General Assembly, July 30, Nov. 29, 1833, co 31/51.
6   Smith to Stanley, May 23, 1833, co 28/111; Smith to Spring-Rice, July 28, 1834, co 28/113. Smith to Stanley, January 22, 1824, co. 28/113; Smith to Spring-Rice, July 31, 1834, co 28/113.
7   Parliamentary Papers, 1837-1838, vol. 44, pp. 154-155; Smith to Stanley, July 8, 1833, co. 28/111. 'An Act for the Abolition of Slavery . . .', April 8, 1834, Barbados Laws, co 30 /21.
8   'An Address of the Governor to the Apprenticed Labourers', July 27, 1838, co 28/123.
9   J. Sturge and T. Harvey, *The West Indies in 1837,* (London, 1838), 12, 151.
10 J. Sturge and T. Harvey, *The West Indies in 1837*, 332.
11 The *Liberal*, August 1, 1838.
12 The *Liberal*, October 27, 1838.
13 The *Liberal*, October 27, 1838.
14 Quoted in McGregor of Glenelg, Aug. 16, 1838, co 28/127., no. 2.
15 The *Barbadian*, Aug. 10, 1838.
16 George Belle, 'White Power in Barbados in 1838', unpublished Seminar Paper, UWI, Cave Hill Campus, Barbados.
17 George Belle, 'White Power in Barbados in 1838'.
18 Bentley Gibbs, 'The Emergence and Development of the Tenantry System in Barbados, 1838-1860', unpublished Seminar Paper, History Department, UWI, Cave Hill Barbados.
19 Evidence submitted to the Select Committee on Sugar and Coffee Planting, (Lon. 1848), p. 51.
20 Evidence submitted to the Select Committee on the West Indian Colonies, (Lon. 1842), p. 117.
21 Enclosure, no. 12., Greg to Stanley, April 19, 1842, Evidence submitted to the Select Committee on the West Indian Colonies; p. 758.

22 MacGregor to Lord Glenelg, Sept. 8, 1838. co 28/125.
23 'Meliora' [Rev. Edward Pinder]. Letters on the Labouring Population of Barbados (1858, London), pp. 12, 13, 28.
24 See John Gilmore, 'Episcopacy, Emancipation, and Evangelization', Department of History Paper, UWI, Barbados.
25 Bishop W.H. Coleridge, *Charge* (Bridgetown, 1838), p. 31–32.
26 John Poyer to Governor Seaforth, 22 June, 1801, Seaforth Papers, GD 46/5, Scottish Records Office.
27 John Waller, *A Voyage in the West Indies* (London, 1820), p. 19.
28 J.A. Thome and J.H. Kimball, *Emancipation in the West Indies* (NY 1936), p. 77.
29 G. Sewell, *The Ordeal of Free Labour in the British West Indies* (London, 1862), p. 67.
30 G.J. Chester, *Transatlantic Sketches*, (London, 1869). 99. Rev. Austin, cited in K. Davis, *Cross and Crown in Barbados* (NY. 1983), p. 85–86.
31 Sturge and Harvey, *The West Indies in 1837*, 144.
32 The *Times* [Barbados], June 29, 1870.
33 C.J. Latrobe, Report on Negro Education in the Windward and Leeward Islands (Lon. 1938), pp. 43, 96-7.
34 Cited in J. Gilmore, Episcopacy, Emancipation, and Evangelization, op.cit, 39.
35 The *Liberal*, Feb. 5, 1840.
36 The *Barbadian*, Feb. 6, 1839.
37 The *Liberal*, Sept. 12, 1840.
38 Police Magistrate Report, Jan. 11, 1840, co. 28/133.
39 Minutes of Council, May 15, 1840, co 28/124.
40 See J.P. Mayers to Vernon Smith, 14 Dec., 1839, co 28/132.
41 Police Magistrate Report, Nov. 1842. co 28/133.

- *Three* -

Emancipation Betrayed:
Struggle For Freedom Begins
1838–1897

Samuel Prescod and Mass Consciousness

$\mathscr{T}$he political forces that informed Prescod's leadership emerged from the protest actions of workers in relation to the provision of the Contract Law. Workers expressed their grievances beyond the plantations at the community level. Prescod's primary contribution, therefore, was not in the initiation of such parochial protest, or formulation of radical thought, but in giving islandwide leadership of popular opinions at the highest institutional levels of society.

Prescod challenged the persistence of white supremacy government. In a series of newspaper articles, public speeches, and memoranda, he represented the workers in their struggles against those sections of the elite who sought to derail the emancipation project. The plantocracy and their imperial supporters saw him as their principal enemy, and sought to discredit his voice. He endured and survived 30 years' invective, such as indicated by the language found in this editorial in the planter newspaper, the *Barbadian*:

> Every man, of every class, of sober sense and reflection, must read with most righteous indignation, the arrogant, insolent, lying and mischievous document called, *Proposals for Colonial Union of the Colored Classes* Samuel Jackman Prescod, that most mischievous damagogue is supposed to be

the chief instigator of this wonder working association. The object of
Prescod can be no other than that of shutting out from the pale of society,
every man who has no African blood in his veins, and in fact of extirpating
if they can the whole race of purely white people. The attempt, therefore,
now to kindle discontented, a rebellious spirit in the colored population
is so injustifiable. [1]

The Blacks, however, were first to recognise the extent to which the
Contract Law attempted to perpetuate slavery aspects of labour relations,
though it was Prescod who had been identified with the articulation of
this theme within official circles. In a memorial written on behalf of the
'Central Negro Emancipation Committee' addressed to Lord Glenelg,
Secretary of State for the Colonies, which was also published in the *Liberal*
of Wednesday, October 27, 1838, Prescod stated:

> That the majority of the colonies have abolished the apprenticeship system,
> and thus destroyed the last vestige of legalised slavery is a matter for
> unfeigned thankfulness; that they have clogged the infant liberties of the
> Negroes with unjust and illegal restrictions and thus destroyed the grace
> of this act, is a matter for deep regret. The Committee will not stop to
> inquire into the motives which induced the local legislature to terminate
> the existence of slavery – whether they arose from a sense of justice or
> whether from the manifest impolicy and danger of its continuance; but
> they cannot fail to remark in the legislative acts which preceded it, and
> which had in view its termination as well as in those measures which
> accompanied and succeeded it a fixed determination to coerce labour
> under the new system and as much as possible to bring the Negro freeman
> under the tyranny of his old master. [2]

Governor MacGregor was also accused by Prescod of plotting with
planters to reduce the civil rights of Blacks by means of repressive
legislation, and he suggested that they should withdraw their labour until
Lord Glenelg at the Colonial Office offered a clear opinion on matters
concerning labour laws. Whereas several black leaders were arrested for
the expression of these and similar opinions, Prescod remained free to
write his critiques of the Contract Law in the *Liberal*.

The July 8, 1839 edition of the *British Emancipator*, published a letter by Prescod in which he clearly demonstrated that the white community had used its enormous legal, social and economic power to keep slave-like conditions as the norm for the employment of Blacks. Freedom, he noted, had been compromised and undermined. The colonial government, an instrument of planter power, was not committed to freedom for Blacks, and was determined to maintain the culture of slavery. The letter generated enormous controversy in England as well as Barbados, and forced the colonial government to respond.[3]

It was a lengthy letter. Prescod was comprehensive in his assessment and sought to illustrate that the historic emancipation act had failed because of white racism in Barbados, and the persistent refusal of white community leadership to accept that emancipation had come. That they had resisted and rejected freedom for Blacks was demonstrated fully. Their strategy was now to frustrate the law. Prescod stated:

> My objection to the present scheme of plantation management are; first, that it improperly interferes with the rights of the labourers, leaving them *less free* than any other class on the island – less free than he may be with complete safety to the community; secondly; that it puts off indefinitely the period when he shall be wholly under those moral influences, by which alone his character can be raised, and his social condition bettered; thirdly, that it excludes a proper market for labour, subjecting wages to improper influences, alike injurious to planter and labourers; fourthly, that it exposes the labourer to fraud and oppression, hinders him from becoming settled, and thus perpetuates the elements of evil, which may some day endanger the peace of the island; and fifthly, that it renders almost necessary the system of ejectment, which, inhuman in its mildest form, is most infamously abused to the disquietude of the whole labouring population.[4]

He ended the letter with reference to the 'spirit of opposition to freedom' that exists within the white community of Barbados, and other West Indian colonies. The result, he said, was an attitude of 'indisposition to admit the freed Negro to his full rights' that guides the 'fraudulent, oppressive policy'.[5]

Case of Betsy Cleaver

Attached to Prescod's letter to the *British Emancipator* was an account of the case of Betsy Cleaver which shows that the power of ejectment was against the spirit of the Emancipation Act. The reality of freedom for the majority of workers, says Prescod, was the constant fear of being ejected from the plantation. Ejectment meant, in most cases, further descent into destitution. Prescod noted:

> This is the mainspring of the whole scheme – on the influencing dread of this terrible infliction the planter solely depends for the labour that is to cultivate his fields; he has most unwisely left himself without other means to influence this labour, and if a dozen labourers prefer this ejectment to bad usage – it may be fraud and oppression – an estate may be left without the quantity of labour necessary to its cultivation . . . this power of ejectment is alone a sufficient objection, had I no other to the scheme. It is a most terrible scourge in the hands of an unprincipled body of men; and it is applied for anything or for nothing, with a most villainous delight in the application of it. [6]

Betsy Cleaver was an estate labourer attached to the property known as Neale's Plantation. As part of the labour arrangement established with the manager of the estate, Betsy rented half an acre of the land belonging to the estate. Her husband was a located labourer on a neighbouring plantation. When the time came to cut her canes, the manager of her estate insisted that they could not be harvested until the estate had completed its own harvest. Betsy's argument was that this would destroy the value of her canes, and proceeded to make arrangements with the neighbouring estate where her husband was employed for the harvest and grinding of her crop.

Betsy's estate manager considered her independence an act of insubordination and ejected her from the estate. Not only was she ejected but the manager ordered her

> House unthatched, and her things thrown into the road, and her infirm uncle's house, in which she had taken shelter, unthatched, after ten o'clock

at night, while the poor man slept; and before the Magistrate he boastfully admitted that he had ordered these things to be done, because the woman, his tenant, had disobeyed his orders in having her canes cut. The same thing he thought should be done upon every estate in the island, to every labourer who similarly offended.[7]

This, concluded Prescod, 'IS THE SYSTEM OF MANAGEMENT IN BARBADOS'. The attorney who represented Neale's Plantation against Betsy, provided such legal services to other properties that employed 1,200 labourers. 'Every labourer in the island,' said Prescod, 'who is a tenant like this woman, is exposed, without legal protection to ejectment for no greater act'.[8]

Prescod's judgement was that the sugar barons could not legislate for a free society, and were incapable of imagining the black worker as a social equal with a right to freedom and justice. He made reference to Prime Minister Canning who, in a contribution to the abolition debate, had outlined the principle: 'trust not to the masters of slaves in what concerns legislation for slavery'. The slave owner's mind was a danger to freedom itself, to the prosperity and happiness of the colonies, to their peace and safety. The colonial government of Barbados, then, according to Prescod, had done all it could to make a 'mockery of freedom'.[9]

It has been suggested that Prescod was probably at his most effective in assisting Blacks to resist the imposition of the emigration laws which were designed to prevent their movements into other colonies. He had accepted the role as sub-agent for Thomas Day, the Chief Emigration Agent for British Guiana, who arrived in Barbados to encourage emigration to that colony. He charged the Legislative Council with attempting to control the movements of workers in the manner that slave owners had done. In a hard hitting speech he warned the Council: 'One of the rights of freemen . . . is that of going wheresoever they please . . . Now that the people are free, some of them . . . to escape the evils of their condition here . . . are leaving the island of their own free will . . .' but there is nothing you can do, for 'the people will go!' When Prescod and other prominent Blacks attempted to form a Barbados chapter of the Anti-Slavery Society, Governor MacGregor referred to them as 'unhappy imitators' seeking 'outlets in the Colonies for the diffusion of their revolutionary poison.'[10]

Prescod was also accused by officials within the Colonial Office of attempting to orchestrate the triumph of Blacks over Whites in Barbados. He rarely referred to racial struggle within his campaign but spoke endlessly of the privileges of the propertied classes, and the misery of the landless within the context of Christian theological precepts. As leader of the 'Popular Party' (or Liberal Party) he attempted to win the support of middle class Whites, especially the more liberal urban mercantile community. This group was also in need of an effective political lobby, and Prescod hoped to provide it by also carrying the mass support. One prominent white person who joined Prescod's movement was F.B. Goodridge, a Speightstown property holder, who was a powerful speaker in his own right. The manifesto of the Party called for the protection of Black's civil rights, reduction of race/colour prejudice within institutions of governments and elsewhere, and the extension of the franchise.

Determined to ensure that the 'labouring classes' be given 'all the civil rights and immunities of free men', Prescod agitated for the extension of the franchise. On June 6, 1840 the Legislature finally agreed to a Franchise Bill which Robert Boucher Clarke, then Speaker of the House, considered 'as liberal a measure as will ever be obtained from the representatives of the present constituency'. The new constituency of Bridgetown was created, but the juggling of reduced property qualifications made a minimal difference in terms of the extension of the franchise to Blacks. Prescod referred to it in this regard as only the 'postponement of the question'. The Colonial Office agreed with Prescod and disallowed the law, though this ruling was later reversed by Lord Stanley who took over at the Colonial Office. In effect, there was no meaningful increase in the number of voters. Before the Act in 1840 there were 1,153 voters, and in 1849 there were 1,322 – less than five per cent of the population. At his death in 1871, the franchise qualifications still rigidly excluded the vast majority of Blacks.[11]

Out of Africa: Emancipation and Bussa's Heroes

Following their defeat in the fields of central and southern Barbados, by April 19, 1816, many hundreds of enslaved Blacks and a few who were free, were arrested and imprisoned for extended periods of time without trials. At the end of the month those identified as core participants in rebellions had been executed. By August 1, many were still untried and imprisoned. On August 31, the *Barbados Mercury* and *Bridgetown Gazette* issued the following statement:

> We have understood that the House of Assembly on Wednesday last, upon taking into consideration that measures ought to be adopted with regard to those slaves who are at present in confinement upon suspicion, or charged with being concerned in the late rebellion, was decidedly of the opinion that an investigation of the circumstances which led to their apprehension should take place, so that they may be dealt with accordingly: that those who have been already condemned to corporal punishment shall receive that which they are sentenced, and then be restored to their owners. With respect to those who have been capitally convicted, it was judged admissible that they shall be transported with the exception (we believe) of some of the most atrocious offenders, whose execution might prove a warning to others.[12]

Of those imprisoned, 124 were sentenced to transportation. At about 1.00 p.m. on Saturday, January 25, 1817, they were removed from the Bridgetown jail, escorted by the flank companies of the Royal Regiment to the Bridgetown wharf, where they were conveyed on board the ship *Francis and Mary* in which they were transported to Honduras. The Lt Governor of that colony, however, refused to accept them permanently on the grounds that his internal security system was insufficiently developed to effectively contain such a large number of revolutionaries. Those who survived this experience were shipped out to Sierra Leone in West Africa in 1819, the ironic punishment for attempting to gain their freedom. But the African voyage was not seen by the rebels as 'homeward bound' since the majority of them, if not all, were born in Barbados, and their views and visions of Africa had long been blurred by the rapid pace of creolisation which Barbadian slave society underwent during the eighteenth century.[13]

On arrival in Sierra Leone, Governor MacCarthy found employment for them on government work, primarily as artisans. Over the years, they showed no signs of hostility to local government, but settled as 'respectable persons' in the colony. Christopher Fyfe, in his book, *A History of Sierra Leone,* noted that these Barbadians 'had trades and found employment easily as superior servants or artisans'. Cain Davis, the free coloured man, a tailor by profession, was employed as a village superintendent, while Jacob Thomas, a horse doctor, according to Fyfe, 'grew rich as a publican, bought valuable house-property, redeemed his daughter left behind as a slave in Barbados, and sent his sons to school in England'. Simon Priddy, a stone mason, married and had children. Most seemed to have achieved an elevation in their social status and accumulated much capital. But Barbados was home, and the turmoil of being in exile was experienced by these rebels.[14]

In January 1841, the exiled rebels petitioned Queen Victoria of England requesting permission to return to their 'native island'. That permission was not initially granted, but as Jamaica was in the process of recruiting Africans to serve under contracts of indenture, the rebels were offered the opportunity to emigrate there. They refused outright Her Majesty's offer and informed her that as Barbadians, only Barbados, their homeland, would be acceptable:[15]

> *To Her Most Gracious Majesty, Victoria*
> *Queen of the United Kingdom of Great*
> *Britain and Ireland, Defender of the Faith.*
>
> *Sierra Leone, 13ᵗʰ May, 1841*
> *The Humble Memorial of your Majesty's most dutiful Barbadian subjects being inhabitants of the colony of Sierra Leone: That your Most Gracious Majesty has asked whether your Memorialists feel a desire to emigrate to Jamaica, one of your Majesty's West India Islands.*

Your Memorialists having taken into consideration your Majesty's Royal wish, begs most respectfully to say that your Memorialists duly appreciate the kind mark and condescension shown by your Majesty, yet your Memorialists cannot but feel it their bounded duty to express with extreme sorrow and regret that as the boon is not held out by your Most Gracious Majesty by which your Memorialists can return back to their own native island, they decline going to the Island of Jamaica in consequence of your Memorialists being totally ignorant of the manner and customs of that place.

In conclusion, your Memorialists most respectfully crave that should your Most Gracious Majesty be pleased to grant that your Memorialists be allowed to return back to Barbados, the place of our nativity, your Memorialists will feel extremely grateful for the same, and by which your Memorialists will endeavour to avail themselves of doing so without causing any immediate expense to your Majesty, and thus by that means it will save your Majesty from any further trouble for our transportation from this colony to any of your Majesty's West Indian Islands...

John Proverbs

John Morgan

Robert Chapman

J.Thomas

Acting for and on behalf of the other Barbadian subjects who have agreed to the foregoing statement.

Governor MacCarthy was then asked to submit character evaluations of the rebels, who by then had been living in Sierra Leone for 22 years. Acting Governor Carr commented on the rebels' conduct in the colony, and enclosed another of their memorials requesting permission to return to 'native land'.[16]

To: The Right Honourable Lord John Russell
Sierra Leone, 5ᵗʰ July, 1841

My Lord,
I have the honor to transmit to your Lordship a Memorial addressed to her Most Gracious Majesty from the Barbadians deported to this Colony in the year

1819. Their object is to obtain the sanction of Her Majesty's Government to return to their native island, Barbados. They seem to have no desire to emigrate to any other Colony. I owe it, however, to them to state to your Lordship that I have always found them an orderly and well conducted body of individuals. I would therefore beg to recommend their case to your Lordship's favourable consideration:

    I have the honour to be

    Most respectfully my Lord

    Your Lordship's Most Obedient and Most Humble Servant

                         John Carr

                         Acting Governor

In September 1841, the Colonial Office finally gave the exiles permission to return to Barbados. The letter from Secretary Russell of the Colonial Office was as follows:[17]

                         Colonial Office

                     30ᵗʰ September 1841

John Carr Esq., or

The Officer administering the Government of Sierra Leone

Sir

I have to acknowledge the receipt of your dispatch No. 14 of the 5th July with the memorial therein enclosed addressed to the (Office) by certain persons native of Barbados, who pray that they would be allowed to return to that Island from whence they were deported in the year 1819 and I have to desire that you acquaint the memorialists that Her Majesty's Government have no objection to their removing themselves to Barbados.

                RT Honourable John Russell

An extensive search through the documents reveals no evidence that the rebels ever did return to Barbados. No mention is made of them in the newspapers or in the governor's correspondence. No discussion of the subject took place in the Council or the Assembly, and no reference has been found in colonial office records. The timing of the rebels' request for repatriation is important. As anti-slavery leaders they had no intention of returning to Barbados during the slavery period. When slavery was finally abolished in 1838 they began to take measures to terminate their exile in Africa. They were rebels with an anti-slavery ideology, but they were also nativist Barbadians.

1863: Famine and Fires in the Land

The full effects of the landless emancipation of 1838 were felt by the black community in the famine of 1863. Tied to the estates, experiencing reduction in wages, and excluded from all public institutions, the black community was easy prey to the drought and disease that produced untold death and suffering. Powerless to acquire land to support their own subsistence, and with a planter class determined not to absorb costs associated with the volatile sugar market, the black community sank deeper into despair and hopelessness. By the summer of 1863, the full reality of their condition was everywhere to be seen as measured by standard indices of well-being.

The *Barbados Times* newspaper carried an editorial story in its issue of Friday, July 17, 1863, with the headline: 'The protracted drought and its consequences'. The editorial appeared under its masthead that proclaimed its motto: 'sworn to no party, of no sect am I; I can't be silent, and I will not lie.' The drought, the newspaper reported, had been 'productive of intensive suffering to man and beast'. The labouring poor is experiencing 'severe distress', it said, 'the rate of wages too having been reduced by an extension of the quantity of work allotted as a task.'[18]

The editor informs readers that the consequences are altogether quite predictable:

> Unfortunately, there have been incendiary fires in various parts of the country; and some instances of marauding. Incendiarism has long existed, and is but a savage mode of reeking vengeance on the proprietor for wrong, real or imaginary; and is justly entitled to severe punishment. That the majority of our labouring population are enduring great privation at

the present time is a fact that few, we believe, will be found bold enough
to deny; and having no prospect of improvement.[19]

The growing sense of hopelessness, the editor noted, cried out for
an action of compassion from those who monopolise the land and have
the power of government within their grasp. 'Almost everyday,' the editor
states, 'adds to the number of those who are out of employment: and
how many do exist without the opportunity of maintaining an honest
subsistence we do not attempt to divine.' The shopkeepers in the
countryside, the editor goes on, 'have openly asserted that it is utterly
useless to purchase goods, as the people have no money to buy.'[20]

The answer, suggested the newspaper, was emigration. There was no
possibility of a land reform by which a peasantry could be created. Neither
were social welfare measures to be expected from a landed class that had
opposed emancipation and continued to see labourers as chattel, in the
same category as their animal livestock. Jamaica was the place preferred,
even though it was recognised that thousands had already gone to St
Vincent, Grenada, and Demerara, and were not missed. The 'thirty
thousand of the population swept away by a fearful scourge (1854 cholera
epidemic) have not been missed', so massive have been the unemployment
and destitution. 'The signs of the times are pregnant with forebodings
of evil,' concluded the editor, 'which cause anxiety to every reflective
mind.'[21]

The preference for Jamaica as a prime site for the Barbadian poor
was based on two important observations; both of these would have
been attractive to workers, but one anathema to the planters. The *Times*
stated that 'rich land lying idle for want of cultivation, and soils which,
hitherto, produced the fat of the earth are now unutilised'. The report,
however, did not explain that an important reason for the state of affairs
in Jamaica had to do with the abandonment of lands by slave owners who
were terrorised by black rebellion, and the refusal of workers to accept
the terms of labour offered by those planters who stayed on to 'rough it
out' during the post emancipation decades.[22]

Neither did it explain that the Jamaican peasantry was an empowered group, having acquired land by means of lease, rent, purchase, and occupation, by which they secured a meaningful degree of independence from the plantation. Here, the rule of the 'great house' was broken, challenged and reduced by an independent peasantry that saw its future outside the scope of the white planter tradition. Readers were informed in respect of the Jamaican labourer:

> There is no lack of enterprise among the people of this island, as will be proved by the unceasing effort they make to improve their condition in making purchases of land, houses, stock, etc; . . . Barbados is but an Indian black hole – there is scarcely any breathing room . . .[23]

The reference to enterprise and access to land in the Jamaican context serves to illuminate the extent to which the Barbadian worker remained enslaved by their landlessness. The Jamaican black farmer was not only sufficiently independent of the 'great house', he also used his land to acquire the political franchise and exercise electoral power. This was the dread of the Barbados planters – the fear that one day black workers would be economically independent and politically enfranchised.

The following letter appeared in the *Times,* August 4, 1863:

> Sir, I noticed a spirited article in your impression of last Friday, relative to the emigration of some of the labourers of this country to Antigua, in which you refer to Jamaica as capable of holding 'the entire population of all the British colonies in the Caribbean group,' and express a wish that Jamaica may soon be in the field. As a well-wisher of Quashee and his dear Quasheba, when they are honest and industrious, I cannot but say a few words on the subject . . . almost every labourer in Jamaica is a freeholder, and is a bit of a politician 'to boot'. On election days his poney, that would cost $100 [has] only cost £7, is saddled, and he is mounted, either to support his Busha or oppose his interest at the poll; this he does fearlessly, for he has perhaps three acres in yams, plantains, and cocoa. I have known the labourers of Jamaica to work for six months without receiving a penny. But this does not affect him; he goes to his ground on Fridays, or gets a few cuts of yams which his wife takes on a donkey to the nearest market town,

and that will bring him more saltfish than Quashee should like to eat in a week. Quashee is no spendthrift. In many cases he is to be seen with his wife on Sunday on horseback, especially in the parish of Metcalfe, going to church. I am in a position to assert that the Jamaican peasantry have not their equals in the West Indies. And it would be a great blessing to the honest and industrious surplus of the population of this island, if an asylum were offered them there. You are in a position, Mr. Times, to advocate this; do so for you would be conferring lasting benefits on your needy countrymen. I shall be most happy to give you . . . information on the subject.

> In haste, yours truly,
> a Jamaican.
> 2nd August, 1863.[24]

The Barbados planters would have nothing of it. They feared the mentality herein described and did all within their power to ensure that their labourers develop a keen sense of their 'subordinate station'.

The spread of distress, leading to famine and spiralling crime, moved Governor Walker to request a full report of the state of affairs in the colony – parish by parish. These reports were published in the *Times*, and represent a useful reference with which to assess the situation. It is necessary, though, to bear in mind that the authors of these parishional reports, not wishing to hold themselves responsible for the extensive destitution around them, had reason to minimise the extent of suffering:[25]

St James
The provisions on the ground are potatoes, yams, and Indian corn; the former are few in number, and the latter in their first stage of growth. Labour-supply is reported abundant. Our correspondent says there has been a restiveness among a certain few, which, as may be inferred from the recent act, has caused some alarm . . ., for if I am bold to assert, with the exception of potato-stealing . . . there is no disorderly conduct. . .one case of potato stealing has been tried by the magistrate, and two justices, as provided by the recent act; but only one man having been convicted; he was not flogged, but sent to prison for three months, and the party to whom he sold them (a white woman) on the same night of their being stolen, was acquitted.

St Peter

Of the labourers, if I could I would fain not write at all; but my duty compels me, when they can obtain employment, I have every reason to believe that they are peaceable at work; but incendiary fires – these beacons of dissatisfaction and discontentment – have taken place, from which I imagine there is no want of the desire to retaliate for any fancied or real grievances. Desultory efforts have been made by some proprietors to keep the labourers located on their estates, continuously employed, but this I hear has been extorted by means of anonymous letters. Very many cases of suffering and want amongst the labourers have come to my knowledge.

St Lucy

Another distribution to our numerous suffering poor fellow creatures took place at the parochial school. . . It was really distressing to witness the miserable appearance of many, particularly those who are on the verge of the grave, the place appointed for rich and poor ... The following provisions were distributed: 3 barrels of meal; 4½ dozen crackers; 1½ dozen herrings; 640 lbs of rice – all at hand at the time.

St James

Labour supply is reported as plentiful as ever. Petty theft continues – many a labourer having been convicted for an ear or two of corn. This seems to be a general crime, for during the past week I saw on three occasions women to the number of eleven passing by from a neighbouring parish, tied together, and being carried to district E. police station. . . ; the only prospect open to them of improving their condition is that afforded by emigration – the benefits of which are two fold – the employer would, for their own interest, treat their work people more considerately, and the supply being less, the industrial portion would be able to command remunerative prices for their labour . . . On Saturday night last three entered a potato-field at Porters, and being overtaken by the watchman, they barbarously beat him – taking away what they required... 'Many children are being convicted for petty theft – a circumstance which calls loudly for a Reformatory School.'

St Philip

The labourers are still leaving this district for Antigua. I am very apprehensive we shall feel the want of them in the crop season for a great number has left this quarter. It may not be felt generally but in districts where they have left in great numbers the want of them will be experienced . . . There are a few potatoes on the ground, but the villains are making away with them . . . On Saturday night a whole field of potatoes, less two rows, were plundered from Mount Pleasant. At Rices, last night, the buildings were broken and a quantity of yams stolen. There was also a fire there.

The response of the planters to workers' destitution were to urge the magistrate courts and police constables, to increase the severity of punishment. The call for stiffer punishment was accompanied by an assertion of the undeserving character of most workers, who it was said, carried deep resentment to their former slave owners.

The case of the potato-raid at Holder plantation in the parish of St James generated considerable controversy. Two boys were convicted and sentenced to three months' imprisonment. The boys had sold the stolen potatoes to a white woman, Mrs Bullen, at 2 or 3'o clock in the morning. Mrs Bullen knew that the boys had no land and wanted cash. She was acquitted. The judgement was considered by Blacks in general as a clear case of racism and white solidarity. Some Whites, the *Times* reported on August 18, also shared this view.[26]

Food Rebellion in St Philip

The July 7, 1863 issue of the *Times* reported a series of events under the title 'Riots in St. Philip'. The story related to a ship named the *Lapwing* of New York that was wrecked off the coast of the St Philip parish. The account of what follows illustrates the overall condition of the working people, particularly their hunger, destitution, and willingness to fight for survival in the death threatening circumstance.

According to the governor the wreck was altogether an unfortunate occurrence, 'for the want of employment amongst the people, owing to an unusually long drought . . . added to a recent scarcity and high price of American breadstuffs, have produced a considerable amount of idleness and discontent among the peasantry and their consequent inclination to mischief found a vent in the plunder of the wreck.'[27] When news was circulated in the parish that food was aboard the vessel, according to the *Times:*

> several thousand persons, composed for the most part of the labouring classes of Christ Church, St Philip, St John, and St Joseph, quickly assembled. When the police attempted to put stop to the taking away of goods for the night, the immense crowd finding it an easy matter to overcome the police, used them severely, and proceeded, most disgracefully, to steal every article that had been saved during the day. [28]

Driven by hunger, many risked their lives climbing down the cliffs to the seaside.

The mounted Cavalry was called out to suppress the starving people, the police having retreated on account of many injuries sustained in the effort. Two men were charged with bayonets, subdued, handcuffed, and taken away as prisoners – attached to the stirrups of horses. These methods of suppression enraged the already angry crowd, who made an effort to rescue the men. The Cavalry drew swords, and turning on the ragged crowd, injured many persons and took more prisoners. Throughout the night crowds of people roamed the parish attacking police whenever they saw them, and destroying young canes in the field. The commander of the Cavalry stated that his swift action had prevented the rebellious workers from taking over control of the entire parish. The *Times* reporter however, responded to this claim with 'what nonsense!', and questioned the integrity of the army's decision to pull out of the parish in the evening when the evidence of rebellion and criminal search for food was mounting.

The suppression of the people in the vicinity of the wreck served, according to the governor, to ignite passions elsewhere. He wrote:

> Although the immediate cause of this excitement has been removed by the disposal of the wreck, and the minds of the people on the spot quieted, the disposition to turbulence which there originated has been communicated to other portions of the labourers in the same parish of St. Philip, and has even extended to the neighbouring parish of St George,

where large gangs have been entering on the provision grounds of several of the estates and helping themselves.[29]

Wage Riots in St Thomas

On July 25, Governor Walker in his weekly intelligence report to the London Colonial Office informed of the rebellious state of workers in Barbados, and added a twist to his previous reports. He regretted having to inform the Secretary of State for Colonies that 'altho' we have succeeded chiefly by night patrols and other means in repressing the disturbances in St Philip's Parish, there has arisen in another district of the island a spirit of lawlessness and disaffection which I find considerable difficulty in checking.' He was making reference to the parish of St Thomas where numerous 'bands of people have been going about by night from one estate to another digging up provisions in large quantities'. These bands of labourers, he said, travelled with 'arms in their hands in such numbers as to overpower or overawe the ordinary watchmen of the grounds'.[30]

Walker, however, was no longer satisfied that the assault of the workers upon the plantations was confined to the search for alleviation from the famine in the land. In his judgement the workers were expressing additional sentiments. He noted: 'There is no longer any pretence that these robberies are committed by the people to satisfy their want, because many of the plants have been wantonly torn up and strewed about the fields. There is undoubtedly a question of wages mixed up with this movement.'[31]

Walker was aware of the significance of this statement, so too were the planters who immediately responded by attacking the governor for taking his analysis beyond the common discourse of food stealing. The governor wrote that:

> The planters are very angry with me when I say so. They aver that there has been little or no reduction of wages, but whatever it may have arisen from, whether from the inability of the planters to give the same quantity of work, or from the difficulty with which the labourers on account of

hardness of the soil accomplish his ordinary task, or from the task having been increased, the labourer is undoubtedly not earning the same amount of money which he has been accustomed to do. I can trace the dissatisfaction to no other source.[32]

In order to strengthen his case, Walker informed the Secretary for Colonies that in many cases the robberies were not confined to provision grounds. In several instances, he said, there has been a destruction of other property, and the incendiary has been busy at work in firing trash, cane pieces, and megass heaps. Last night, he added, a fire at Mount Hillaby Estate did enormous damage to buildings. It is important to note, he surmised, 'for some time past there has been some misunderstanding between the manager and the labourers, and the police and the people came into collision'.

The Mount Hillaby situation escalated, and according to the governor, the details of the events suggest that hunger-driven attacks upon food supplies were an insufficient explanation. He wrote:

> The Police, having been pelted with stones, and two shots fired from the mob, the Magistrate of the parish, having in vain exhorted the people to refrain from further violence, was at last obliged to give orders to the Police to fire, but to do so over their heads. This having no effect, and the people becoming indeed more outrageous in their attack upon the police, the Magistrate ordered the latter to protect themselves, when they again fired upon the mob who there upon withdrew.[33]

To maintain the suppression of workers in St Thomas, Walker assembled a stronger force of police who were dispatched and stationed at strategic points within the parish. He also informed the people that any further turbulence would be met with the deployment of 'Her Majesty's troop' in the parish.

The tensions between the governor and the planters with respect to the cause of workers' rebellion deepened as newspapers reported his account of events. The planters in turn accused him of stimulating rebellion by giving workers' a sense of their moral right to protest their condition. Some were outraged by the implications of the governor's explanation, and saw it as a break in the ranks of the white supremacy rule over Blacks.

The logic of their reasoning was that their class dictatorship depended upon keeping Blacks on the moral and material defensive. That is, by explaining the destitution of Blacks in terms of their own social failings, compounded by 'acts of God', such as the drought, they would have no legitimate cause to mobilise as a moral force seeking justice. Their experience was that Blacks were quick to mobilise into rebellious movement when they believed that moral authority was clearly on their side. The other aspect of this reading was that workers' rarely rebelled solely because of material hardship and destitution, but primarily when these conditions were accompanied by additional injustices such as wage cuts, brutal use of military power, and the cruel and inhumane judgements of courts.

But Governor Walker was not allowing the planters to define him as sympathetic to workers' rebellion. For this reason he threatened Blacks by calling out the soldiers, and deploying more constables in the areas identified as 'hot spots'. These sites were many and increasing daily, forcing the governor to complain of the absolute shortage of police within the colony.

Walker, furthermore, was not retreating from his position that workers' rebellion was not entirely confined to food stealing, lacking ideological focus and distinct political objectives. He knew that some workers, whom he considered a minority, wanted more than access to food, but desired to confront and engage the structural basis of their deprivation and the famine that threatened their communities. In a statement read to the House of Assembly dated July 28, 1863, he made this much clear, and urged the planters to become more alert to the wider damages posed by a few workers.[34]

The document stated:

The Governor regrets very much to inform your Honourable House that in one or two Districts of the Island there have been repeated robberies of provision grounds and other acts of lawlessness.

He has reason to think that these outrages have not been committed by the regular labourers on the several properties, but by idle and mischievous persons who congregate from various quarters, and march from place to place in large gangs for purposes of plunder.

Every effort has been made to repress these proceedings, and with that view all the appliances at the Governor's disposal have been strained to their full extent. The police generally have behaved with a steadiness and temper highly creditable to the force. With their continued exertions, and the blessing of more reasonable weather, which will bring with it an increased demand for labour, and by the good sense of the large mass of the people operating upon the turbulent vagabonds who may come into their neighbourhood, the Governor is confident that there will be an early return to a more wholesome state of things.

But he is glad, nevertheless, of the opportunity afforded by the meeting of the Legislative bodies today of bringing the state of the island to their notice, and of receiving from them any counsel which they in their wisdom may think fit to give him.

J. Walker, Government House
28, July, 1863

The House was heartened by the governor's statement which seemed to indicate a willingness to toughen his moderate views on the subject. They noted that he had made no mention of reduced wages as the trigger to rebellion, and complimented his judgement in this regard. They were also satisfied with his analysis that did not lump all workers together, but made a clear separation between the 'good' and the 'bad' within their ranks.

The 'good' workers according to the governor, were in pursuit of alleviation; the 'bad' workers wished to inflict harm and damage to the rule of the Great House, and those who lived in it. That the Governor was not willing to countenance any perspective emanating from 'bad' workers also satisfied the Assembly, and in this spirit leading members considered it necessary to respond to his call for suggestions with respect to how to deal with spreading rebellion.

It was business as usual. The planters who dominated the House could imagine no other way to deal with the social and political effects of the famine other than by an application of sterner legal measures, and more brutal policing methods. The governor was told in clear terms by elected officials that this was the only effective way the white community could deal with rebellious Blacks. But the governor had four days earlier, very strategically timed to precede the meeting of the House, issued a proclamation in the name of Her Majesty to the effect that he intended to 'punish to the utmost extent of the Law all such Thieves and Vagabonds . . . and mischievous men who show themselves to be so totally unworthy of living in a free country'. The text was unequivocally in line with what the planters had wished:[35]

PROCLAMATION

WHEREAS it has been reported to the Governor that in several Districts of this Island lawless bands of people have been moving from one Estate to another and robbing and destroying the provision grounds, and have been otherwise manifesting a disposition to turbulence, and that these acts of plunder and outrage are committed not by the regular and steady labourers on the different Properties, but by idle and mischievous persons who do not work and will not work themselves. And whereas it is the Governor's duty to see that the Law is enforced and that such wanton and wicked practices are put an end to, and that the industrious and peaceable Laborers are protected against the evil consequences of such crime and outrage which must end in no further provisions being planted, and in the poor being thus deprived of the cheapest and best article of food which they now enjoy, I do in Her Majesty's name proclaim that it is my firm determination to repress all such acts as I have referred to, and to punish to the utmost extent of the Law and such Thieves and Vagabonds, and I do hereby call upon all the good and well conducted peasantry in the Island, as well as upon the Inhabitants generally, to support me in this determination, and to assist me in apprehending and bringing to justice the idle and mischievous men who show themselves to be so totally unworthy of living in a free country.

Given under my Hand and Seal at Arms at Government-House this 24th
day of July, 1863, and in the twenty-seventh year of Her Majesty's reign

Having satisfied the planters' thirst for validation with respect to the
causes of rebellion and measures for its cure, Governor Walker wasted
no time informing the Colonial Office of the true state of affairs. It is not
that he was afraid of planter criticism, but rather that he recognised it
was impossible to rule the colony without their support. But at the
same time, he was answerable to The Colonial Office, and as a professional
civil servant sought to present accurate information to his employers.

Less than two weeks after his statement was read to the House, Walker
wrote to the Secretary of State. His letter dated August 9, 1863 sets out
a comprehensive account of the crisis facing the black people and the
reactions of their employers. He wrote:

> In my dispatch No. 165 of this day's date, I have confined myself to a
> report of the measures which have been taken for repressing the
> turbulence which has lately prevailed in the island. It is no part of my
> business to interfere in any such question as that of wages. But still it is my
> duty to inform Your Grace that there has been without doubt a great
> amount of privation and distress throughout Barbados during the last few
> months, and that there has been in many quarters a considerable reduction
> of wages. I am not at all disposed to blame the planters for this reduction
> . . . but it is unfortunate that they should have felt themselves compelled
> to resort to the step at a time of peculiar pressures on the poor. [36]

The governor ended his account with reference to an emigration
scheme being put in place to relocate Barbadian workers to Antigua.
Three members of the Antiguan Legislative Council were on the island
making shipping arrangements. Forty-two workers departed in the first
shipment, and another ship was due to depart the following week with a
similar number. The arrangement was for each worker to be provided
with a free passage, and to receive ten pence per day for wages. They
were also to receive free medical attention, 'a small lot of land for their
own cultivation, and a bounty of five pounds on their undertaking to
enter into a contract for three years service'.

The year ended with the governor making further references to hunger and destitution in the land, and calling upon the Colonial Office to further enable emigration. The discussion on wage reduction and landlessness retreated as the emigration option took centre stage. If planters were not prepared to maintain wages, it was folly to expect them to engage in land reform to favour the poor. Over 200 workers headed for Antigua in the year, and 69 to Guiana. For the remainder of the decade, emigration to Guiana increased dramatically, as destitution showed no signs of abating.

Flight from Barbados to avoid starvation was the predominant feature of the decade. Workers fled in all direction to save their lives. By 1871, there were 3,155 workers in Trinidad, 1,273 in St Vincent, 757 in St Lucia, 491 in Antigua, a total of 5,676 in addition to the 9,775 who had emigrated to Guiana.

The Economic Crisis

Immediately following the termination of the Apprenticeship System in 1838, the colony experienced a sudden drop in levels of sugar production and food cultivation. The toll of black lives occasioned by these developments was noticeable to many observers. Planters attributed the cause of declining economic activity to the anti-plantation stance of labourers. Reflecting planter opinion on this question, Richard Schomburgk in his 1848 book, *History of Barbados*, stated that though the prolonged drought was a significant factor 'the chief cause of the deficiency was the relaxed labour of the peasantry, and the great injury which the cultivation and manufacture of sugar suffers by want of continuous and regular labour'. One clergyman suggested that in the summer of 1841, for instance, 541 working class children died of malnutrition and nutritional related illnesses, compared with an average of 185 for the previous three years.

The decline, however, was short-lived; so too were fears among the plantocracy that the sugar industry was, in their own words, 'fast dying a sort of natural death.' From 1844, the statistics show that sugar production

Table 1

Emigration of workers to Guiana, 1863–1870

YEAR	NO
1863	69
1864	4,297
1865	2,482
1866	757
1867	559
1869	980
1870	631
TOTAL	9,775

Source: *Dispatch from Government House,* June 5, 1871, co 28/215

and exports had picked up and were rapidly increasing to new record levels. Production in 1847 amounted to 33,111 hogsheads, in 1850 to 35,302, and in 1858 to 50,778. The explanation for this remarkable recovery had to do with planters' assertion of effective control over the labour force, increased acreage placed under sugar, and increased yields resulting from improved cultivation techniques. Widespread use of chemical fertilisers and more efficient factory techniques also contributed to greater yields.

Sugar planters, therefore, despite the 1846 Sugar Duties Act, which provided for the gradual removal of all protection for West Indian sugar on the London market, and the 1846 collapse of the Bridgetown based West Indian Bank which was a major supplier of credit to the plantation sector, were able to expand production and maintain their market share.

The collapse of London sugar prices in 1848 to a mere 23s. 8d, the lowest level since 1832, did not produce panic among planters; they responded by temporarily shifting greater acreage into food provisions and cutting their import bill by over £90,000 in 1849. More importantly, they were able to transfer the pressures of falling sugar prices onto the shoulders of workers by means of wage reductions during the 1850s. By slashing the size of their labour bill, planters were able to withstand the sharp edge of competition from slave-owning sugar producers, especially after 1854 when the Free Trade Act of 1846 was put into full effect.

Table 2
Exports from Barbados, 1848–1858 (£)

Year	Total Value of All Exports
1848	659,073
1850	831,534
1852	951,726
1854	945,849
1856	971,028
1858	1,468,449

Source: *Barbados Blue Books, 1848-58* C.O 33/58-68.

Reduction in wages, without violent rebellious responses from workers, also gave planters the room and confidence to implement certain technological adjustments within their industry. During the late 1840s, Governor William Reid had urged planters to modernise their production, and on one occasion insulted them by making references to the 'bad state' of their working cattle, the dilapidated condition of their windmills, and the disgust experienced on seeing their 'weak oxen drawing a wagon'.

Whereas in 1841 there was only one steam factory on the island, in 1859 there were at least 12, and 95 in 1890. Steam factories were estimated to produce between 12-18 per cent more sugar than the traditional windmills, and this development greatly assisted those few planters who were able to raise the capital for modernisation. On the whole, nonetheless, technological backwardness remained a feature of the post-slavery sugar industry.

Table 3
Wages in the West Indies, 1846-1850

Colony	Average wage per day (pence)
Trinidad	24
Br. Guiana	20
St. Lucia	16
Jamaica	15
St. Vincent	10
Grenada	9
Antigua	8
Barbados	6

Source: *Barbados Blue Books, 1846-1854,* co. 33/55-68 *Earl Grey to Governors of West Indian Colonies,* Sept. 15, 1848 co 854/4.

The period between 1854 and the mid-1880s was one of uncertainty compared with the previous decade. Though sugar prices remained stagnant output increased slowly. Planters' confidence in the industry was not undermined by market trends, and between 1860 and 1887 few estates were sold, and the average price of these remained above the satisfactory rate of £50 per acre. In those years when sugar prices declined, profit levels were maintained by the increase in volume of sales.

It was during this period, also, that Barbadian sugar planters were able to take advantage of openings within the North American market. Since the 1840s the balance of trade with the United States had been negative; exports to the United States in 1845 were valued at £1,750 while imports were valued at £188,686. The increase in sales of sugar to this market was slow and inconsistent until the mid-1850s, since Barbadians sold their sugar mainly to English merchants to whom they were indebted. Available data show that between 1855 and 1858 the value of Barbadian sugar exports to the US jumped from £8,865 to £60,000. Since lower-cost Cuban and Puerto Rican sugar producers had captured a sizeable portion of this market, English West Indians did not consider themselves competitive, and in 1893, the value of Barbados sugar and molasses exports there amounted to only £755,465.

The deep end of the sugar crisis was reached in 1884 and continued until the turn of the century. For the first time since emancipation, planters sincerely expressed their inability to cope with market trends, and confidence in the industry declined rapidly. The root cause was the sudden drop in European sugar prices – the result of rapidly increasing subsidised domestic sugar beet production. Between 1884 and 1897 planters reported the disappearance of their small profit margins. Production levels fell marginally and even then most major producers were operating at cost levels above what was required to make a profit. The volume of exports did not show any appreciable decline, though with collapsing prices, returns fell off sharply. In 1886, for example, the values of exports were about 40 per cent below the 1884 level. The crisis within the industry was reflected in the collapse of sugar estate values; estates sold in 1884 at between £65-70 per acre while in 1887 sales were recorded at £25-30 per acre.

The worst years of the crisis were the mid-1890s. Though property values fell sharply, few, if any, estates were abandoned, unlike Jamaica for example. In 1896, a Royal Commission was appointed to investigate the sugar crisis. The Agricultural Aids Act of 1887, which was passed to allow the government to provide short-term financing for sugar planters, had had little positive effects, and the economic crisis was seen to be leading to social unrest among the increasing impoverished labouring poor. As usual, planters slashed wages in response to falling prices, and evidence of rising mortality and general malnutrition caused much concern to law enforcing agents.

Finally, in a desperate attempt to shoulder up the industry and ease, indirectly, the social crisis within the colony, government assisted by the establishment in 1902 of the Sugar Industry Agricultural Bank – the result of a grant of £400,000 from the British government. It was not until during the First World War [1914-1918] that profits returned to the sugar industry, as many of the beet sugar zones of Europe were destroyed. These years, and shortly after, were periods of great prosperity, and for a while memories of the crisis of the last part of the nineteenth century were pushed into the background.

Table 4

Sugar Exported from Barbados, 1883-1897

Year	Tons	Price per cwt (£) £ . s. d.
1883	46,242	19. 0
1884	54,263	13. 3
1885	52,649	13. 6
1886	40,047	11. 9
1887	60,263	11. 9
1888	63,882	13. 0
1889	57,106	16. 0
1890	74,606	13. 6
1891	44,226	13. 6
1892	51,849	14. 3
1893	58,765	11. 3
1894	57,967	10. 0
1895	33,331	10. 9
1896	45,170	9. 3
1897	51,257	9. 6

Source: _Barbados Blue Books, 1880-1897_

Strengthening the Club

Economic consolidation was associated with strategic political adjustments. Tinkering with the constitution was all well and good, but paving the way for genuine representative government was not what the political leadership wanted. They called the political machinery under their command the 'Old Representative System' but in effect it was an 'old self-serving club' that tolerated no dissent within or engaged criticism without. Conrad Reeves, the distinguished black lawyer was brought in, but to protect and consolidate their interests.

Ironically, the failed workers' revolution of 1876 boosted confidence in the planters' perception of their right to rule. There was hardly any critical reflection on the political messages of the battle. They agreed that the constitution was in good shape and that the Blacks should be further repressed. The former required, for its protection, the elevation into government of the finest establishment of legal minds on the island; the latter called for more police, more stringent laws, and the retention at all costs of the Imperial Garrison.

The planters could not imagine any other social group effectively sharing the political process. They believed that no other group possessed the qualities required for viable public administration. Two major rebellions of workers (1816 and 1876) and persistent popular resistance, in addition to formidable intellectual challenges and ridicule of their rule, internally and abroad, did not produce meaningful self-criticism and reflection. They alone understood what was good for Barbados because for them, their interests and the public good, were one and the same. Sugar was the past and future of Barbados, and anyone who did not know this, or understood its significance, was not fit to hold public office. This excluded the black community, which saw the sugar plantation as a place worse than hell, and the sugar planter in the light of someone thrown out of heaven.

Anthony Phillips has argued that 'as the owners of the land and directors of the economic enterprises, the political elite were inclined to adapt the view that what's good for us is good for Barbados,' and that 'they conducted the business of the State on the same basis as their own private business'. When they spoke of representative government, he noted, the concept was one which tied their material and social interest to the reproduction of public political institutions.[37]

Furthermore, Phillips illustrates, 'the Assembly was basically like a club. Elections were held annually, but there were seldom any electoral contests. Sometimes the identical membership was returned, and the changes which did take place were from resignations, retirements and deaths'. The black community showed none or little interest in the politics of the club, not because they were excluded from membership participation, but because they saw the arrangement as a corrupt dictatorship of the sugar planter and his mercantile allies. They knew that Prescod, after decades of constitutional advocacy on their behalf, had not impacted the membership of the Assembly. The conclusion they had drawn from this aspect of his effort was that only civil conflict could open up the system and enable the democratic impulse.[38]

The social composition of the 'political club' was effectively homogenous. It was the place of the white male elite, whose occupations included the professions of the planter, merchant, doctor, lawyer and administrator. Half of the members were planters, and those who were not, aspired to be, and idealised the world of the 'Great House' as the symbol of achievement necessary for the conferment of honours and titles. They dominated both the Assembly and the Legislative Council. Constitutional changes such as that which took place in 1876 whereby the Legislative Council was divided into two chambers, one legislative and the other advisory (Executive Council), did not expand the social range of political selection.

The profile of the Pile family is illustrative of the standard accepted as the social benchmark for the white elite. Phillips sets out their circumstance as follows:

> The largest land owner to have a seat in the Assembly was G. Laurie Pile who represented St. George for 18 sessions, from 1884 to 1905. In that year he was appointed to the Legislative Council following the resignation of his father, Sir George Pile. He also inherited from his father in 1905 the attorneyship of the plantations owned by the Earl of Harewod – The Belle, The Mount, Thicket and Fortescue. The plantations owned by G. Laurie Pile were Boarded Hall (318 acres), Bulkeley (390 acres), Buttals

(209 acres), Brighton (393 acres), Carmichael (250 acres), Clifton Hall (401 acres), Jordans (235 acres), Valley (250 acres), Windsor (250 acres) a total of 2,955 acres. He was also a part-owner of Claybury (303 acres). These estates were situated variously in St. Michael, St. George and St. John . . . G.L. Pile was also Vice President of the Agricultural Society and established Bulkeley Central Factory, one of the first modern sugar factories in Barbados. He also had a range of business interests, being connected with several companies and with the Chamber of Commerce. He was Chairman of the Barbados Fire Insurance Company and of the Railway Board. A cousin of G.L. Pile, Archibald Jones Pile, was representative for St. Peter from 1871 until his tragic death in 1898. A.J. Pile was owner of Green's St. George (109 acres), part-owner of two others, and one of the largest agricultural attorneys in Barbados, having control of thirty estates. A.J. Pile was Speaker from 1882 until his death.[39]

There were many other families who aspired to the reality achieved by the Piles who came to represent the epitome of the idealised white Barbadian mentality. For example, the Haynes, Sealy, Clarke and Parris families were among the principal aspirants, and together they constituted the political dictatorship over Blacks that was called representative government.

Phillips analyses their political and economic ownership and presents a graphic image of the network of domination and terror maintained with respect to the emancipated community. He noted that:

Another large planter was A. Percy Haynes who represented St. Andrew for seventeen sessions, from 1894 to 1912 when he was appointed to the Legislative Council. He was the owner of Fruce Vale (225 acres), Fruithall (13 acres), Hopewell (62 acres), Mellowes (250 acres), Parks (262 acres), Seniors (150 acres), Spring Vale and Mellards (187 acres) Vale (12 acres) – a total of 1,161 acres in St. Andrew and St. Joseph. Richard Haynes of Easy Hall and Saltram, St. Joseph (354 acres) represented that Parish from 1894 to 1902 when he was appointed to the Legislative Council. G. Elliott Sealy was the owner of the five plantations, three in St. John and one each in St. Philip and St. George – Bowmanston (245 acres), Lemon Arbor (179 acres), Mount Pleasant (317 acres), Todds (255 acres), Woodland (147 acres) – a total of 1,143 acres.[40]

Another very influential planter, said Phillips, was Frederick James Clarke who represented Christ Church continuously from 1887 for 47 years:

> Clarke inherited Coverley Plantation from his father, and also became the attorney of a number of plantation owners, including many absentee proprietors. He was an agriculturalist of prominence, becoming President of the Agricultural Society in 1905. Succeeding A.J. Pile as Speaker in 1898, he held the post for 36 years. He was knighted in 1911. And finally, another example of large landowners was James W. Parris who represented St. Andrew until 1882 and was then appointed to the Legislative Council, serving until 1899. He served on the Executive Committee from its formation in 1881, eventually resigning in 1893 from failing health. Parris was the owner of Walker's (70 acres) in St. Thomas – Ayshford (165 acres), Duke's (181 acres), Fortress (87 acres), Highland (158 acres), Lion Castle (234 acres) – a total of 1533 acres.[41]

The elite was sustained by a small cadre of electors who were dependent on it for economic survival, social validation, and cultural legitimacy. The electors included managers, public servants, small property owners, and a range of professionals. According to George Belle, in 1876:

> The vote could be exercised by those who (i) had freehold possession of an estate valued annually at nor less than £12 16s 6d sterling for life or in right of marriage or as a dower of wife; or if himself or his wife had a life interest in the rents and profits of lands of a similar annual value; (ii) were leasees or assignees of land or of tenements paying rent of not less than £64 2s 0d sterling and the term of the lease was in its original creation not less than five years; (iii) occupied any house, warehouse, store, counting house, shop, or other building in a town, parochially rated at not less than £32 1s 0d sterling rent per annum or (iv) paid parochial taxes for two years of the least £3 4s 1d sterling.[42]

A total of 1,664 voters elected 24 members from 12 constituencies to the House of Assembly for one year. Belle continues:

New Elections were held annually with very much the same results. This elected Assembly was the lower house of planter government; the upper house consisted of the Legislative Council made up of nominated members, usually highly influential and experienced planters. Colonial authority of course stood above these local institutions, the governor representing the imperial government. The executive of the government consisted of the governor and the Legislative Council combined who formed the Executive Council. The colonial secretary, the attorney general and the officer commanding Her Majesty's troops also sat in the Legislative and Executive Councils. The Legislative and Executive Councils were made up of eight and nine persons respectively at the beginning of 1876.[43]

Table 5
Registered Voters in 1876

Constituency	Population	Electors
St Michael	27,000	215
Bridgetown	21,000+	398
Christ Church	18,000	102
St Phillip	17,000	221
St George	14,000	125
St John	10,000	65
St Thomas	10,000-	115
St James	9,000-	97
St Lucy	9,000-	107
St Andrew	7,000+	38
St Peter	7,000+	69
St Joseph	6,000-	94

Source: *Blue Book 1876, George Belle, The Abortive Revolution of 1876 in Barbados.*

Phillips has noted that after the mid-nineteenth century, an important feature of the political dictatorship was its higher education in prestigious local schools and British universities. This was politically pursued as a strategic response to the post-emancipation charge that the elite taking the colony into the new dispensation was characterised by academic illiteracy, ignorance of letters, and cultural crudity. In 1869, for example, Grenville Chester, an Englishman who spent time among them wrote:

The total want of interest in literature, art, and science which prevails amongst the well-to-do classes is exemplified by the fact that for years past there has been only a single book society in the island; that this society, now broken up, numbers less than a score of members, and that some of these were Englishmen. The destruction of the rest of the universe would interest the true Bim only as the catastrophe would affect the price of sugar![44]

The image painted of planters during the emancipation discourse was that they were lacking the cerebral skill necessary to imagine a new order based on social equality and justice, and that they were a culturally degenerative bunch who enjoyed the petty despotism of their little sugar kingdoms.

Reacting to these descriptions, which were politically effective in that they assisted British public opinion to move against them, they made a conscious effort to improve their educational profile by enrolling their sons in the finest British universities, and inducting into their ranks persons who had attained academic or professional distinction. This agenda was driven in part, by the appearance in society of black and coloured men who had acquired higher education and were able to mount an intellectual challenge with the aim of discrediting their political dictatorship.

Prescod was leader of the intellectual vanguard that demonstrated the moral, intellectual and political bankruptcy of the planter dictatorship, and held it up to metropolitan scrutiny. The power of his rhetoric and the authority of his research was unmatched by those who sought to counter his influence. His conceptual flair set him apart as arguably the greatest orator of his time. On the other hand, Conrad Reeves, another black man who was able to blend his formal training as a lawyer with the gift of oratory and ethical persuasion, surfaced as the man of the moment for the members of the club. He was the man in the middle, at the centre of things, situated there because of his political compliance as well as his intellectual brilliance.

The elite, however, could not rely upon the social system to produce many of Reeve's kind. Rather, they imagined a possé of Prescods coming through. It was their response, then, to produce their own thinkers in

large numbers to serve their cause. It was important for them to project
the kind of mind that could win the respect of those they claimed to
represent. The university education was the finishing touch required to
secure membership in the elite, and an invitation to serve on the
Legislative Council.

A.J. Pile, Phillips noted, was educated at Leamington College, and
Exeter College, Oxford University where he obtained a Bachelor's degree
in 1867. F. J. Clarke was educated at Caius College, Cambridge University
where he graduated in 1879. James A. Lynch graduated from Trinity
College, Cambridge, J.W. Carrington at St Edmund Hall, Oxford, and
W.K. Chandler at St John's College, Cambridge. Thomas O'Neal attended
Trinity Hall, Cambridge, and H. Walter Reece, University College,
London. Most became lawyers and politicians, and consolidated their
position within the plantocracy. These were all distinguished men whose
academic and professional training set them apart as outstanding
personalities working in the service of the colonial establishment. By
1900, the Barbados elite comprised many highly educated planters,
merchants, and professionals. In effect, it had reinvented itself to emerge
as a modern class with sufficient intellectual equipment to defend and
protect itself.[45]

Merchant Elite to the Rescue

The economic depression of the 1880s and 1890s eroded the minimal
material gains which workers had slowly attained in previous years, and
produced significant changes in the ownership of arable land. These
developments influenced the social composition of the elite. The most
important feature of this period was the rise of the indigenous merchant
class as a new force within the social elite – merging with, and to a large
extent pushing aside, sections of the traditional plantocracy.

The political ascendancy of the merchant elite was characterised by
their forceful entry into the financial arrangements and family structures
of the plantocracy. This development had to do with two important
features of the post slavery order. First, the ability of planters to retain

the old representative system, and hence their control over the Legislature. This meant that planters were able, by means of manipulating the organs of government, to ensure that estate ownership, even in the most difficult of times, stayed in local (their) hands and not transferred to English merchant houses to which they were indebted. Second, the development of local financial institutions and merchant companies that were able to purchase many estates before 'foreign' interests were able to do so.

Unlike the case in Jamaica, for example, the Barbados Legislature had refused to accept the imperial Encumbered Estates Act of 1854 through which bankrupt plantations were put up for sale on the London market. Generally, such estates did fall into the hands of English merchant consignees who held liens on them, a process made legal by the English Chancery Court. The Barbadians resisted this solution to plantation indebtedness, and implemented, with Colonial Office approval, their own Chancery Court system which was manipulated to ensure that indebted estates were resold to (white) locals. Between 1854 and 1870 the majority of estates sold in chancery in Barbados, unlike other colonies, went to the merchant class.

Bridgetown merchants had long been consolidating their economic base with an eye to buying into the plantocracy which they recognised, in spite of its economic decay, as the legitimate social elite. This, of course, had to do with planters' firm grip over the political machinery. In 1840, for example, the Barbados Mutual Life Assurance Society (BMLA) was formed by a section of this merchant group, and by the 1860s this institution had become a major supplier of short and long-term finance capital to sugar planters. The general policy of the BMLA was to allow planters to use their crop as security for short-term loans and to obtain a lien on estates for long-term loans.

The development of a local capital market resulted in the planter class having to lean heavily upon merchant finance, with the result that by the early twentieth century, Bridgetown merchants had taken over a considerable number of sugar estates. By the end of the nineteenth century the BMLA appeared in the Chancery Court as plaintiff in more than 30 cases. By 1905, Bridgetown merchants were clearly the leading force in sugar plantation modernisation. After this date the number of estates falling into their hands increased as they suspended loans to planters unable to resolve their financial difficulties.

In 1905 most prominent Bridgetown merchant families were considered an integral part of the plantocracy. Families such as the Cavans, Austins, Camerons, Brydens, Wilkinsons and DaCostas consolidated their financial links with the traditional plantation sector, through marital ties with old planter families such as the Chandlers, Piles, Sealys and Haynes. While the merchant class rose 'phoenix-like out of the ashes of the depression', the urban-based poor Whites were also enjoying some socioeconomic upward mobility. Indeed, it seems as if the circumstances of this late nineteenth century provided the context for loosening the rigidities which had formerly kept static the white community. Some traditional poor-white families, such as the Goddards, Dowdings, Seales, and Emtages, emerged also as substantial Bridgetown merchants, joining the mercantile network that assisted them with contracts, loans and financial information.

Traditional planter families, nonetheless, continued to dominate both the Assembly and the Legislative Councils, though the most prominent of them were now linked financially and maritally to the new merchant elite. The success of the political challenge of the Bridgetown merchants, however, was not as comprehensive as their financial strategy. Merchants tended to represent Bridgetown and St Michael, while planters held on to their rural seats. James A. Lynch was probably typical of the new merchant politician. He represented Bridgetown during the early 1880s and sat on the Legislative Council. His elevation had to do with his role as founder of the firm, James Alsop-Lynch and Company, and ownership of the 164-acre Friendship Estate. His son James Challenor Lynch, built upon this foundation, and as a planter, merchant and lawyer, also won a Bridgetown seat in 1888.

Other merchants such as John Gardiner Austin, senior partner of Michael Cavan and Company, whose sons founded Gardiner Austin and Company after his death in 1902, also represented Bridgetown from

1895 to 1911. Arthur Sydney Bryden, an English born commission agent, and founder of A.S. Bryden and Sons in the 1890s, represented St Michael from 1894 to 1899. He was also a director of the BMLA and of the Barbados Fire Insurance Company of which G.L. Pile was Chairman.

Some merchants also succeeded in winning rural seats that were traditionally held by resident planters. For example, J.O. Wright of the firm Collymore and Wright, later Plantations Limited, represented St Andrew between 1899 and 1904. On the whole these merchants were white, though a few Jews such as E.I. Baeza who represented Bridgetown in 1908 and H.W. Lofty, a coloured representative of St Michael between 1899 and 1905, and Bridgetown in 1910, were able to rise to prominence within the political community.

In general, then, merchants used their economic power to infiltrate the political institutions of the colony, and had become a significant lobby by 1900. They sat on vestry and statutory boards, as well as in the Assemblies, Legislative Councils and the Executive Committees. Commercial Hall, the Bridgetown Chamber of Commerce, was never unrepresented in the making of important political decisions. In fact, it was generally stated that the merchants at Commercial Hall had similar access to governors as members of the Agricultural Society, an indication that their political power exceeded their physical representation in government.

The overall result was a strengthening of the plantocracy as merchant families generally aspired to the socio-ideological standards and values that had been established by planters since the seventeenth century. This meant that though the economic depression led to structural change in the social composition of the plantocracy, it certainly entered the twentieth century as a financially reinforced elite, confident in its ability to rule the labouring classes even during the difficult times.

White Corporate Consolidation

The decision by the Colonial Office to send off a Royal Commission to investigate conditions in the depressed West Indian sugar industry in

1897 reflected imperial concern that the economic crisis was structural and long-term, and that the social implications, particularly for the labouring class, would be severe. It was the first comprehensive investigation of the sugar industry in fifty years, and the appointment of commissioners familiar with West Indian conditions also suggests the seriousness with which its report would be received.

When the findings were submitted there were few surprises for Barbadians. The conclusion that the sugar industry would continue to decline and that alternative export crops would have to be found, did not comfort plantation owners, but the idea was not original. That bounty beet sugar was the principal factor in the market dislocation of cane sugar was also not a new idea; though Barbadians were less than pleased with the recommendation that no discriminatory taxes or duties should be imposed on beet sugar since the British consumer was benefiting from cheaper sugar.

It was, nonetheless, pleasing to the working classes that the Commissioners endorsed the imperial government's social responsibility towards them, and recognised that they were absorbing a disproportionate share of the economic crisis. More significant were the recommendations that peasant expansion be encouraged so as to allow a greater proportion of the black community to establish their own culture of subsistence independent of the sugar sector. More importantly for white Barbadians was the recommendation that the imperial exchequer should offer a loan to the colony for the establishment of modern central factory equipment and facilities.

Sir Henry Norman, Chairman of the Commission, a former governor of Jamaica, was determined that the recommendations be quickly implemented. In 1902, Parliament approved a grant of £80,000 for the modernisation of the Barbados sugar industry. In addition, because of the hurricane of September 10, 1898 which killed 112 people and destroyed the homes of over 10,000 black workers, a grant of £40,000 was allocated for working class assistance, and £50,000 for sugar plantation repairs.

Planters considered the grant to the sugar sector modest, given the backwardness of the industry, but were not willing to bargain on this matter. They were, however, not prepared to consider the question of black peasant development as a strategy for socioeconomic rationalisation. In fact, during the hearings in Bridgetown, a resident watchmaker, Walter Marston, gave evidence which suggested that W.K. Chandler, Master of Chancery since 1882, was engaged in a system of over-appraising estate values so as to exclude Blacks and Coloureds from purchasing land.

When, in 1903, £80,000 was made available to the Government of Barbados, disputes arose as to the manner in which it should be disposed. The resolution of the debate came with the establishment of the Barbados Sugar Industry Agricultural Bank, which granted loans from the fund to individual planters. A series of Plantation Aid Acts assisted the management of the funds, and in 1904 at least 107 of the colony's 411 estates had borrowed under these provisions. It was not until the 1910s that central factories began to appear, though planters remained concerned that the implications for the traditional style family operation would not be all positive.

The Commissioners had no difficulty in illustrating to planters the relationship between economic decline and social unrest. The Report stated that the British Government had 'placed the labouring population where it is, and created for it the conditions, moral and material, under which it exists and cannot divest [itself] of responsibility for its future.' Planters interpreted this concern to mean that workers had to be encouraged, by means of education, to respect and appreciate plantation labour, rather than pursue peasant development. The Agricultural Conference which was held in Barbados in January 1900, had given support to the idea that working class black boys should be discouraged from seeking clerical work and should be 'trained in an atmosphere favourable to agriculture'. Also, that they 'should learn that tilling the soil and caring for crops is . . .worthy of being studied by intelligent minds.'

Planters, furthermore, considered that the context for such a development was already established, especially as J.E. Reece, the

Barbadian Inspector of Schools, had reported in 1899 that the children
of most agricultural labourers tended to continue in that occupation.
This was in spite of the fact that the 1878 Education Act, and the
recommendations of the Bree Commission Report of 1896, had called
for compulsory education for working class children under the age of
12. Typical of planter opinion on this question was a report entitled
'Are the masses responsible?' published in the planters' newspaper, the
Barbados Agricultural Reporter, October 26, 1905:

> It is admitted that the Negro, if properly handled, is an excellent labourer.
> The question then is one of proper handling. Handle the negro properly,
> and there would be no lack of workers . . . Such handling would involve,
> amongst other . . . things, the giving of a sound practical education. Some
> book learning is of course essential, but the mistake of conveying to the
> child the idea that such education as he acquires at school is calculated to
> make him eligible for the highest honours in life must be avoided.[46]

At the village levels, planters had ready social allies in the Anglican
clergymen. The official clergy had long merged with the plantocracy
and had also made their inputs into the evidence collected by the Royal
Commissioners. Planters saw them as providing assistance in shaping the
consciousness of villagers in such a manner as to be amenable to
agricultural labour. The parish priest was a very powerful figure in the
black villages and could determine the fate of families by severing or
creating bridges to plantation resources. The 1891 census showed that
from a total population of 182,867, some 147,000 were Anglicans, and
the respect which black Anglicans conferred upon the church, and its
ministers, they were also required to confer upon plantation owners
and managers. Though Methodists, Moravians, and other denominations
accounted for some 19,000 Barbadians, their presence in the rural villages
did not counter the alliance between the established Church and the
plantation.

The Royal Commission had heard countless statements from witnesses
that the 'ambition' of every working class person was 'to own a piece of
land.' It also heard that very few had succeeded in obtaining freehold,

and that the vast majority of those who had access to land were plantation tenants – whose material subsistence had been much reduced by the 'potato raid' on plantations, a form of redistribution larceny in which workers expressed the ideological notion of 'justified appropriation'.

On July 1, 1898, for example, shortly after planters had vocally rejected the call of the Royal Commissioners for an extension of the peasantry, a group of some 400 men and women raided the potato fields of Bowmanston Plantation in the St John parish, and took provisions for several days sustenance. Nineteen of these persons were convicted and sentenced. Such events were as common in the 1890s, as reports of starvation in the countryside. The Commissioners also heard evidence from labourers who stated that starvation hunger in the tenantries was leading to the widespread criminalisation of workers, since food scavenging was their principal survival response. But planters were able to deflect such discussions by focussing the attention of the Commission upon the problem of sugar marketing, and the industrial modernisation of the plantation.

For sugar planters, then, the existence of rural poverty enhanced their effective grip over the labour of villagers. Indeed, the 1878 Commission on Poor Relief had indicated, in response to a suggestion that wages be increased to alleviate poverty, that 'more money per day would, in by far the majority of cases, probably mean more idleness per week'. Wages remained inadequate, and the Royal Commission, when informed by planters that the daily wage for estate mechanics was 2s., for adult male field hands 10d–1s., female adult field hands 7 1/2d., and children under age 16, 5d., knew that these rates were exaggerated. The official Colonial Blue Books for the period 1901 to 1911 quoted 8d per day as the norm for male field hands.

The high mortality rate among workers immediately after the 1898 hurricane was due in part to outbreaks of typhoid and dysentery. Adding to their plight was the smallpox epidemic of February 1902 which lasted until April 1903 and claimed 118 lives. On this latter occasion the island was quarantined by neighbouring colonies. Then there was the yellow fever epidemic of 1908, the first since 1881, all of which contributed to the economic depression in the colony by reducing trade levels and government revenues. In 1910, a medical officer noted that 'chronic pauperism . . . like a chronic disease is . . . undermining the population of this island.'

Meanwhile, planters' hopes of economic recovery were pinned upon Joseph Chamberlain's campaign to abolish the sugar beet bounties. When Chamberlain became Secretary of State for the Colonies in 1895, he expressed great concern for the plight of West Indians and was hailed in Barbados among planters as a hero. At the 1902 Brussels Convention he managed to persuade the Europeans to remove the bounties on beet sugar, but his assistance was insufficient to generate renewed enthusiasm among planters, who at this critical stage found that they were losing ground on the American market.

Since the 1880s, sugar planters had been looking more to the United States for markets, and the indices of exports illustrate the changing pattern of the colony's trade. By 1902 when the bounties on beet sugar were removed Barbados was exporting more in value to the United States and Canada than to the United Kingdom. In that year the value of exports to the United States of America was $1,359,888; to the United Kingdom $109,420 and to Canada $586,355 – 63.5 per cent, 5.1 per cent and 27.4 per cent of the total value of exports respectively. The expansion of the sugar industry in Cuba and Puerto Rico, however, which were structurally and financially linked to the United States, represented the basis of Barbadian displacement. The slump in Barbadian trade with the United States was sudden and substantial, and though this was partly compensated for by expanding trade in syrup and molasses to the United Kingdom and Canada, the overall level of exports showed a downward trend until the First World War.

In 1903 molasses exports were valued at £136,548 and rose to £232,920 by 1907. This export item brought measurable relief to sugar planters, whose spirits were also lifted by good crops in 1910, 1911 and 1914. Labourers and tenants, however, continued to experience severe hardship. There was prolonged drought from 1910 to 1912 which suppressed ground provisions production. Rising sugar output, then, was associated with diminishing food production and inflationary prices for scarce items.

The responses of the impoverished Blacks to the economic depression were not uniform. There were food riots, social restlessness and political turmoil – and these caused some *concern to* legal and political officials. But on the whole, the nature of the responses of most was summed up by Dr J.F. Clarke testifying before the 1897 Royal Commission:

> Through all the hardships the labourer endures he assumes a pleasant demeanour, and which is mistaken by his employer for comfort and happiness . . . He is often taken to the magistrate of his parish and punished for breach of contract, or for taking a few points of sugar cane from the plantation . . . and yet he returns to the very plantation and resumes his work peaceful and quiet.[47]

Such was the consolidated power of the planter-merchant elite and their control of economic resources which ensured social order even when living standards around them were falling.

Cricket and Cultural Apartheid

If the establishment of central factories constitute proof of the survivalist economic attitudes of the transformed sugar plantocracy, then organised cricket was symbolic of its need for a sophisticated social instrument of cultural domination and distinction. From the 1870s, the game was not seen by the planter elite as simply a form of recreation; there were visions of its role as a force in social cohesion, as well as an index by which social classes could be clearly distinguished during this time of unprecedented restructuring to the social order. While merchants were rapidly becoming planters, and some coloured and black men emerging as professionals, merchants and politicians, the still dominant traditional planting families sought to maintain their class distinctions within the area of social culture.[48]

The establishment of cricket clubs and competitions during the late nineteenth century gave rise to the use of sport as a mirror image of the old order. According to Brian Stoddart, 'plantation owners, merchants, bankers, clerks, and civil servants came to competition matches categorised by their place in the hierarchy of sugar production; and from its organised outset cricket was a powerful agency in the preservation and promotion of that hierarchy'. Certainly in 1892 when the Barbados Challenge Cup competition was established, the sugar planters were the cricket elite and clubs were ranked by the class of their membership.

In 1877, Wanderers Cricket Club was formed, and for the remainder of the century its membership was drawn exclusively from the white merchant-planter elite. The leading players and administrators of this club were the most prominent politicians and businessmen of the day; one long-serving president was J.O. Wright, a leading planter, merchant and politician D.C. DaCosta, J. Gardiner Austin, and A.S. Bryden, symbolic of the new merchant-planter elite, were also members of this club, so too was R.S. Challenor, whose son, George Challenor, rose by 1914 to become the leading West Indian batsman of his time. The merchant-planter elite, then, saw the Wanderers Cricket Club as a social institution through which they asserted the cultural authority of their race and class at a time of rapid social change. Most of the club's prominent members had been supporters and activists of the Barbados Defence Association during the confederation crisis in the year prior to its formation, a fact which enhanced the image of the club as representative of traditional elite conservatism.[49]

Other cricket clubs which were formed later, such as Spartan and Pickwick, were the preserve of the professional upper and middle classes. Spartan, the propertied coloured man's club, boasted the fact that Sir Conrad Reeves, the coloured Chief Justice and respected lawyer, was its first president, while Pickwick, a whites only club, had as a player and president, G.A. Goodman, the colony's Solicitor-General. These clubs took pride in their support for the English standard of sport ethics, and considered offenders of regulations and values as traitors to country and empire.

In general, the members believed that the principles of the cricketing culture were admirable guidelines for social behaviour and held these up as standards to be emulated by an impoverished, oppressed, and mostly landless working class. In the schools the children of the white upper classes and black and coloured middle classes were inculcated with these concepts. Harrison College and The Lodge, schools for the white elite, exposed students to cricket as a social institution of great magnitude. Combermere, the school of the small but rising black middle classes, did not question these values, but mimicked them in a manner which suggested profound acceptance.

Meanwhile, the illiterate children on the tenantries and in the urban ghettoes played their adapted version of the game in a robust spirit which signified some measure of cultural resistance and autonomy. They transformed the spirit and structures of the game, reduced its degree of formality, and hammered it into a shape best suited to urban alley and plantation tracks. While all social classes played the game as popular recreation, it also served to enhance the rigid structure of social distinctions. At the organised level, the game emerged as a social institution which was shaped by race, colour and class forces, while its advocates consistently described it as an agency of social cohesion.

The white and coloured propertied classes, however, never attended the matches played by black labourers on the tenantries. For many elite players the aggressive and sometimes violent nature of the game played by the lower orders was an affront to their authority and evidence of cultural insubordination. They were, nonetheless, impressed with the way in which the labouring classes had developed a great enthusiasm for the game, though the remark was frequently made that, as was the case with Christianity, Blacks did not grasp its finer conceptual points.

Blacks, on the other hand, turned out in their thousands to watch the upper classes compete among themselves, and against other regional elites in the inter-colonial games. By 1930, cricket in Barbados was a mass game. Whites continued to dominate its financial and organisation structures. No such status, however, was enjoyed by Whites in the department of technical skills on the fields; this aspect of the game went increasingly to the Blacks, as represented by the great player Herman Griffith, and the formation of the black middle class club, Empire.[50]

Company Power

In order to take advantage of the wartime boom in the sugar industry, and to withstand the pressures resulting from the growing domination of plantation ownership by the mercantile elite, the remaining elements of the traditional plantocracy were forced to adopt strategies for survival. In 1917, they established a large corporation, Plantations Company Limited, with the intentions of increasing the size of capital funds available to the industry, and to enable them to purchase and retain plantations, thus minimising the land engrossment tendency of the Bridgetown merchant houses. In addition, the company was designed to pilot the planters' entry into the commercial sector, thereby taking competition to the merchant class, and to capitalise on investment funds being accumulated in the non-sugar sectors.

Since the 1880s, planters had been complaining that the market manipulations of wholesalers and retailers was a critical factor in their inability to share the economic benefits accruing to businesses that revolved around the supply of goods and services to their plantations. Commission agents, in particular, who controlled price levels, credit lines, and the pattern of commodity supply, were identified as their main aggressors. These agents dominated the Commission Merchants Association, as well as the Barbados Life Assurance Company – a major credit supplier. Plantations Company Limited, therefore, was designed as an instrument of planter defence and counter-aggression within the 'cut throat' competitive market of the depression years.

In 1920, the leading families in the merchant sector, realising the effectiveness of the planters' corporate innovation got together and formed their own company. The family names – Manning, Gardiner Austin, DaCosta, Musson, Challenor and Wilkinson, and Haynes – were all known. The formation of this company, Barbados Shipping and Trading, was both a response to planter consolidation, and the inevitable response to the threat of accumulation posed by the depression. The presence of these two corporations signalled the origins of monopoly capitalism in

Barbados, and the final stage in the successful economic domination of the colony by the merchant class.

During the 1920s, these two companies competed for trade, arable land, and control of government policy. But the threat of black militancy, which emerged after the mid 1920s, forced their directorates to consider strategies for the consolidation of their power within the polity. The development of organised radicalism in the workplace following the defeated dockworkers action in 1927, presented the context for the abandonment of outright competition between the two groups. In 1934, they established between themselves the Barbados Produce Exporters Association [BPEA] which, at least symbolically, represented the consummation of the planter-merchant economic alliance, and the triumph of corporate organisation within the economy.

NOTES

1   See MacGregor to Normandy, Oct. 9, 1839, 10.28/128; MacGregor to Russell, Dec. 5, 1839, co 28/129.
2   The *Liberal*, Oct. 27, 1838.
3   Letter to the British Emancipator, July 8, 1839.
4   Letter to the British Emancipator, July 8, 1839.
5   Letter to the British Emancipator, July 8, 1839.
6   Letter to the British Emancipator, July 8, 1839.; see also Governor MacGregor's response to Prescod's Letter, co 28/132-4.
7   Letter to the British Emancipator, July 8, 1839.; see also Governor MacGregor's response to Prescod's Letter, co 28/132-4. Prescod's Letter.
8   Letter to the British Emancipator, July 8, 1839.; see also Governor MacGregor's response to Prescod's Letter, co 28/132-4. Prescod's Letter.
9   The *Liberal*, 3 Sept. 1842.See also J.A.Thome and J.H. Kimball, *Emancipation in theWest Indies* (NY, 1936), 332.
10 C.Levy, *Emancipation, Sugar and Federalism: Barbados and theWest Indies* (Gainesville: University of Florida Press), 82. Also Prescod to Tregold 1840, May 29; Prescod to Lord Russell, Nov. 21, 1840; Rhodes House Library, ms. S22. The *Liberal*, March 25, 1840; August 15, 1838.
11 See 'A Message of the House of Assembly of Barbados to the Governor', March 13, 1838, co 28/122; 'An Address of Robert B. Clarke to the Assembly of Barbados', *Journal of Barbados* General Assembly, April 24, 1838, co. 31/51.
12 *Barbados Mercury and Bridgetown Gazette*, August 31, 1816.
13 *Barbados Mercury and Bridgetown Gazette*, August 31, 1816.

14 C. Fyfe, *A History of Sierra Leone*. (Lon. 1963), 136.

15 Governor MacCarthy to Colonial Office, co 267/164.

16 Carr to Colonial Office, co 267/164.

17 Russell to Carr, co 267/164.

18 The *Times* [Barbados] July 17, 1863.

19 The *Times* [Barbados] July 17, 1863.

20 The *Times* [Barbados] July 17, 1863.

21 The *Times* [Barbados] July 17, 1863.

22 The *Times* [Barbados] July 17, 1863.

23 The *Times* [Barbados] July 17, 1863.

24 The *Times* [Barbados] August 4, 1863.

25 The *Times* [Barbados] October 9, 1863.

26 The *Times*, August 18, 1863

27 The *Times*, July 7, 1863. See also, Governor's correspondence, co 28 series July, 1863.

28 The *Times*, July 7, 1863.

29 The *Times*, July 7, 1863.

30 Governor Walker to Colonial Office, Government House, July 28th, 1863.

31 Governor Walker to Colonial Office, Government House, July 28th, 1863.

32 Governor Walker to Colonial Office, Government House, July 28th, 1863.

33 Governor Walker to Colonial Office, August 9, 1863 co 28/196–8.

34 Minutes of the House of Assembly, July 28, 1863.

35 Proclamation, Governor Walker, Government House, Barbados 24 July, 1863.

36 Governor Walker to Colonial Office, August 9, 1863, co 28 series.

37 A. De V. Phillips, 'The Political Elite in Barbados, 1880–1914: Aristocracy, Plantocracy, or Bureaucracy', History Seminar Paper, Department of History, UWI, Barbados, 1977.

38 Phillips, 'The Political Elite in Barbados, 1880–1914: Aristocracy, Plantocracy, or Bureaucracy'.

39 Phillips, 'The Political Elite in Barbados, 1880–1914: Aristocracy, Plantocracy, or Bureaucracy'.

40 Phillips, 'The Political Elite in Barbados, 1880–1914: Aristocracy, Plantocracy, or Bureaucracy'.

41 Phillips, 'The Political Elite in Barbados, 1880–1914: Aristocracy, Plantocracy, or Bureaucracy'.

42 George Belle, 'The Abortive Revolution of 1876 in Barbados', *Journal of Caribbean History*, vol. 18, 1984.

43 George Belle, 'The Abortive Revolution of 1876 in Barbados'.

44 G. J. Chester, *Translantic Sketches* (London, 1869).

45 Phillips, 'The Political Elite, in Barbados, 1880–1914: Aristocracy, Plantocracy, or Bureaucracy'; see also by Phillips, 'The Racial Factor in Politics in Barbados, 1880–1914', History Department. Seminar Paper, UWI, Barbados, 1973.

46 Barbados Agricultural Reporter, Oct. 26, 1905.

47 Dr J. F. Clarke, Testimony before the West India Royal Commission, 1897.

48 See Hilary Beckles, *The Development of West Indies Cricket*: Vol. 1, *The Age of Nationalism*, (The University of the West Indies Press, 1998, Kingston), 20–46.

49 Beckles, *The Development of West Indies Cricket*, 20–46.

50 Beckles, *The Development of West Indies Cricket*, 20-46.

Four

The War of General Green: 1876 Rebellion Against Post-Emancipation Slavery

*T*he 1876 workers rebellion, or the War of General Green, took place on the 60th anniversary of the 1816 anti-slavery rebellion – described by the *Barbados Times* newspaper as the 'War of General Bussa', the name and title of the principal military leader in the struggle.[1] As was the case in 1816, Barbadian workers in 1876 led into battle by their own peers, General Green and Colonel Baird, sought to overthrow the dictatorship of the planter elite and establish a society along more democratic, egalitarian lines. Importantly, their concern was to uproot the rule of the Great House, its class and race oppression, and the determining power of white supremacy ideology. The political thinking of workers indicated the maturity of their vision, despite the tendency of the white chroniclers of the time to minimise the magnitude and clarity of their agenda.[2]

A telegram sent from Barbados to London with news of the rebellion sought to inform rather than alarm. It stated: 'Riots throughout the island. Plantations and houses sacked, animals destroyed, enormous destruction of property, over 40 rioters shot, troops actively employed, city threatened, business suspended, families seeking shipping, rioters report they have governor's sanction, immediate recall necessary, save colony.'[3] The rebellion, according to historian Alana Johnson, was organised on the ground by the Dottin brothers who were in command of 1,000 labourers grouped into ten regiments of 100. These units went from estate to estate waving a red flag, securing food for the people by raiding plantation provision grounds, destroying the property of their employers, and threatening to murder those with a known record of abusive relations to Blacks. They were in effective control of large sections of the island, and drove fear into the souls of the Great House folks.[4] The Dottin brothers, took instructions from a central command, individuals whom they recognised as their leaders.

The official reports of the rebellion submitted to the Colonial Office by the governor, suggest that there were two principal military leaders who received formal rank from their followers. According to these reports the commanders of plantation-based military units recognised a labourer by the name of J.P. Green as their 'General'. Green was shot in the right lung during the battle at Applewhite Estate, and was removed to the General Hospital as a prisoner where he died.

General Green gave orders, the official report stated, to another labourer, a man named 'Smith Baird, whom the military units recognised as their 'colonel', or second in command'. Little more is said of Colonel Baird. General Green, it was said, led the sacking of the Hinckson's Great House at Applewhite Estate. It was here that he was shot by Mr Hinckson who had received beforehand security reinforcements in the form of six policemen who stationed themselves at strategic points on his property. Three of the six policemen fled during the attack of General Green's unit; two of them were found in hiding at Locust Hall Plantation, and the other was captured and tortured by General Green's men.[5]

Political historian George Belle, who provides a rigorous assessment of the war against the sugar planters, sets out in a lively fashion the ideological context and political content of the workers' actions. He wrote:

> The political events of 1876 represent a critical juncture in the political history of Barbados. The 1876 political crisis was the most serious the society had experienced since the 1816 slave rebellion and the adjustment problems of the emancipation years of the 1830s. Indeed, it is reasonable to argue that the 1876 political crisis was the most serious in the history of Barbados. For those reasons alone 1876 presents itself as a nodal juncture

in the political development of the island. However, besides this, the 1876 crisis facilitates the analysis of three features critical to the politics of development of Barbados and to an understanding of that politics: oligarchy, democracy, and revolution. By 1876 slavery had been abolished for some forty years. Changes, of course, had occurred since the 1830s, but the early post-emancipation period remained intact. The island was still ruled and economically controlled by a rigid oligarchy. No extension of the franchise had taken place since 1842, and the planter class with some exceptions was still elected by the planter class to the House of Assembly. With a population of some 162,042 persons in 1876, only some 1,664 were recorded as registered electors . . .[6]

The 1876 rebellion, then, was an attempt to restore the integrity of the emancipation promised, but compromised in the years after 1838. Freedom from enslavement was the political objective of the struggle.

The *London Times*, June 24, 1876 reported that the rebellion was caused by low and falling wages, insufficiency of education and social relief, oppression, taxation, stark poverty, rising vagrancy and destitution, high and rising infant mortality rates, social suffering and spiralling crime, and the general cruelty associated with the Contract Laws. In short, war was declared by a post slavery generation not willing to accept slave-like conditions and opting for the revolutionary cause.[7]

Influence of General Bussa

The symbolic power of the 1816 rebellion is established in the reports of 1876. Newspaper commentaries, and official investigations indicate that workers were deriving political sustenance from the 1816 'War of General Bussa', and were determined to succeed on this second occasion.

The War of General Bussa took place during the Easter period [April 14-17] 1816. The war of 'General Green' erupted on Easter Monday, April 17, and lasted for nine days. The Easter period, the time of resurrection and ascension, was once again chosen by Blacks as the spiritual time to rise from oppression and forge the freedom. The significance of an Easter Revolution in Barbados weighed heavily on the consciousness of the white community. Kortright Davis noted that 'the planters had always stood in fear of Negro uprising every Easter time, and there appeared to have been consistent rumours that rioting would break out during the Easter Season'.[8]

Not surprisingly, Easter Monday was marked by tension and the chill of expectation. Rev A.H. Moore reported that few people attended his church that day, and according to Davis 'very few persons had been present at the traditional Easter Monday entertainment at the school house at Mt Tabor for fear of uprising'. Rev Moore also noted that two of his lay preachers on their way to Clifton Hall on Sunday were stoned by young black men as they passed through Russia Gully, and a white bookkeeper was attacked at the same site. Moore reported, nonetheless, that the day itself 'passed off without anything noteworthy'. The night, however, was marked by extensive cane fires, and a few incidents of attacks on white persons. By early Tuesday morning general rebellion had broken out.[9]

Memory of the 'War of General Bussa' was strong within the black community, exercising a powerful hold over its imagination. The community knew of Bussa's achievements and failures in organising the war for freedom. At the same time, they understood the reasons for Bussa's defeat and held a desire not to repeat military errors. The evidence shows the 1876 war as a planned follow-up to the 1816 war, and sets the nineteenth century apart as an age of revolution in the political traditions of Blacks.

The *Barbados Times* made the following report on Monday morning, April 24, 1876:

> Since the publication of our last issue, the whole island has been suddenly thrown into a state of excitement and confusion, absolutely unprecedented in the annals of Barbados, as is attested by the oldest livers among us. The 'War of General Bussa' was a comparatively partial affair, and the anticipated slave retaliation at the period of emancipation ended in smoke, whereas the present riotous movement has extended its contagion from St. Peter's parish in the north to Christ Church in the south. The dissatisfaction fermented among the labouring classes . . . has arrived at its legitimate climax, and the storm of rebellion has burst forth with an avalanche of savagery. For some days past there had been sinister rumours about an

intended 'rising' at or about Easter which threw the country's residents into a ferment of consternation and alarm.[10]

An official report filed in the British Parliamentary Papers for the period 1871-1876, contained a letter signed 'a white man', dated July 20, 1875, in which two important references were made to the 'War of General Bussa'. First, the action taken by the governor which suppressed the rebellion was referred to as 'Bussa's Marshall Law'. Second, it indicated that the 'Negroes in this time' were more 'enlightened', and skilled in the use of firearms, which was not the case in 1816. The author was explicit on this issue, and stated that the Blacks no longer 'put shot at bottom and powder at top'. This statement serves to draw attention to humorous references to Blacks injuring themselves while seeking to use shot guns and cannons against the militia and imperial troops in the battles of 1816.[11]

The invocation of Bussa in the reports on the 'War of General Green' had to do also with the use of political rhetoric and propaganda by leaders in an effort to mobilise workers for mass action. In 1816 the rallying call was that the British Parliament had legislated emancipation in 1814, when the Registry Bill was debated and passed in the Commons, and that the slave owners were hiding news of this development rather than implementing the imperial will. Rebel leaders, then, saw it as their duty and honour to carry out the royal wish and overthrow slavery.

From early January 1876, rumours circulated on the island carrying the message that sugar planters intended in short time to restore slavery, abolish wages, and confine Blacks to the plantations. The July 20, 1875 letter by 'a white man' made reference to a black who had said 'kill we will . . . if slavery again came'. The following month, acting Governor Freeling had notified the Earl of Carnarvon, that during a meeting of the Executive Council, July 24, 1875:

> Sir G. Briggs (of Farley Hill) rose to say that he thought it his duty to bring to my notice certain rumours that had been circulated that Government intended to change the Constitution and to introduce slavery, that he, Sir Graham Briggs, was the cause, that the lower classes had been led to

believe this, and the result was a general feeling of alarm, with threats against himself.[12]

Freeling expressed concern about the state of anxiety in the country with respect to notions of restoring slavery, and dispatched Rev Cleaver, temporary head of the Wesleyan Mission, to Speightstown, and Rev Edgehill, head of the Moravians, to 'calm the people'. He attached a copy of the letter received by Sir Briggs. The threat to him was explicit. It stated:

> I write to tell you that a woman living down the road who has, as she expresses it, 'done for me for the last 15 years,' had made it 'her business' (her own words again) to come and tell me to write and let you know that the Negroes all up and down this road swear, that if they ever catch you after dark, they 'will lick you up side down in our carriage'; they say you are trying 'to bring back slavery,' that at the late meeting in Speightstown Mr. F. (Foderingham) stated that you wanted to begin by reducing wages to 15 cents per day, and that Mr. F. said 'I will consent to that.'[13]

In addition, the sworn statement of E.H. Grant before Justice of the Peace, J.H. Leacock, also makes reference to Bussa within the 1876 rebellion. Grant, a bookkeeper at St Nicholas Plantation in the parish of St Peter, was attacked by a gang of Blacks. 'One of them,' he said, 'held a stone towards my face and threatened to knock me down, saying that he would not do like Bussa.' The reference here to Bussa points to the policy pursued in 1816 not to violently assault white civilians, but to confine combat to the militia and imperial troops.[14]

On March 18, Fred Cook, overseer at Hennessey's Estate in Christ Church, commenting on the changed attitude of workers, said:

> . . . when we give the people their usual instructions respecting their work in the field and buildings, we find them insubordinate, and they say they need not bother with work as the Governor has given orders that they shall have two shillings a day and as much land as they wish to plant and they can't be certain when it is to commence, it may be next week. The work of the plantation is being retarded in consequence of this impression on the people's minds. I was coming to town yesterday morning

when I was met by five men, one of them called to me by name, and said, 'We know you are going for money, make haste and return, and we will take away your money and horse and send you home with a good licking. You may have a revolver, but we have one too . . .'[15]

Confederation Politics

Since emancipation the Colonial office had sought to replace the Old Representative System of elected assembles with executive authority (Crown rule) throughout the West Indies; Jamaica resisted this policy adamantly during 1839, and Parliament backed off to reconsider strategy. The events surrounding the workers' rebellion at Morant Bay in Jamaica in 1865, however, enabled this policy to be implemented. By 1875, the Colonial Office's political policy for Barbados was twofold (a) a confederation with the Windward Islands (b) direct Crown rule. The Barbados Assembly prepared to resisted this policy by suggesting that the loss of the Representative System would be the denial of ancient rights, and a triumph of imperial interests. Trinidad and Guiana were already crown-ruled colonies, and the Jamaica planters, in order to prevent Blacks and Coloureds taking over the Assembly under franchise reforms and undermining white authority, had finally asked for the imposition of Crown rule and the Executive System. The Barbadian planter class had no such fear, and considered that there was no political crisis deep enough to warrant such an imposition.

The precedents for confederation were ample. Barbados had been involved in such a structure during the late seventeenth century with the Leewards, and after 1834 with the Windwards. In 1871, also, the Leewards were successfully confederated. For these, and related reasons, the Colonial Office believed that Barbadian confederation, coupled with crown colony rule, would not result in any major political resistance. At the end of 1875 John Pope Hennessey was appointed governor with the duty of implementing these aspects of Colonial Office policy. Hennessey failed. In the process the colony was torn by rebellion and bloodshed.

The Colonial Office sought to legitimise its policy on the grounds that a confederated executive system would be efficient, economical, and the only way to achieve political representation for the wide cross-section of free society. On these points the Barbadian ruling elite was divided, and for the first time since emancipation, sections within it pitted against each other. In March 1876, Governor Hennessey had received reports, which he passed on to the Colonial Office, that the anti-confederate defenders of the status quo had begun to organise themselves to resist, even if violently. The vanguard organisation of this group was the Barbados Defence Association (BDA) which pledged to defend the 'constitution' and protect the social order. The principal leaders of this group, according to Hennessey's report, were S. Yearwood, J. Smith, J.A. Lynch, Thomas Sealy, Sir John Sealy, J.H. Shannon, J. Spencer, S.H. Collymore, J. Innis, B. Innis, T. Gill and D.C. DaCosta.

The BDA drew up a list of prominent persons whom they considered confederates and supportive of the governor in the 'destruction of the colony's ancient constitution'. This list of over 20 names was published in the the *Agricultural Reporter*, and was headed by Bishop Mitchinson, Lord Bishop of Barbados, and Sir Thomas Graham Briggs, member of the Legislative Council (owner of Farley Hill Plantation). With the 'enemy' identified, the BDA mounted an island wide political campaign to strengthen opposition to Governor Hennessey. It held mass rallies and used the oratorical skills of Thomas Gill, a former Speaker of the Assembly, and Joseph Connell, owner of Oughterson's plantation, to attract the attention of Blacks and Whites alike. At a mass meeting held at the Promenade Gardens in Bridgetown, speakers accused the confederates, among other things, of plotting to restore slavery, removing the political rights of inhabitants, imposing heavy taxes on property owners for the financing of government in the Windward Islands, and seeking to gain their ends by orchestrating disruption and violence within the society. Variations of these themes were published in the *Agricultural Reporter* and the *Times* – newspapers of the planter class and the middle class coloureds respectively.

The confederates also attempted to mount a mass campaign, both to defend themselves against the BDA, and to present the merits of their case to the populace. To assist in the attainment of these ends, they established the *Barbados People and Windward Islands Gazette*, a newspaper designed to reach those sections of the community which, for various reasons, stayed away from political meetings, as well as to present political information clearly and simply for the labouring classes.

It was the first time that Blacks found themselves at the centre of ruling class conflict. The *West Indian*, a conservative newspaper, particularly in the early part of April, suggested that Governor Hennessey had sought to lodge his case at the lowest social level with the result that a class war had been unleashed within the society. Such conflict, the paper argued, would lead to mob politics, mob violence, and a cult of destruction. In addition, the confederates were accused of misleading ill-informed working people with 'communistic' doctrines about equalitarian distribution of land, and the 'utopian uplifting of the poor to the material and social standard of their employers'.

Though the confederates did not openly suggest that Crown rule would lead to any major distribution of wealth and power in favour of the poor, labourers had already adopted the position that any movement which sought to break the dictatorship of the sugar barons could only assist them to attain greater civil rights. As such, working class spokesmen sought to win mass support for Hennessey, while sections of the black and coloured middle class rallied behind the Barbados Defence Association. By the middle of April working class leaders, ahead of their small armies, attempted to resolve the impasse with a strategy of open warfare aimed at toppling the recalcitrant planter class. The accumulation of grievances by workers since the dreaded Contract Law of 1840, had convinced them that the planter class was the enemy. As such, the constitutional debate provided the political context in which they saw the possibility of expressing their disapproval of post-emancipation 'slavery', and for offering the imperial government the perfect opportunity to implement policies for genuine socioeconomic emancipation.

Resurrection Rebellion

Late in the night of Easter Monday, April 17, 1876, the workers began their war for freedom within the wider context of an imperial crisis associated with developments in constitutional politics. The leaders of the rebellion considered their cause to be just and legitimate. They were fighting for more than justice, they were fighting for survival itself. Famine was on the increase, and landless emancipation had rendered them incapable of an effective strategic survival response. There was no place to retreat; and to strike at the source of their oppression was the only way forward. They had reached desperation level as wages were being cut weekly, and unemployment was increasing within the context of inflationary prices for food.

George Belle examined the schedules of wages and prices in the colony, and indicated the inevitability of widespread hardship, even among the employed. He wrote:

> The cost of consumption goods and the wages worked for by the labouring class additionally give some indication of the material burden on that class. Praedial labourers worked for eight pence a day or, if working per ton or job, an able bodied labourer could earn from 10d to 1s 8d within ordinary working hours. Domestic servants who were hired by the month had wages varying from 8s. 4d to £1 17s 6d. A tradesman would earn 2s 6d per day and masons and carpenters 2s to 2s 6d per day. It must of course be remembered that there was no job security for any of these workers and work could be very irregular. The sugar crop for instance lasted six months and the employment of many of the labouring class depended on crop work . . . The 1876 Blue Book of Statistics gave the following prices for articles of use for consumption: wheaten flour, £1 13s 4d per barrel of 196 lb; wheaten bread, 3d per lb; horned cattle, £15 per head; horses, £40 per head; sheep, £1 13s 4d per head; goats, £1 5s per head; milk, 1s 4d per gallon; fresh butter, 1s per lb; salt butter, 1s 8d per lb; cheese, 1s 6d per lb; beef, 10d per lb; mutton, 1s per lb; pork, 6d per lb; rice, 3d per lb; coffee; 10d per lb; tea, 3s 4d per lb; refined sugar, 7d per lb; salt, ½d per lb; wine, per dozen £1 13s 4d; brandy, 16s 8d per gallon; beer 10s 6d per dozen; tobacco, 2s 6d per lb.[16]

An analysis of these circumstances by Bruce Hamilton suggests, furthermore, that in addition to prices moving ahead of employed workers' ability to cope, there were other charges upon their falling wages, such as taxes. He stated:

> . . . In times of stress . . . the labourers were the principal sufferers. Hennessey reports in May 1876 the dismissal of labourers, the reduction of wages and the demand of more work for the same wages . . . Combinations to raise wages remained, apparently, illegal . . . Although it was claimed that the working classes paid no taxes except indirectly as consumers, and that these were infinitesimal, as the import duties on food were so low, £24,330 was levied on imported foodstuffs of the sort used by the poor in 1873. Hennessey quoted the . . . West Indian newspaper in 1874 as calling attention to how taxes on provisions used by labourers had been largely substituted for taxes on land . . . [17]

Archdeacon Grant E. Thomas broke ranks with the Anglican clergy and spoke on behalf of the poor. In his opinion, peace and social advancement were 'indispensable elements in a Christian and civilised community'. Since 1859, Thomas claimed, many governors of the colony, including Grey, Colebrook, Hincks, Walker, and Freeling, had petitioned the imperial government and the local Assembly to address the question of growing poverty and destitution among Blacks. According to Kortright Davis, Bishop Mitchinson supported the view of the Archdeacon that poverty and destitution were increasing, and that the case was 'apparently hopeless'.

The evidence of spreading famine resulting from landlessness could be found in the coroner's reports of inquests that made 'shameless disclosures' that 'the Bishop and many of the clergy have avowed that not a day passes without its one or more victims to starvation in this island, no bigger than the Isle of Wight'. The condition of the poor, Thomas concluded, 'was no better than it was in 1845'. The situation gave no reason to be optimistic. Destitution was linked to landlessness and the planters' determination to keep wages below subsistence level while considering the poor not worthy of social welfare provisions. In his judgement the local oligarchy was incapable of seeing the workers as fellow members of a community, and therefore could not rule with public consent. Their removal from power, and the substitution of royal government, was the answer.[18]

The political elite was divided with respect to the question of Barbados forming a Federation with the Windward Islands. By Tuesday afternoon, April 18, news of isolated incidents, described as triggers to workers' rebellion, were being reported by Police Magistrates, and discussed widely. The *Times* [Barbados] carried a report which described growing rebellion in the southern parishes:

> By Tuesday afternoon, certain notorious proceedings were commenced in St. Philip's parish, at Byde Mill, by certain crowds demanding liquor, digging up potatoes, and setting fire to the cane fields. Mr. Sealy, Magistrate of the district, read the Riot Act, but to no purpose, as the rioters refused to disperse until the police were brought up. On the two next days, the same wanton acts were perpetrated, and the saturnalia continued up to the present time (24th), to such an extent that the government has found it necessary upon being urged by repeated deputations to call out the military.[19]

Initially, it was thought, on account of such reports, that the incidents constituted a 'mere potato riot'. But it was realised by Wednesday 19, that there were grander considerations behind the assault on the plantation. By Wednesday evening, said the *Times*' report, the rebels had 'prosecuted their work in all directions . . . down to the very outskirts of Bridgetown.' Along the way 'houses have been completely sucked of their contents, cane fields fired, potato crops destroyed, in some cases to the estimated value of a thousand dollars and more, and estates' stock have been wantonly hacked to pieces with cane bills and cutlasses'.[20]

The human aspect of the rebellion was also detailed in the *Times*' report. Readers were informed that 'proprietors and managers have been obliged to hide for their lives, and whole families have abandoned their houses and been obliged to remove to Bridgetown for protection'. Blacks were determined to take possession of the colony, and to give effect to their vision of emancipation. The landlessness of their freedom had been understood since the 1830s as a fraudulent act of deeper exploitation perpetrated by the colonial government, its local and imperial supporters. Seizing the land, then, was the critical act that indicated the developmental vision of Blacks in respect to economic and political enfranchisement, and cultural freedom.

The *Times* also reported on this aspect of the rebellion. Its report of April 24, 1876 presented the following details:

> The notions have been systematically organised by ringleaders who, on entering a field, read a paper and formally gave their followers possession of the soil, openly referring to Pope Hennessey as an authority for the aggression. In this way Joes River, Drax Hall, Rose Hall, Bank Hall, Bush Hall, The Pine, Waterford, Lears and other places have been invaded.[21]

The following month a group of the island's clergy was concerned with the issue of black landlessness. After considerable fact-finding exercises among the poor, they wrote to the Secretary of State for Colonies, the Earl of Carnarvon, through the offices of Bishop Mitchinson and Governor Hennessey. They informed the Secretary that the rebellion was due in large measure to the belief that they were entitled to land, and a general redistribution of the economic resources monopolised by the planters. Furthermore, their leaders had informed them that a royal order was sent to the Governor instructing him to give them land. In conclusion, the cleric indicated that the workers' feelings against all land owners and property holders 'owing to the belief noted above, is one of intense bitterness and hostility, that will require firmness and judgement on the part of all in authority to remove, if it is removed in this generation.'

In a number of confrontations many police constables were injured, including Colonel Clements, the chief in the Force, and 'others have mysteriously disappeared'. The rebellion 'reached a culmination on Saturday morning (22nd). By this time 'all stores were closed, trade was entirely suspended, and a detachment of the military, including artillery, was again in requisition.' The merchants of Bridgetown organised themselves into a defence posse, and sought permission from the governor to patrol the streets with arms. James A. Lynch was commissioned to carry the proposition into effect. During the day, there were crowded meetings on Broad Street, where several hundred unlisted white men were enlisted as special constables, and were divided into companies under different commanders – all under the supervision of J Gardiner Austin as Adjutant. These companies mustered in the public buildings, separated in different directions, and patrolled the various thoroughfares of Bridgetown until morning.

On Sunday, 23rd, according to the *Times*,

> the riots continued, and a large number of prisoners were captured, carried to the main guard, and tried by sitting Magistrate, Captain Delamere. Ashton Hall Great House in Speightstown was burnt, and large numbers of residents in the town took refuge in Bridgetown, travelling by boat. Many white ladies and children also fled aboard ships lying at anchor in Carlisle Bay.[22]

Accounts of the build-up to the rebellion are detailed and graphic. There was considerable rage within the black community with respect to the sabotage of the objectives of emancipation legislation. Blacks wanted their freedom from the bondage imposed by the contract laws and related judicial provisions. They wanted land, fair wages, and respect. The white community was not prepared to offer any of these concessions. That is, they were not willing to consider emancipation as a social and economic reality for the black community. Furthermore, they were prepared to further consolidate the racist culture of white supremacy ideology as the only legitimate framework for Barbados' development.

On March 23, an Anglican clergy who did not sign his name, sent a letter to Governor Hennessey deploring the racism of the planters, and calling attention to the workers' grievances. The spirit of rebellion in the air he attributed to the growing political and social repression of the elite, and its refusal to see Blacks as free persons. In his opinion, the planters had effectively maintained the important features of slavery in the years after emancipation legislation had been passed. With respect to this attitude, the reverend gentleman stated that planters continue to see Blacks as 'Goods and chattel, inferior to their horses and mules, and less to be cared for, for if they die they will lose money, whereas those are no less to them when they die; therefore when the labourer becomes impaired by age or use, they cast him aside, as a useless encumbrance'.[23]

He called upon the governor to show consideration to the labourers by 'bettering their position' and add 'a bright lustre' to his administration. The governor, however, was already in receipt of the details of a letter written by another clergyman, Rev Austin to a Mr Chambers in which it was stated 'the growing excitement and discontent amongst the Negroes show themselves by cane burning every night, and in muttered insolence as you drive along the road'.

The testimony submitted by Evans Grant, bookkeeper at St Nicholas Plantation in St Peter, in which he made reference to a rebel's invocation of Bussa, also sets out the nature of a violent event at Prospect Plantation the month before the Rebellion started. Grant's testimony contains the following statement:

> On the 28th of March last I attended at Prospect Plantation, in the said parish [St. Peter], where it was advertised that an anti-Confederation meeting was to take place. I reached the place about 10 minutes to 5 o'clock p.m. I found a few gentlemen collected in front of the dwelling-house. I overtook Mr. Bourne in the road and went to the place with him. About 5 o'clock Mr. Pedder, manager of Prospect, and the Rev. Mr. Greenidge, Mr. Deane, and two or three others, went towards a platform erected on a pasture near the house, and I went with them. Mr. Greenidge was, before we reached the platform, turned back by a man with a stick, and I and the others, too, were turned back, and as our backs were turned the mob commenced to pelt stones at us most furiously; we had done or said nothing to excite the people. Mr. Deane was riding alongside of me and he was knocked from his horse. I believe that it was done by a stone pelted by the mob, and I saw blood flow from his head. He appeared to me to be senseless, and I assisted to take him to the house. I did not see who struck him. Some of the gentlemen tried to get away, but the better part were turned back to the house, and eventually nearly all that did not return were driven into the house and the house was pelted. From the time the pelting commenced it was continued until I left at a quarter to 6;

I, with Mr. Bourne, got shelter in the stable. Some time after we were in
the stable many of the mob came in there and threatened to kill us; they
accused Mr. Bourne of having a revolver, and searched him and found that
he had none.[24]

The workers were not short on organisation, but needed guns in
order to strengthen their offensives. Many were armed with muskets,
and as indicated in the letter to the governor signed by 'A white man',
they boasted knowing how to use them. Unlike the 1816 affair they
were not prepared to confine their aggression to the militia and imperial
military. All property owners were the oppressors who were responsible
for the famine and social destitution. The post-emancipation system of
slavery that made them desperate men and women was administered by
the wider white community, and as such it was the enemy.[25]

Death and Destruction

As in 1816, the militia was ineffective. The white men and boys in
the community, including police constables and magistrates, were not
prepared to confront the armed masses. In fact, most of them fled with
their families for cover, leaving their properties at the mercy of the rebels.
It was the intervention of the imperial troops from the Garrison in
Bridgetown that made the critical difference. This was also the case in
1816.

The field reports of the military contain considerable evidence to
support this view. Some planters went in search of the military while
their families fled to forts, ships in the harbour, and public buildings in
Bridgetown. A military commander, Major Blythe, describes three days
in the field with striking graphic imagery that conveys the human and
material destruction associated with the armed conflict. He wrote:

I marched with the detachment under my command from the garrison,
and arrived at Gun Hill about 6:30 p.m., 21st instant. On our way the
people appeared to be much excited, and the planters we met on our
march alarmed, but their confidence was restored by our appearance. We

passed through three estates which had been previously plundered that day by the rioters, but these depredations were confined to robbing provision grounds, no stock having been touched, or houses entered. On Saturday morning, 22nd instant, our attention was attracted by crowds of people collecting all round this station, and we had several applications from managers of estates in the neighbourhood for assistance, they being threatened with violence. I therefore marched 40 men in the direction of Grove's Estate, about one and a half miles to the north of Gun Hill; on our arrival we found that about a quarter of an hour previously the mob had dispersed, having first destroyed and taken away with them the under-mentioned cattle, viz., six pigs, seven goats, one calf, six sheep. We observed that the ground in the vicinity of the house was covered with blood from the slaughtered animals. Being informed that the rioters had gone in the direction of Applewhite (Mr. James Hinckson's) Estate (about two miles to the west of the above-mentioned estate), we followed them, and I may say arrived not a moment too soon, as the rioters had gutted the house, and threatened the lives of the inmates; on our road we met several gentlemen on horseback, who had been sent to hasten our arrival; on our approach we noticed a number of people dispersing in various directions, some of them carrying what I now conclude was plunder, but a large portion (perhaps two or three hundred) were loitering about, most of them appeared to be armed with bill-hooks and long cane knives, who on being questioned explained that they were the usual tools for their daily work, cutting canes.[26]

The destruction of life and property was extensive. Dead bodies, almost entirely those of Blacks, were scattered all over the countryside, surrounded by gutted buildings, burnt fields, and the rotting carcasses of farm animals. Major Blythe reported that along the avenue leading up to Applewhite 'Great House', he found a dying man, 'shot through the right lung'. On getting to the house his men found large stones strewn all round in the verandah which:

Had evidently been used as missiles, and for breaking in the doors. All glass smashed, doors, windows, sashes, and Venetians hacked and broken as if by hatchets or billhooks; in this way an entrance appears to have been made. The house was completely gutted of all portable articles, and the heavier furniture destroyed; for instance the piano smashed, chandelier pulled from the ceiling and broken to pieces, also marble tables shattered in pieces, and lock-up places for the reception of papers and money burst open, and in fact the lower part of the house a complete wreck, as was the case with the upper part, where the family was in hiding, and the rebels had just gained access to when the report reached them of the army's approach, which caused them to decamp. Another rebel was found lying dead, shot through the forehead in rear of the house.[27]

As was the case in 1816, however, the number of fatalities were overwhelmingly those of Blacks, a distribution that speaks to their technological disadvantage within combat. Blacks were killed and injured by gunshots and bayonets. Most Whites injured sustained wounds from stones and other missiles thrown at them. It was a one-sided affair in terms of the use of guns. The tables below show the names, numbers, and cause of death and injuries sustained by Blacks for the 21st and 22nd of April. The list is not complete but it is a fair sample.

Table 1
Blacks Killed in Battle, April 21–22, 1876

Name	Age	Domicile	Details
Robert Sendhouse	35	St Joseph	Bayoneted by Police; died on the spot
London Bird	33	St George	Shot in head at Applewhite Estate by Police
Charles Cummins	24	St John	Shot in thigh by Police at Halton; lost leg and died
Joseph Went	17	St George	Shot in leg by Police; died after amputation
Joseph Brathwaite	30	St Philip	Shot by soldier of 35th Regiment
J P Green	27	St George	Shot in right lung by Mr Hinckson, owner of Applewhite Estate
Murray Clarke	20	St Joseph	Shot in groin, found dead on April 26

Blacks Wounded in the Rebellion, April 21–23, 1876

Name	Age	Domicile	Details
Rebecca Daniel	19	St Philip	Shot in stomach
John Bayley	26	St Philip	Shot in thigh, leg amputated
Isaac Ward	23	St Philip	Shot in leg
Herbert Sealy	10	St John	Shot in instep
Rebecca Alleyne	21	St John	Shot in arm, amputated
William Hill	26	St George	Shot in thigh
Joseph Hoyte	30	St John	Shot in leg
Mary Belle	33	St John	Shot in foot
Mary Taylor	46	St Philip	Wounded by bayonet
Margaret Shepherd	26	St Philip	Wounded by bayonet
R.W. Crichlow	15	St Joseph	Shot by Police in arm and knee in Halton battle
Mary Forde	?	St Michael	Shot in bowel by Mr Haynes, owner of Staple Grove, in battle there
Henry Jones	23	Christ Church	Shot in back by manager of Fairy Valley Estate
Hardy Clarke	45	St Joseph	Shot in arm by Police during battle at Crab Hole
George Thomas	34	St George	Shot in back
John Carrington	25	St Thomas	Shot in thumb, amputated
John Holder	40	St Michael	Shot in face
Mary Blackman	38	St George	Shot in arm by Mr Whitehall, manager of Rowan's Estate (son also shot)
Alexander Small	19	St George	Wounded in head by stone
James Griffith	19	St Michael	Shot in chest
William Blackman	12	St George	Fractured skull

Source: British Parliamentary Papers, Vol. 1871–76:
Papers relating to the West Indies. George Belle, *The Abortive Revolution of 1876 in Barbados.*

It is possible that officials minimised the number of police and soldiers who were injured in battle. In each case of Black rebellion during the colonial regime, a policy was enforced to under-report police and militia fatalities and injuries, and to over-estimate the magnitude of damage to property. There is no reason to believe that this was not the case in 1876.

Using the official records Belle surmised that only eight policemen were injured during nearly two weeks of rebellion in at least eight parishes. His analysis shows that Sergeant Taylor, 36, of St Philip received wounds to the head, arms, and feet in the battle at Byde Mill estate; Constable Harrison, 30 also of St Philip, unable to dodge a stone hurled at him had his chin opened; other police who received injuries from stones hurled at them were Constables Mapp, 30, Griffith, 43 and Acting Corporal Ashby, 39. Colonel Clements, Inspector General, 48 of St Michael, suffered blows to the body and had a temporal artery severed in a battle; Constable Forde 32, was hacked in the face with a cutlass, and Sergeant Lyder, 40, of St Andrew, had his head opened by a stone during the Crab Hole battle in St Joseph.

The Blacks, then, once again, paid a dearer price in terms of life but declared their position in the strongest possible terms. They were not prepared to accept the new slavery that Emancipation Legislation had created. Instead, they were prepared to fight bloody battles in order to win the civil rights promised but resisted by the planter elite that clung to the traditions of slavery. In effect, they had declared war knowing themselves to be out-gunned by the local militia and imperial troops garrisoned on the island. It was do or die time, as famine was on the increase. They decided to 'do', and many died in the effort.

The rebellion was short-lived – though it lasted much longer than the revolt of 1816. It began on the night of April 17 and lasted until the morning of April 26. Mobilised in units of hundreds, Blacks carried flags and professed to be agents of Governor Hennessey. They moved through the town and country confronting police with guns and an assortment of agricultural weapons and stones. Plantation properties were destroyed and foodstuffs removed from ships and stores, while many Whites fled to safety wherever it could be found. It was on the night of the 20th, when the governor received reports that several prominent Whites were threatened with execution by Blacks, that he called out all the troops in the Garrison to assist the retreating militia and battered police force which had failed to impress. Within six days the rebellion was effectively suppressed.

Unlike the rebellion of 1816, however, the mortality among Blacks did not reach the thousand mark. Seven or eight Blacks were reported to have lost their lives, but no Whites. Hundreds of Blacks, however, and eight policemen were wounded. The rebellion was defeated, partly because the mass participation was not effectively armed, and also because of confusion arising from perceptions of the governor's true position in the matter. A letter which is alleged to have been written by a worker, addressed to the governor, illustrates, perhaps, the fact that Blacks saw themselves as the final catalyst in the conflict between Parliament and Assembly. Also, that they alone could remove oligarchical government in the colony. It is also interesting to note that, like the 1816 revolt, Blacks believed that they could defeat the planters' militia and police, and that the imperial troops, who on both occasions they hoped might assist them, emerged the victorious force. Summing up the situation in the colony, Colonel Sarjeant reported to the Colonial Office:

> There can be no doubt that since the commencement of those riots, a great amount of wanton destruction of the property of planters and others has been perpetuated throughout the country . . . from the 21st instance and during the 21st, 22nd and 23 instance . . .,sufficient in itself to create the greatest and most intense alarm in the minds of landed proprietors . . . There can be no doubt whatever that after the experience gained by the present transaction that Barbados can never be left without the presence of European troops. I am fully convinced that if we had not sufficient force to stem the spirit of riot and disorder openly and unreservedly shown by the evil disposed on this occasion, that the white population, and I have no doubt, would have met with consequences of the most grave and painful character.[28]

Governor Hennessey was praised by the Colonial Office for his effectiveness in putting down the rebellion, though officials were not prepared to dismiss the Assembly's view that he was not to be far removed from the political rhetoric which had informed the uprising. Parliament, however, decided to reconsider their confederation policy, though many members were of the opinion that some planters had deliberately sponsored and stimulated the violent upheaval as part of their campaign against the imposition of Crown rule. It is also true that there were suspicions within the BDA that confederates had encouraged the riots so as to provide Parliament with the context for firmly imposing executive authority. As part of Parliament's policy retreat, Governor Hennessey was 'promoted' to the post of Governor of Hong Kong in November, while members of the disbanded BDA celebrated their victory.

Hennessey was replaced as Governor by Captain George Strahan. Under his administration Parliament entertained the possibility of imposing Crown rule, though without the confederation. But the Colonial Office, receiving reports that Barbadians would continue their resistance, proposed a new line of action which represented an attempt at conciliation. Lord Carnarvon at the Colonial Office offered the Barbadian Assembly the option of keeping their representative system on condition that they allow two members appointed by the Crown to sit in the Legislature. The proposal was rejected outright.

NOTES

1   The *Times*, April 22, 1876. The 1816 Slave rebellion is described in the editorial as 'The War of General Bussa'.

2   See for the most detailed assessment of the workers' struggle in 1876, George Belle, 'The Abortive Revolution of 1876 in Barbados', *The Journal of Caribbean History*, vol. 18 (1984), 1–34; see also Bruce Hamilton, *Barbados and the Confederation Question, 1871–1885* (London: Crown Agents, 1956); W.A. Green, 'The Creolisation of Caribbean History: The Emancipation Era and a Critique of Dialectical Analysis', *Journal of Imperial and Commonwealth History*, vol. 14, no. 3, (1986).

3   Telegram dated April, 24, 1876; Defence Association to Colonial Office. Cited in Hamilton, *Barbados and the Confederation Question, 1871-1885*, 80.

4   Alana Johnson, 'The Abolition of Chattel Slavery in Barbados, 1833–1876', unpublished PhD thesis, Cambridge University, 1994.

5   See British Parliamentary Papers: Correspondence Relating to the Federation of the Leeward Islands of the West Indies and Recent Disturbances in Barbados, 1871–1876.

6   George Belle, 'The Abortive Revolution of 1876 in Barbados', *Journal of Caribbean History*, vol. 18 (1984), 1.

7   *London Times*, June 24, 1876.

8   See Kortright Davis, 'The Church and the Confederation Crisis', Seminar Paper, History Department, UWI, Barbados, 1976.

9   Kortright Davis, 'The Church and the Confederation Crisis'; see also Kortright Davis, *Cross and Crown in Barbados: Caribbean Political Religion in the late Nineteenth Century* (Frankfurt: P. Lang, 1983).

10 The *[Barbados] Times*, April 24, 1876.

11 British Parliamentary Papers: Correspondence Relating to the Federation of the Leeward Islands of the West Indies and Recent Disturbances in Barbados, 1871–76.

12 British Parliamentary Papers: Correspondence Relating to the Federation of the Leeward Islands of the West Indies and Recent Disturbances in Barbados, 1871–76.

13 British Parliamentary Papers: Correspondence Relating to the Federation of the Leeward Islands of the West Indies and Recent Disturbances in Barbados, 1871–76.

14 British Parliamentary Papers: Correspondence Relating to the Federation of the Leeward Islands of the West Indies and Recent Disturbances in Barbados, 1871–76.

15 British Parliamentary Papers: Correspondence Relating to the Federation of the Leeward Islands of the West Indies and Recent Disturbances in Barbados, 1871–76.

16 Belle, 'The Abortive Revolution of 1876 in Barbados'.

17 Belle, 'The Abortive Revolution of 1876 in Barbados'.

18 See *The West Indian*, June 30, 1876.

19 The *[Barbados] Times*, April 18, 1876.

20 The *[Barbados] Times*, Apri 19, 1876

21 The *[Barbados] Times*, April 24, 1876.

22 The *[Barbados] Times*, April 23, 1876.

23 Hennessey to Carnarvon, March 22, 1876, c.1539, no. 77. Parliamentary Papers: Correspondence Relating to the Federation of the Leeward Islands of the West Indies and Recent Disturbances in Barbados. 1871–76.

24 Parliamentary Papers: Correspondence Relating to the Federation of the Leeward Islands of the West Indies and Recent Disturbances in Barbados 1871–76.

25 Parliamentary Papers: Correspondence Relating to the Federation of the Leeward Islands of the West Indies and Recent Disturbances in Barbados 1871–76.

26 Parliamentary Papers: Correspondence Relating to the Federation of the Leeward Islands of the West Indies and Recent Disturbances in Barbados 1871–76.

27 Parliamentary Papers: Correspondence Relating to the Federation of the Leeward Islands of the West Indies and Recent Disturbances in Barbados 1871–76.

28 See the report of Colonel Sarjeant, Parliamentary Papers: Correspondence Relating to the Federation of the Leeward Islands of the West Indies and Recent Disturbances in Barbados 1871–76; also, Belle, 'The Abortive Revolution of 1876 in Barbados', 15.

Five

Democracy From Below:
The New Grassroots Politics
1876–1937

Response of Famine and Destitution

$\mathscr{T}$he further collapse of the sugar industry in the decade after the 1876 Workers' Rebellion deepened the mass unemployment of the labouring classes. Everywhere, the signs of destitution and hopelessness were evident. In country and town, workers faced starvation and famine. The sick, the infirm and the aged were hardest hit. The women and children too, carried with them in the street drawn faces and sunken eyes as they begged alms. There had been outbreaks of 'potato raids' on the plantations during most of the 1880s, reaching a crescendo in 1895 and 1896. Early in 1897 when a Royal Commission on the Depression in the West India Sugar Industry to investigate the crisis arrived, potato raids and other acts of desperation seemed insufficient and ineffective in redressing widespread starvation.[1]

The 'Potato Riots of 1895' dominated the rural landscape and signalled the workers' continued intention to take things in their own hands in order to survive. C.J. Lawrence, Inspector of Police, said that the riots were 'due to dissatisfaction felt by the labourers at the reduction of wages, and took place directly after the reductions were made'. These acts of grand appropriation of plantation foodstuff, the Inspector stated, were called 'potato riots' because the labourers assembled in large numbers, and looted the potato fields, chiefly at night.

The editorial of the *Times*, January 2, 1895 focussed on the Potato Riot at Boscobel Plantation, but took the opportunity to inform readers of the general tide of food appropriation that was sweeping the island:

> A Report reached Bridgetown a couple of days ago that some labouring people belonging to the district of Boscobel, in the parish of Saint Andrew, had taken it into their heads to institute a potato scramble. The reason assigned for this unusual behaviour on the part of those labourers is that their wages, already quite low, were about to be made lower, at the instance of the Receiver of the Boscobel Plantation. We regret exceedingly this labour outbreak. We know very well that there is at this moment, a vast deal of suffering amongst all classes of toilers on the Island. And we also know that recourse to rioting will in no way cure the disease. Some other and more successful remedy must be applied. What that remedy should be, we are not now attempting to propound. Sufficient to say, that we regard with no little concern the disturbance to which we have referred above. It seems, just the beginning of a graver and sadder state of things to follow, perhaps, in the near future – the contemplation of which stirs, with the deepest emotion, every fibre of our being.[2]

The naming of the Commission indicates some of what there was to know of its intention. It was not a Commission sent to investigate the famine among the labouring poor. It was given terms of reference that indicated imperial concern for the sugar planters whose economy had not been sustainable for near a century, but who clung to the land as a symbol of social status and an instrument of political and economic terror over the dispossessed poor.

The Commission began its business on Wednesday, February 17, 1897, in the Council Chamber at the Public Buildings in Bridgetown. The Chairman, Sir Henry Norman, a former Governor of Jamaica, indicated that 'The object of the Commission, briefly stated, is that we should, after very full inquiry, suggest such measures as may seem to us best calculated to restore or maintain the prosperity of the West Indian colonies'. With this in mind, not surprisingly, the first witnesses were the Hon A.J. Pile, C.M.G., Mr C.P. Clarke, and M.F.F. Clarke, described as 'representatives of a Joint Committee of the Agricultural Society and the Mercantile Body'. Collectively they set out the context of their mismanagement of the economy, and the consequences for themselves as a ruling class.[3]

The Hon A.J. Pile, who sat at the top of the pile of sugar barons in the island, stated that many plantations were now carried on by loans under the Agricultural Aids Act, which made money advanced for working plantations a first charge on the growing crop. He stated that if from any cause such advances should be no longer obtainable, then there would be no alternative but to cease cultivating the plantations so dependent.

The number of dependent plantations was computed at 44, constituting a total of 10,824 acres. These plantations were all in Chancery and had borrowed £32,141. Then there were another 94 plantations with a total of 20,674 acres, still in the hands of their owners, but which had borrowed £64,727. C.P. Clarke assisted the Commissions with an account of the planter's responses to their financial condition. Wages, he said, had been reduced since the early 1890s, as had been the case in earlier times. The workers who were also confronted with an absolute shortage of food, found their capacity to purchase slashed by up to 25 per cent.

Pile, however, was concerned with the effects of the sugar crisis upon future generations of white planters. He stated that there were some 'local corporations, like the Barbados Mutual Life Assurance Society, for instance, which advanced to planters and held a great many of the mortgages'. Most of these mortgages, said Pile, 'arose from legacies being left to younger children by former proprietors, and the estates to the son; and according as the younger children came to age the mortgages passed into other hands'. F.S. Clarke stated: 'labour is plentiful; it is fairly efficient, that is to say, an employer obtains a fair day's work for a fair day's pay; the cost is moderate, and most of the farming operations are done by piece work.' He suggested that male agricultural labourers receive between 10d to 1s per day, and females 7½d per day; children under 16, receive 5d per day.

Admitting that these wages were significantly reduced from the previous decade Pile stated that most workers were not in a position to grow their own food. He estimated that there were 42,000 labourers available to the sugar industry, and that an estate of 500 acres would not employ more than 250 of them, including men, women, and children. The plantation system, he added, occupied about 65,000 acres of farm land, operating therefore with a significant and burdensome structural surplus of dependent workers.

The result of this circumstance was that Blacks could not be catered for to their satisfaction within the sugar sector, and that petty larceny had become 'the curse of the place'. C.P. Clarke added that 1895 was a 'hard year' and that 'petty larceny was about 1,000 higher in consequence of the hard times'. Wages, Pile stated had been 'reduced about 20 per cent' Mr J. Gardiner Austin stated that this reduction was related to the effort by planters to cut the operation cost of production. In 1894, said Austin, when wages began to be reduced, the working expenses of Barbadian planters were £29,635; they fell in 1895 to £22,476, and in 1896 was £24,426. Mr A. Cameron, one of the attorneys for Thomas Daniel and Company, stated that the reduction in wages was brought about in different ways, but were beneficial to the sector.

Table 1
Summary Convictions

Year	Larceny and Serious Offences Against Persons	Minor Offences	Total
1893	4250	4586	8836
1894	4551	4588	9139
1895	5743	3098	8835
1896	4787	3742	8529

Source: Report of the Royal Commission, 1897/98 App.C, Part III

Austin disagreed with the 'surplus labour' argument, and told the Commissioners: 'there were not more labourers in the island than we can provide employment for. We were overburdened with mechanics and loafers. The town was crowded with men who did not and would not work'. Cameron supported Austin and added: 'I may say that labour is cheap and plentiful. We do not wish the agricultural labourers to emigrate, but what we do want to be relieved of is the thousands of loafers and idlers about the town and wharves who do not apparently work for their living'. C.J. Lawrence, Inspector of Police, also supported this line of reasoning and informed the Commission: 'I do not think the actual number of agricultural labourers in Barbados is beyond the requirements of the colony. The number of idlers to be found in the country districts is not very large. In Bridgetown, of course, there are a good many idlers.'

The views presented to the Commission by the clergy varied, though not considerably, from the planters and their mercantile allies. Rev Canon Sealy (Anglican), Rev J. Payne (Wesleyan) and Rev C.T. Oehler (Moravian) were examined and spoke of the social effects of the depression in the sugar industry upon the labouring classes. They indicated that the poor were suffering, especially in Bridgetown, where the population had almost doubled within the last few years on account of the 'large proportion of which has gravitated from the country'. Rev Oehler related the story told him by his wife of a 'man somewhere near his district who has gone half-crazy, and she attributes his condition to the want of support.' 'I suppose', the Rev concluded, 'a great many people lose their senses in consequence of not being properly fed.' The conclusion of Canon Sealy, importantly, was that 'further depression of the sugar industry would lead to a considerable reduction in the cultivation of cane', and that would mean, he emphasised, 'starvation'.

The medical practitioners were called upon to make submissions with regard to the physical health of the poor. Drs F.B. Archer, H.J. Wolseley, C. Hudson and C.G. Gooding engaged the commissioners on the range of public health issues. Gooding's submission showed that there had been 'an increase in the death rate' among the workers. The increase in infant mortality, he said, could not be avoided because mothers were out seeking work, leaving their babies with older children, and the food supply 'is very often improper and unsuitable'. The evidence showed, he said, that the infant mortality rate had 'steadily gone up during the past ten years', even though in some years it had decreased. The oveall death rate, Dr Wolseley stated, 'is enormous – sometimes reaching 50 per cent'.

Dr Hudson stated that 'there is a very high death rate . . . that arises from the struggle for existence in this large population'. Statistics, he said, were collected in 1896, and showed that infant mortality was 35 per cent of the total deaths. The children, he said, were dying 'from want of suitable food', and the rate had increased from 21 per 1000 to 29 per 1000 over 1896. Death and destitution were everywhere, and the planter dictatorship could find no answer to the rising human misery.

The Commission received submissions from many sources in which the evidence of rising vestry poor relief between 1890 and 1896 reflected the spread of starvation and famine. In 1889 some 4,022 persons received outdoor food or money from the parishes and another 7,170 were visited by parochial officers. By 1895, these figures had risen to 4,788 and 12,677 respectively. In the same period the number of persons receiving indoor relief increased from 2,699 to 3,334.

Table 2
Barbados' Death Rate, 1861–1896

1861-1870	21.54
1871-1880	23.64
1881-1890	27.01
1891-1895	28.65

Source: Royal Commission Report 1896/97, Submission No. 226.

The cause of both rising death rates and poor relief expenditure, noted Dr Gooding, was that many workers were finding it 'difficult to keep soul and body together'.

Dr F.B. Archer submitted a memorandum which showed that the planters' attitudes to the black population, 50 years after emancipation legislation, remained aggressive and racist. Despite the famine all around them, and the growing wretchedness of the workers who were carrying the greater human cost of the economic crisis, Dr Archer saw them 'as happy, peaceable, and contented as any similar classes in any part of the world'. Other submissions detailed the woes of reduced wages, rising infant mortality rates, and increasing crime, yet Archer describes workers as 'improvident' and willing 'to work for as much as will supply their immediate want', lacking regard to the 'idea of putting up for a rainy day'. Furthermore, he said, 'labour is abundant and cheap, and well that it is so, for were the cost of production of sugar increased by a rise in wages, matters would be much worse than they are now'. Society is plagued, he said, with 'roughs and scum' who it 'would gladly get rid of'. They stay behind and constitute 'a nuisance in the island'.

Workers' Submissions

Workers organised for the submission of memoranda, and in some instances sent representatives to address the Commission. On February 19, Fitzdonald Dowridge spoke 'On behalf of the 'taxpayers and labourers'. He informed the Commissioners that the 'labouring classes of the country, both agricultural and industrial, have a wide and well deserved reputation for efficiency'. Labour, he stated, 'is almost entirely recruited from the Negro population, and they have displayed aptitude for acquiring skilled proficiency in every calling, their ability being only limited by opportunity'.

Widespread starvation in the community, he said, was because 'the labourer is under paid', and the injury is compounded by 'arbitrary and unjust deductions' from their wages and 'abnormal rent charges'. The prospect of 'further reduction in wages', he concluded, would be greater 'starvation, and probably disorder'.

George Daniel, a journalist, speaking on behalf of 'A joint Committee of Artisans and Labourers', reiterated that 'the labourers are fearfully underpaid.' The wages paid in many parishes of 8 to 10d per day for an able-bodied worker, from 'sunrise to sunset', cannot keep life within these toilers. Only rebellion, he concluded, could follow a further reduction in wages. Washington Harper, also giving testimony on behalf of the 'Joint Committee', added:

> The present pay of the labourer is absolutely inadequate to a proper state of living, being hardly sufficient for maintenance, and the labourer cannot be said to be contented therewith, in as much as those perquisites which he was allowed or permitted to enjoy when sugar paid well have since the depression been absolutely restricted...Owing to the poverty of the labouring classes, which is the direct result of the low state of wages, no savings for comfort can be provided, and consequently their housing is of such kind as to effect their morals adversely, with families being crowded into mere huts.

Workers, then, articulated their own position on the sugar crises and its social consequences. Many of them wished to appear before the Commission but were 'unable to meet the formalities of written evidence', stated George Daniel. They did not share responsibility for the mismanagement of the sugar industry, neither did they trust the sugar planters, whose financial accounts they believed the Commission should investigate. Indeed, Daniel was instructed by the workers to inform the Commission that 'justice may be done the labourers by the planter in allowing the Commissioners to have a peep into the estate books for the last five years'.

The distrust workers held towards the sugar planters ran deep. It was rooted in the knowledge that slave owners had fought to maintain slavery, were racist in social outlook, and determined to keep slave-like relations within the colony despite the Emancipation Acts.

Distrust was expressed in fear, and an unwillingness to enter contractual arrangement that required verbal agreement, a mark, or signature. The pain of their relationship with the Contract Law remained a living reality, and the results were obvious, especially to emigration agents who sought to finance their relocation to other colonies. Massiah Gaskin, an emigration agent operating in Barbados, made this point clear to the Commissioners. When asked about contracts being signed with respect to emigration to Trinidad, he replied:

> The Barbadian labourer had the fear of slavery in him, and he therefore disliked a contract. At Demerara and Trinidad able-bodied labourers could earn from 1s 4d to 2s 8d per day. Cane cutters could earn at least 4 dollars or 5 dollars per week, very often they could earn more. Trenching was done by the rod, and his impression was that a labourer could earn not less than 2s 6d per day for the same. Drilling and trashing was also remunerative work to the labourer in that colony. The minimum wage was 1s 4d per day and every child up to a certain age got 8d per day.

When asked more specifically about a system of indenture 'as is done in the case of the East Indian emigrants', he replied:

> Such a system to Barbadian labourers would be like holding a red rag to a bull. They would regard it as a reversion to slavery. He, however, thought a contract for 12 months would be accepted, although even now labourers sometimes did not keep such a contract after making it. Sometime ago he carried 100 labourers to Trinidad to Mr. Agostini, on a signed contract, and although those labourers signed the contract before a police magistrate here, when they reached their destination and were asked to go before a police magistrate there to ratify it, they all repudiated it, denying that they even knew Mr. Seon before whom the contract was signed here. A similar thing occurred with some labourers whom he took to Tucker Valley.

Barbadian workers, then, in the midst of their destitution, were not prepared to engage in any system of labour arrangement that resembled slavery. They were aware that since the 1838 Emancipation legislation, employers had made concerted efforts to deny them their due. As a result they prepared for long-term resistance and struggle. Daily protest was the norm, with occasional eruptions of violent warfare. But within the confines of these contestations, they knew how to avoid and reject efforts to further erode their precarious position.

Not even famine and persistent planter-sponsored harassment and violence could get them to soften on the issue. They continued to demand new forms of freedom, and pressed for opportunities to advance their cause for justice and betterment. Considerable tenacity was shown in the face of rising mortality rates and general hunger. In effect, what they were saying to the planters was that the desire for freedom could not be suppressed by the confines of a 'starvation wage'. The result, then, was a deepening of the war against bondage.

1897: What the Workers Wanted

The workers wanted in 1897 what they wanted in 1837. This much was made clear to the Royal Commission. They knew that the landless emancipation imposed upon them by the Abolition of Slavery Act was designed to assure their continued slave-like subordination to the white elite community. At the same time they understood that land ownership was the basis of economic independence, social status, cultural rootedness and empowerment.

Prescod spoke on their behalf in 1838. In 1897 they were in the less favourable position of having to hire spokespersons as the formal procedure of the Royal Enquiry demanded written submissions. The dream of a landed emancipation had not died, as planters had hoped it would. Rather, workers continued to challenge and reject the white community's right to monopolise the land and to use it as a weapon of institutional dictatorship

The planters, and their allies in the high and low church, commercial chambers, and political councils, set out their argument before the Commissioners. The workers rejected their claims with the same certainty that their forbears had done. Planters were unanimous in the view that the plantation should be untouchable as it was the only vehicle on which the colony could journey to progress. This view was asserted within the context of a critique of the viability of small farming and peasant development. To this end, two principal rationalisations were presented: (a) that lands were not available for small-scale farming among the Blacks (b) that Blacks lacked the financial ability to participate meaningfully on the land market. These views dovetailed in the conclusion that only the emigration of the 'surplus' labour force – meaning workers who were radical, ill, and aged – could assist the development of all sections of the society.

The exchange between the Chairman of the Commission, Messrs Pile, Sealy and Clarke, speaks to this ideological contest. It also illuminates the Chairman's scepticism with respect to the planters' hostility to the landed economic enfranchisement of Blacks.

The recorded exchange in the Commission's reports is set out as follows:

212.   The next printed question was as to the disposition on the part of the labouring classes to engage in agriculture on small holdings, either rented or purchased. The Secretary read the following rep*ly:-*

   (i)   The number of small holdings, both freehold and rented, is considerable. A large number of the cultivators of such holdings plant canes. The small holders seldom make a living out of their land alone...; the holders of rented land are generally agricultural labourers. The number of freehold owners of five acres and under is about 8,000.

(ii)   There is no excess of the demand for small holdings over the supply.

213.   In reply to the Chairman, Mr. Pile said that there was no increasing demand on the part of the labouring classes for small holdings, nor did they cease to work in the estate when they became freeholders, unless they possessed about an acre or more of land.

214.   *(Chairman.) I see you have about 8,500 freehold owners of five acres and under.*

215.   Mr. C.P. Clarke explained that that return was taken from the books of the parochial treasures, because the poor rate is assessed on the land. In addition to the statement in that paragraph, he might mention that about 4,500 of the total acreage of plantations were in the hands of renting holders, who were agricultural labourers.

216. (Chairman.) What rent do they pay? – (Mr. Pile.) About £4 a year per acre.

217. And you think there is no excessive demand for holdings? – (Mr. C.P. Clarke.) I think not at present, because one or two small plantations have been recently sold out in small holdings.

218. And what would a man pay for such a holding? – (Mr. Pile.) He pays at a very high price; about 350 dollars an acre.

219. How do they pay that? – (Mr. F.J. Clarke.) They generally pay down so much on purchase, and pay the balance by instalments.

220. Then that puts them in debt. Do they ever go elsewhere and earn money and come back? – (Mr. F.J. Clarke.) I do not think so. I do not think that a man who has purchased an acre or two of land would go to any of the other islands to work. We would always find him here.

221. He may go to the other islands to work for money and come back? – (Mr. F.J. Clarke.) I do not think that would tempt him.

222. But if he had not a holding and he earned money elsewhere would not he come back to get one? – (Mr. F.J. Clarke.) Yes.

223. In reply to St. David Barbour, Mr. Pile said that the small holders of land grow chiefly cane and ground provisions; nothing else. They sent their cane to the neighbouring estates to be ground and manufactured into sugar. They also raised a little feathered stock.

224. (Mr. C.P. Clarke.) We say ground provisions; they grow maize and Guinea corn in addition to potatoes and things of that sort.

225. (Sir David Barbour.) They do not attempt to grow anything for export? – (Mr. Pile.) No, except such things as go to Demerara.

226. (Mr. Sealy.) There is not a very large number of holdings as high as five acres. A great many of the holdings are very small pieces of land. The statement in the reply read by the Secretary is 'five acres and under.' That gives rather a wide margin. The majority of holdings is about half an acre. Holdings consisting of five acres will only be found in parts of the island where the land is cheap.

227. In reply to the next printed question as to whether general distress would be entailed in the event of a disastrous failure of the sugar industry, the Secretary read the following:-

(a.) In the event of a general failure of the sugar industry, distress would be universal. Everything in Barbados depends immediately or ultimately on that industry. No other industry known to us would afford employment for the dense population.

This final statement by Sealy, then, represented a kind of closure, a final expression of the narrowing of the arteries, so to speak, that had begun a pace with the emancipation discourse.

But there had always been opposition within the white community to Blacks owning land. The Rev E.S. Thorne, Rector of the St Joseph parish, spoke against the planters, and signalled the views of Blacks, how their commercial culture worked, and their demand for land. He told the Commission:

> The population of my parish is estimated to be about 5,000, and these people are for the most part employed in agricultural pursuits. But there are many who employ themselves by carrying fruit to town day by day. They grow the fruit themselves. Some of them who do not own land rent land from the plantations, and they grow breadfruit, bananas, oranges, and other fruit, which they seem to sell fairly well in town, and they are thereby enabled to live. The men on the seacoast employ themselves by catching fish, which form a considerable portion of their diet, and they also sell some to the other inhabitants.

Rev Thorne's Exchange with the Commissioners went as follows:

431. What rent would a person pay for a piece of land on which he could grow fruit to sell? – Land is rented at various prices according to its value. I do not know of anyone renting more than an acre of land, and the rent of an acre is about 10d per week.

432. There has been a reduction in wages during the last two years? – From the answers which I have received, with one exception, I gather that the wages have been reduced about 20 per cent.

433. Has that reduction been gradual or sudden? – I heard of the reduction nearly three years ago. I do not think there are many

recent reductions. From any account which I have received I think the average wage of adult male labourers is 10d per day, and that of adult female labourers 7½ per day.

434. Is there a great desire on the part of labourers to rent land? – I am sure there is. They prefer to rent land, and they rent it whenever they can get it, and they help themselves by working otherwise in addition to tilling their plots. They often plant canes in their land, and they generally have them reaped and manufactured at the estate on which they live.

435. Do they ever sell them for money? – They get them converted into syrup and, when they are very good, into sugar.

436. If there was a considerable decrease in the production of sugar with existing prices, what would be the result? – I think the suffering in the island would be very great. Sufficient provision could not be grown to maintain the people with food.

The plantation system, then, was structurally flawed from the perspective of its economic rationale, and was maintained primarily as a guarantor of white elite privilege and authority. The Blacks knew this to be true, and within the context of its rejection, developed counter-proposals and visions which they placed before the Commissioners. Their unrelenting demand for a 'landed' emancipation was evident from their proposals which were elegantly set out within the framework of a development alternative for the wider society.

Three persons spoke before the Commission with respect to the written submissions of labourers and artisans. Each document stated clearly the workers' perspective on the crisis of the economy, and ended with the offer of 'Possible Remedies and Palliatives'. This latter section contained a number of proposals, and in all cases the issue of economic enfranchisement via land ownership was central.

George Daniel, the journalist, submitted on behalf of the Joint Committee of Artisans and Labourers. He was given a brief by the Committee to address the land issue in a frontal fashion. He stated: 'Estates in Chancery should be cut up into small lots of five and ten acres at an average, say, of $60 per acre. The fancy prices paid for land in this country has been brought about in order to prevent a peasant proprietary body from rising up in our midst . . . It is only under such a system that the idea of central factories could ever be entertained.'

The workers, then, did not accept the views of the planters and proposed an alternative strategy that called for a reform of the plantation model. Washington Harper, a shipwright, deepened the proposal on behalf of a 'General Meeting of Artisans and Labourers'. He stated: 'There is a growing feeling that other commodities than sugar should be resorted to, and if a peasant proprietary body be ever properly established there can be no doubt cultivation of the land will not be solely confined to the cane plant.'

C. W. Alleyne, a builder, speaking on behalf of the Joint Committee affirmed: 'There is no other means of establishing minor industries, but by peasant proprietorship. In Jamaica, although sugar does not keep its usual stand, yet the island is better off through its peasant proprietary, and their fruit trade, say nothing of their cocoa, coffee, ginger, and other industries.'

Finally, Archibald Fitzdonald Dowridge, a master tailor, speaking on behalf of the 'taxpayers and labourers' stated:

> There is, at present, literally no means of acquiring local peasant proprietorship, as it is practically impossible at present wages, no matter how thriftily disposed, to acquire land, owing to ruling prices and methods of sale. When estates, out of speculation, are cut up and sold, or parcels of land put on the market, so eager is the desire to acquire a holding that from 800 to 1,400 dollars per acre have been paid for small allotments. The number of small proprietors engaged in planting in 1891 on lots of five acres or under was only 807. The salvation of the country, after rational emigration, will lay in central factories and small farmers.

The plantations, then, the workers agreed, were not viable, and should become the basis of a land redistribution policy designed to encourage commercial farming within the black community. The larger, profitable sugar estates should be networked with small farms around central factories for efficiency gains. The workers understood the need for modernisation, and factored themselves into the equation as central part of a new agricultural dispensation.

But they wanted more than land. They proposed a series of initiatives designed to uplift the black community as a vital human resource for colonial development. Their vision was a rounded one, rooted in their history. Dowridge, for example, had set out clearly in his submission how land redistribution, an emigration policy, and a federation of the region, would work to the benfit of all:

> Among the remedies I venture to suggest would be a proper system of assisted homestead emigration to the other colonies, notably Jamaica where thousands of acres of exceedingly fertile and accessible uncultivated lands are easily obtainable. Such emigration to consist of families, and under Government aid and supervision for a limited period. To that end I advocate the welding together of all these West Indian colonies in a scheme of consolidated union, with a central government and imperial Parliamentary representation . . . Federation is desired, firstly to economise the cost of administration of these colonies, and secondly, to incorporate us into the body of the nation of which we are proud to feel ourselves a part. Cheaper facilities for transit to and fro between the islands, the present cost of travelling being prohibitive to our peasantry and masses.

The workers also wanted technical education in order to strengthen their skills base and the market value of their work. Dowridge continued:

> Technical education is necessary because mechanics are deteriorating in quality, and it being impossible to re-establish the apprenticeship system, we must advance along the lines found necessary in the mother country, and Europe generally. Trade schools must be established to enable our artisans to compete with the cheap finish of foreign goods. . .

Adding to this request for technical education for workers, George Alleyne called for an investment in the primary education of children, and for a reformatory for vagrant girls. The workers' delegations were effective in that the Commission was persuaded by their call for land reform and the independent entrenchment of workers on the soil. The commissioners, however, were not thinking in terms of ending the landless emancipation inflicted in 1838, but practically, with the need to end the hunger and famine that had engulfed the colony on account of the crisis of the sugar industry.

Recommendations

The Commission admitted that the labouring population was experiencing wide-spread famine, with evidence of further suffering to come:

> The depression of the industry is causing sugar estates to be abandoned and will cause more estates to be abandoned, and such abandonment is causing and will cause distress among the labouring population . . . and will seriously affect, for a considerable time, the general prosperity of the sugar-producing Colonies . . . If the production of sugar is discontinued or very largely reduced, there is no industry or industries that could completely replace it in such islands as Barbados, Antigua, and St. Kitts and profitably carried on and supply employment for the labouring population . . .

It did not accept the view that the crisis was due to mismanagement of the industry by the planter class:

> The crisis is not due in any considerable degree to extravagance in management, imperfection of the process of manufacture, or to inadequate supervision consequent or absentee ownership, and the removal of these causes wherever they exist would not enable it generally to be profitably carried on under present conditions of competition.

They accepted, though, the workers' proposal for landed enfranchisement, and suggested that it was the best way forward for Barbados with respect to poverty reduction. As a result they proposed 'the settlement of the labouring population on small plots of land as peasant proprietors', and 'the establishment of minor agricultural industries and the improvement of the system of cultivation, especially in the case of small proprietors'.

The Commission admitted, furthermore, that the black population had paid a long and dear price in the development of the West Indies. It recognised that entrenched white racism served to oppose the transfer of productive resources to Blacks who were perceived by employers as part of exploitable labour rather than fellow members of civil society:

> The settlement of the labourer on the land has not, as a rule, been viewed with favour in the past by persons interested in sugar estates. What suited them best was a large supply of labourers entirely dependent upon being able to find work on estates and consequently subject to their control and willing to work at low rates of wages.

On this score, the Commission broke ranks with the dictatorship of the planters and supported the workers' vision of their emancipation: 'No reform affords so good a prospect for the permanent welfare in the future of the West Indies as the settlement of the labouring population on the land as small peasant proprietors; and in many places this is the only means by which the population can in future be supported.'

The workers, then, had won a major policy battle. But once again, the planters dug in and prepared to resist reform efforts. As expected, imperial support for the landed enfranchisement of workers as a strategy to create self-sufficiency with the black community did not rest well with planters who were steadfast in preferring a dependent, weak, subservient working force that was there to serve and not to aspire.

The workers had not separated the desire for land from the assertion of a right to the franchise and formal education. Everywhere, Blacks looked to owning land and school lessons as the twin towers of their future trajectory. Education assumed powerful proportions, and elders expected their children to grasp whatever opportunities were available.

Here again, the planters sought to mislead and deceive the commissioners. They did it with respect to the land issue, and also with education. C.J. Lawrence informed then that 'agricultural labourers do not seem to avail themselves to as great an extent of educational advantages offered by the island as the other classes do'. But the Rev Canon Sealy provided a critical context when he stated:

Years ago the labourers took care to send their children to school, because it was their delight to say that while they had been slaves, yet their children were educated. But we have no compulsory education here and the effort to keep the children at school is not so great as it was years ago . . .; they are taken from school early . . ., sometimes at as early an age as 10 or 11 years for the purpose of working to supplement their parents' earnings.

It was C.E. Gooding, MD, however, who touched upon more important reasons why primary education was not encouraged, and had fallen off despite parents' commitment to their children. He noted that when black children 'passed through the primary schools' they emerge with 'the marked distasted for agricultural labour', an attitude they 'display'. The result was that they gravitate to artisan crafts, the ranks of which have become 'professedly overcrowded'.

In effect, the formally educated youth were withdrawing their labour from the sugar plantations; many preferring unemployment to exposure to the cane fields. Planters reacted to this development by withdrawing their support for both formal education and artisan craft training. But the youth were sending a signal into the twentieth century. They were prepared to turn their backs upon the plantation even when a choice was unavailable. They were in flight from the exploitative arrangements that continued to engulf their elders.

All around, then, workers and their children, despite famine and police brutality, were not prepared to surrender to the Great House, and maintained a tension with it despite there being no alternative form of labour. They continued to look to 'land' and 'lessons' as the vehicles for the future journey out of the cane fields.

Panama Money and Migrants

Emigration had long been conceived by the worker as a major strategy for socioeconomic betterment. The economic depression of the late nineteenth century, however, had the effect of expanding significantly that pool of potential migrant. But the emigration outlet that irrevocably changed Barbados and widened the horizons for the black Barbadian working class, appeared in 1904. In that year, the United States renewed the construction of a canal across the Isthmus of Panama. Labour was required, and Barbadian workers having never experienced employment on a large scale in a non-agricultural setting, saw the opportunity to reject sugar planters and plantations, and pursue an autonomous path. When, in 1905, the Panama Canal Agency established a labour recruitment office in Bridgetown, there was no doubt that persuasion was not necessary.

The initial reaction of sugar planters was that the surplus unemployed labour was being siphoned off, a process which in their judgement could only lead to better labour relations. By the end of 1906, however, their vision had changed as the flow of migrants was unexpectedly large and eroding plantation labour supply. The steamers which sailed between Bridgetown and Colon had taken over 10,000 by the beginning of 1908, and by 1914, at least 20,000 contracted men had departed for the Canal. It was the largest wave of migration in the colony's history, and the impact upon economy and society was considerable. It has been estimated that the total number of non-contracted and contracted migrants amounts to 45,000, in spite of the legislative attempts to contain it between 1905 and 1908. The censuses show that between 1911 and 1921 the island's population fell from 171,983 to 156,312, a decrease of some 15,671. Though many factors contributed to this net reduction, there can be no doubt that the Panama emigration was the chief cause.

The migration opportunity was seen by Blacks as a chance to finally cast off the yoke of plantation domination. J. Challenor Lynch, for instance, reported to the Legislative Council that before boarding, Blacks would abuse and aggressively denounce Whites. It was also considered, by those who wanted to stay behind, as an instrument to strengthen their hand on the labour market in bargaining for better wages. Bonham Richardson has recalled that labourers would chant the following song during industrial disputes:

> we want more wages, we want it now, And if we don't get it, we going to Panama. Yankees say they want we down there, we want more wages, we want it now.

He reported the case of a prospective emigrant who was heard shouting to field workers, 'Why you don't hit de manager in de head and come along wid we!'[4] Whereas the drastic reduction of male labourers on the estates should have led to wage increases, planters were able to prevent this by employing women to do what had become 'men's' work at wages below what men generally obtained. As a result, wage levels in the plantation sector did not increase. Black women, who had gradually removed themselves from some of the more physically arduous tasks on estates, found themselves back in the fields as the dominant gender in occupations such as cane holing, trench digging, and cane cutting.

But it was the remittances of money to Barbados from Panama, and the capital brought back by returnees, which were to have a profound impact upon the island. While in 1910, for example, the merchant community had advanced £80,000 to planters to assist their sugar industry, in the same year official sources show that black Barbadians brought and sent back £83,000. Though many migrants died in the Canal Zone (one respected estimate is 15.5 per cent) some of those who returned with capital were able to achieve considerable social and economic mobility. In 1906, 3,501 returnees declared £18,000, and the following year 3,525 declared £26,291. Between 1906 and 1915, some 20,326 returnees declared a total of £171,641. These ex-field hands had hopes of buying land, opening shops, learning a craft, obtaining an education for clerical and business professions. There certainly was a startling appearance of village shops and corner stores in the suburbs that can be attributed to 'Panama' money.[5]

Many planters, by sheer necessity, sold off their properties to 'Panama men' in small lots, and by 1930 the pattern of landownership had been changed marginally.

In 1897, for example, the Royal Commission was informed that there were 8,500 small proprietors who owned 10,000 acres. In 1929 the number of small proprietors had increased to 17,731. At least one estate was bought whole by Panama money, though this was a practice not approved of by the leadership of the white community. In 1910, for example, Dr E.G. Pilgrim, Assemblyman for St James, sold a large proportion of his estates at Carlton, Sion Hill, Reids Bay, and Westmoreland in small lots to 'Panama men'. For the first time, Blacks were making significant inroads into the land ownership pattern of the island.

Table 3
Postal Remittances Sent from the Panama Canal Zone to Barbados 1906–1920

	No. of Postal Orders	£
1906	3,613	7,509
1907	19,092	46,160
1908	26,360	63,210
1909	31,179	66,272
1910	31,059	62,280
1911	24,968	51,009
1912	28,394	56,042
1913	31,851	63,816
1914	22,619	39,586
1915	14,210	22,874
1916	11,241	17,539
1917	10,430	15,194
1918	8,777	12,680
1919	7,747	12,591
1920	5,782	9,173
Total		**545,935**

Source: Bonham Richardson, *Panama Money in Barbados, 1900–1920*, Knoxville, (1985),p. 157

Under the sudden influence of Panama money, land prices rose dramatically, and even in the outlying parishes the price of £200 per acre in 1925 was normal. At these prices only the most successful returnees could purchase land, and many struggling planters took timely opportunities to speculate on the land market by putting their marginal lands up for sale. By all criteria, most returnees had been able to attain a better quality of life, though for the majority of the labouring poor, conditions worsened during the 1920s as the war-time boom in the sugar economy had collapsed. Renewed outbreaks of 'potato raids' were reported and social tensions rose. On May 13, 1921, for example, 14 men who raided the fields of Porters estate in St James, shot at the watchmen, injuring one. Violent armed attacks on plantation food supplies were reported as commonplace as the desperately poor workers sought to feed themselves and their families. Assemblyman for St Lucy, HW Reece, distinguished himself for suggesting that the House should not consider persons who confiscated provisions to 'appease hunger' the same as robbers who sold stolen items on the markets. Violent clashes between police and workers occurred in most parts of the countryside, as planters, refusing to push up wages, marketed their provisions at prices considered by labourers as unreasonable. Panama money, then, had an effect of heightening differences in the material and social standing of black workers; those who struggled to make a living saw the Panama men as symbols of success, and seemed prepared to confront the established order in ways they knew best, for the attainment of a more secure livelihood.

Friendly Societies

The injection of 'Panama money' into working class communities allowed them, for the first time, to develop island-wide financial institutions, designed and managed by themselves. The Friendly Society movement was revived, transformed and popularised as the leading force within the financial culture of the labouring classes during the early twentieth century. Societies allowed workers, on the weekly payment of about ten to 12 pence, to insure for sick and death benefits. Located in rural villages and in the towns, their accounts were managed by treasurers who were bound by law to deposit all funds at the National Savings Banks.

Between 1907 and 1910 at least 110 societies were established, a remarkable increase over previous years. There were few black families on the tenantries and in the urban areas who did not participate in the movement, and the 1921 census showed that some 156,312 persons were covered by over 260 societies. These black organisations attracted the attention of the Legislature for the principal reason that the large sum of capital they collected could be used against the interests of the white community if properly mobilised. For example, societies could purchase land on behalf of members and influence the pattern of land distribution. As a result, the 1905 Friendly Societies Act made it illegal for individual societies to hold 'land exceeding one acre in extent.' This legislation immediately undermined the potential of societies to become agents of social and economic change.

Restricted by this legislation, societies became attractive primarily for the Christmas money 'bonuses' they paid to members. That is, members who paid their weekly subscriptions were entitled to a lump sum repayment in December, in which case societies functioned more like savings banks than insurance institutions. The important fact being, however, that in this way, funds were kept within the hands of Blacks rather than falling into the hands of land speculators who were seen to be capitalising on the 'thirst' for land among Panama returnees. In 1946, a total of 161 friendly societies existed on the island, representing 97,639 due-paying members, who, in that year, contributed £130,217, and paid Christmas bonuses of £93,913.

It was an important institutional innovation from the black community which reflected the general trend of economic rationality during the depressed years after the mid-1880s. Societies were vital to the survival strategies of communities even after, as in 1905, their wings were clipped by planter legislation. It showed the determination of Blacks to keep their hard-earned and scarce capital within institutions they managed, and in this sense the proliferation of societies constituted a level of economic resistance to planter-merchant domination of the monetary and financial structures of the colony.

Landships and Lodges

The social security functions which the early friendly societies had provided the working class were supplemented by the development and expansion of the 'landship' movement, especially during the depressed years of the 1920s. Described as 'voluntary neighbourhood associations', landships provided the working class with a social organisational structure which at once satisfied the need for cultural expression as well as economic assistance for workers at times of severe need. Rather than merely subscribing to friendly societies, workers created 'landships' which were associations whose members were ranked and defined according to the status hierarchy used by the British Navy. Meetings and parades also took on the naval-style display of drill, uniforms, and discipline. Members were referred to as 'crews'. The meeting house, invariably a chattel house on a tenantry or in Bridgetown, was the 'ship'. Male youths who joined the ranks were known as 'blues' while the females who provided medical assistance were known as 'stars'. The flag of the association was affixed upon the house, or 'ship' as a mask, and within, meetings were conducted within the strictest manner by observations of rank, station, and naval protocol. All ships were given names, and 'docked' at frequent intervals. For example, the Rosetta, with its crew from the Bay Street area in Bridgetown, 'docked' every Monday, Wednesday, and Friday between 7:30 and 9:30 p.m.

Many communities developed their own 'landships' during the 1920s and 1930s, and these competed in displays of discipline, uniform, drill, and other naval rituals. It has been estimated that during the 1920s more than 60 ships were established throughout Barbados, with over 3,800 male and female crews. Also, it has been argued that the landship was a 'powerful social factor' in the lives of its members.

The movement was essentially unique to Barbados within the Caribbean context and is said to have fulfilled the need of the unemployed poor for order, discipline, respectability and mutual assistance during the depression. 'Crews' paid their weekly fees, and these constituted premiums for insurance against sickness, unemployment and death, while at the same time forced workers to be frugal with their very limited finance. Members were generally buried in grand military style, with long processions and community attendance.

Like fraternal lodges, and Friendly Societies, the Landship Movement represented a commitment to self-help and survival within the working classes. It reached its highest organisational level in 1933 when most 'ships' were brought together as a 'fleet' in the Barbados Landship Association, which created the naval rank of admiralty for veteran officers. At this stage, the movement displayed its potential for political activity and influence, but which on the whole, was not fulfilled. The movement illustrated the organisational capacity of the working class, and pointed towards the development of its political consciousness; at best it indicated that workers were prepared for the rigour of organised mass politics.

Revivalist Churches

Like friendly societies and the landship movements, the revivalist church made its impact upon black communities during the 1920s, and emerged as an important social institution. During the 1880s and 1890s, when economic conditions adversely affected the material lives of the working classes, religion became another area in which they asserted their cultural independence and self leadership. During this time, the revivalist church emerged as expressive of their general rejection of the established Anglican Church and other 'white controlled' denominations. It also symbolised the denial by villagers that social respectability could only be gained by conformity to the dominant anglicanism, and confirmed that some workers saw social legitimacy in terms of their own autonomous expressions.

A principal origin of the dynamic revivalist church was the United States where Pentecostal and Baptist missionaries, having made substantial inroads within the black communities of the southern plantation zone, launched into the Caribbean to serve the spiritual need not met by the elitist and racist Anglican clergymen. The most prominent among the evangelicals were the Christian Mission, Church of God, Pilgrim Holiness, and the Salvation Army. The Christian Mission began their proselytising in 1891, and led the way for the other groups to establish what became known as the 'people's ministries'.

By the 1920s, these groups had captured the imagination of the Black poor who, throughout the island, built their own churches, threw up their own preachers, and managed their own affairs. This self-leadership was in direct contradiction to the traditional practice of Blacks congregating under white clergymen on Sunday mornings. By 1930, most villages and towns were affected by this fundamentalist Christian proliferation; everywhere would be found the tiny wooden churches of Pentecostalists, Plymouth Brethren, Spiritual Baptists, other Baptists and Brethren which fitted congruously with surrounding chattel houses. Meanwhile, the working class congregations of the Anglican, Wesleyan, Moravian, and Methodist churches declined.

Black Pentecostal preachers, male and female, expounding the gospel in the lively musical and theatrical form of Afro-Barbadian traditions, became a central feature of social life, and represented village autonomy at its most aggressive. The preacher was more than a translator of the scriptures; he or she was the embodiment of respectability, social morality, and community leadership. Conflict and tension between the official church and these groups was common. White clergymen frequently denounced the revivalists from their pulpits and attempted to use their Afro-centric forms of worship as a basis of denigration.

Black Political Mobilisation

The proliferation of black socio-economic organisations after the turn of the century, especially the friendly societies, lodges and the

Barbados Labour Union [formed in 1919], provided many of the prerequisites for the development of a radical political movement. Indeed, these apparently non-political organisations had been the incubators of the spirit of political agitation and the schools in which working people learnt the skills of political mobilisation. At the end of the nineteenth century, the respected black educationalist, Rawle Parkinson, head teacher of the Wesley Hall School, had impressed upon black workers the importance of recognising the relationships between political activity economic survival, and the acquisition of formal educational training. By the early 1920s, these developments had coalesced against the background of Marcus Garvey's Pan Caribbean and international 'black power' movement. Garvey's politics, more than any other single factor, rooted within the consciousness of Barbadian workers the fact that only organised mass political action could deliver in a general way those social and economic objectives which they had pursued through their friendly societies.

It was Clennell Wickham who, after the war, did most to provide the working classes with a theoretical framework for political agitation. He did this by articulating working class interest and frustrations within the context of an aggressive and incisive criticism of planter-merchant elitism. Wickham was a veteran of the First World War, during which his experiences as a black man, contributed to the development of his anti-imperialist consciousness. It was difficult for him to reconcile the facts that as the British sought to impose a firm colonial grip on Africa, the landed elite in Barbados was attempting also to strengthen its control over the labouring poor by means of monopoly corporate organisation.

In 1919, Clement Innis established the *Barbados Herald*, a weekly newspaper which has been described as providing, for the first time in the colony's history, 'biting, acerbic, workingclass views.' Wickham soon became editor of this newspaper, and used its pages to provide working people with information and analyses relevant to their political condition. In the process of debating the crisis of social and economic relations in Barbados, he developed a socialist agenda for action, and came close to being the country's first Marxist theoretician and activist. In Wickham, the emergence of a working class radical intellectual was something new; the politics of the country would henceforth be conditioned by this force from below.

But the man who brought formal political organisation to the working classes for the first time was Charles Duncan O'Neale. As a medical student in Edinburgh during the first decade of the twentieth century, O'Neale had established connections with the British Fabian Socialist Movement which appeared supportive of black radicals committed to the decolonisation process in their colonies. He was a St Lucy man, born in 1879, from an emerging middle class family. On his final return to Barbados in 1924, after short periods of medical practice in Newcastle, England, and then Trinidad, O'Neale decided to organise a socialist forum to give representation to working class interests as articulated by Wickham. As a medical man, he was particularly disturbed by the colony's high and rising infant mortality rates and the generally poor health standards within the black communities. In his estimation little had changed for the better in terms of working-class health and sanitary facilities since his departure from the island as a student in 1899.

In Trinidad, O'Neale had been impressed by the organisational style of Captain Arthur Cipriani, the champion of the 'barefoot men' in their struggle for civil rights. He had also been influenced by the black nationalism of Marcus Garvey, in both its organisational as well as ideological forms. Under these political influences, O'Neale, undoubtedly a radical socialist, projected himself into the leadership of working people. He considered the time right for radical action, since working-class consciousness had been stirred by the 'black power' ideologies of Garvey, as well as the trade unionism which sprang from Cipriani's agitation. According to George Belle, he began to do for the black working class in Barbados what Garvey had been doing for them in Jamaica and the United States — organised them with a clear and viable political agenda.[6]

Within weeks of returning to Barbados O'Neale had been consulting with Wickham on the political situation with the intention of formulating strategies. In May 1924, he had organised along with Wickham, and other labour supporters such as J.T.C Ramsay, John Beckles the Garveyite, and J.A. Martineau, a delegation that petitioned the Governor requesting him to use his executive powers to obtain legislation for the termination of the most backward aspect of plantation culture – child labour. This move was designed primarily to attract public attention to their presence and intentions, rather than obtain results, though this demand was made frequently for another ten years. Out of this and other forms of initially limited political actions, emerged in October 1924, the Democratic League – the first political party in Barbados. Though it was initially considered a black middle-class party with working-class pretentions and a socialist manifesto, O'Neale's leadership was consistently reflective of the wide range of demands put forward by the disenfranchised working class.

The support base for O'Neale's Democratic League was wide and varied. It was supported by black and coloured middle-class professionals as well as the labouring poor. There was a branch of Marcus Garvey's Universal Negro Improvement Association (UNIA) in Barbados since 1920, and the hundreds of active Garveyites threw their support behind the League. The strategy of the League was to contest as many elections as possible and use their base within the Assembly in order to influence the Legislative Council. But the restricted nature of the franchise during the 1920s meant that only a small percentage of the working people possessed the vote. The 1901 Representation of the People Act had placed an income qualification on the franchise of £50 per annum and a freehold qualification in respect to land and properties of rent £5 or more annually. The small but growing black lower middle class could vote, so could some artisans, but these were insufficient in most parishes to give comfortable majorities to League candidates.

In December 1924, Chrissie Brathwaite won a St Michael seat in a by-election on the League's ticket, and paved the entry of the Movement into Parliament. Brathwaite demanded compulsory education for black youths and the banning of child labour. Both O'Neale and other prominent League leaders were branded by the planter press as 'racist', and 'bolsheviks'. In response, O'Neale went to great lengths to illustrate the Christian nature of his socialist philosophy and the moderate quality of his party's agenda. He would frequently state, as did Wickham, that only the most inhumane and unchristian members of the ruling class would seek to oppose measures designed to reduce infant mortality, remove child labour from plantations, and protect working people from the scourge of malnutrition. But the moral appeal of the League was hardly effective within a polity that was dominated by an elite which saw its interests in narrow terms, and had not yet developed a socially holistic vision of its leadership.

Other members of the League were to win seats over the next decade, but defeats came more frequently than successes.

Brathwaite was a favourite with the electorate, and in 1930 he finally got some support in the House when Erskine Ward won the City seat for the League. O'Neale was to eventually win a Bridgetown seat in the 1932 general elections – defeating the prominent merchant H.B.G. Austin by one vote. Until his death in November 1936 he retained this seat, though the strained financial circumstances of the 1930s depression, proved not to be a suitable context for the implementation of his social reforms.

O'Neale had also recognised the need for an organisation to further the economic aims of the working class, to represent them on the labour market, and to assist workers to invest their accumulated savings for their collective good. In 1926 he was instrumental in the establishment of the Workingmen's Association which functioned also as the 'industrial and business arm' of the League. Modelled to a certain extent on the Trinidad Workingmen's Association and the British Guiana Labour Union, the Barbados Workingmen's Association was the parent body for two other working-class economic organisations the Barbados Workers' Union Cooperative Company, and the Workingmen's Loan and Friendly Investment Society. These two organisations had done a great deal to open up avenues in the commercial sector to Blacks – the Cooperative Company ran a store on Baxter's Road, while the Investment Society mobilised workers' savings as a friendly society.

The Barbados Workingmen's Association worked in close association with John Beckles of the UNIA. Both organisations were under constant police surveillance by Governor O'Brien's instructions. Uniformed police corporals attended their meetings, took notes, and kept the Governor informed of their activities and ideas. To counter this situation, meetings generally carried some religious and pro-British overtones. As a result, O'Brien was able to report to the Colonial Office that as meetings began with the National Anthem and much singing and praying, they could not be described as being of a revolutionary nature.

But the political militancy of these groups was well cloaked for strategic purposes, and there was no doubt that workers understood the difference between form and content. For example, Moses Small, a radical spokesman for the Workingmen's Association after singing hymns at the beginning of a meeting on Passage Road, Bridgetown, on December 8, 1927, launched an attack upon the Anglican clergy in the island. He described them as racist, anti-worker, and pleaded with members to reject their 'hypocritical treasures in heaven' theology, but instead to vigorously pursue wealth, property, and general material advance. This was the only way, he argued, that the black race would gain respect and power.

It was during the dockworkers' strike of April 1927 that the Workingmen's Association made its most incisive impact as a workers' organisation. Trade union activities were still outlawed in Barbados, and employers and government readily unleashed backlashes on protesting workers. O'Neale was unperturbed by the aura of criminality which surrounded his decision to support the workers' strike. Less committed leaders of the Democratic League, and the Workingmen's Association which represented the striking workers, dissociated themselves from O'Neale's actions in fear of employers and official reprisals. Grantley Adams, the young lawyer, was perhaps most acerbic in his critique of O'Neale's defence of the workers.

Just back from Oxford studies in 1925, Adams had been politicised in England as a 'Liberal Party' associate as opposed to a Labour Party socialist. The Barbados elite recognised his legal skills and moved to absorb him as a supporter of the status quo. He was made editor of the *Agricultural Reporter*, the planters' paper that had taken an aggressive anti-worker stance since the mid-nineteenth century. It was in this capacity that he attacked O'Neale and other working class leaders during the strike. He described them as hotheads speaking claptrap on political platforms. The strike action was effectively suppressed and the legislature produced the Better Securities Act which provided additional legal machinery for the prosecution of strike leaders and their supporters.

Adams' entry into the political culture of Barbados as the formulator of conservative opinions in the leading planter journal enhanced his image within the workers' movement as a planter-merchant supporter. Wickham used his editorials in the *Herald* to attack Adams, and to illustrate the antiworker stance which his alliance with the elite represented at this critical stage in the struggle for civil rights. Adams, however, with the might of the establishment behind him, was to become instrumental in the final undoing of Wickham, and the *Herald*. Representing the libel suit of a client, W.D. Bailey, a Bridgetown merchant, against Wickham for statements made in the *Herald*, Adams used his legal skills and official support to the full in gaining what Professor Gordon Lewis described as the 'vindictive judgement of the Barbados Grand Jury' in 1930. Damages of £1,450 plus costs were awarded. This judgement was to financially ruin Wickham and led to the change of ownership of the newspaper.

The demise of the *Herald* and the silencing of Wickham represented a major blow for the Democratic League and the workers' movement. Adams continued to critique the policies of O'Neale and to suggest instead that the workers' movement needed to come to terms with the realism of planter-merchant power, and to recognise that only gradualist non-confrontational policies could gain important concessions from employers. Refusing to accept the centrality of race prejudice and domination within the political culture, Adams advocated a brand of liberal pragmatism which seemed out of touch with the social forces that had been represented by the Garveyites, O'Neale and Wickham. At the same time, many sections of the workers' movement saw in him outstanding ability which they recognised as misplaced and a sharp intellect in need of decolonisation.

Adams' criticisms of the Democratic League did much to undermine its potential as a Parliamentary force. By the early 1930s it seemed that the conservative and liberal elements in the country had won out against the assault of the Garveyites and socialists. At this stage a measure of frustration crept into the affairs of the League. Measures introduced into the House by its representatives, such as franchise extension, workmen's compensation, compulsory education, and the abolition of child labour were suppressed or thrown out. For example, between 1930 and 1936, its members in the House sought to reduce the income qualification on the franchise from £50 to £30 per year, and the freehold qualification from £5 to £3, and failed to gain the support of the legislature. Reform efforts were frustrated by Select Committees and the Legislative Council which were still dominated by conservative members of the merchant-planter elite one of whose chief spokesmen was Douglas Pile.

Against the background of Wickham's diminished capacity to agitate the working classes, O'Neale's absorption with Assembly politics, and frustration within the Democratic League, Grantley Adams made his entry into the House. The year was 1934, and his debut represented a triumph for the liberal black middle-classes who were now confident that they had found a leader who could withstand the pressures of Garvey's black nationalism and O'Neale's socialism on the one hand, and white racism and conservatism on the other.

Both O'Neale and Chrissie Brathwaite extended a welcome to Adams when he entered the House. They were of the assumption that if he remained true to his liberal principles that these would soon be transformed into radicalism on encountering the rigid conservatism of the planter interest. The events of the next two years showed that there was some truth in their assumptions. In defence of middle class interest, and in protecting the rights of the 'respectable' working-class, which were threatened by the corrosive forces of the 1930s economic depression, Adams became increasingly supportive of measures which were designed to assist the working-class. For example, in the debate over the 1936 Franchise Bill he emerged as the leading critic of Douglas Pile who had consistently resisted the extension of the franchise. Adams argued that the qualifications had to be reduced otherwise, the economic depression would disenfranchise many persons, who hitherto had only marginally qualified, by reducing their income levels. He also declared himself supportive of many of the items that had been on the League's agenda since its inception – such as compulsory education for black children, abolition of child labour and workers' rights to combine in trade unions.

O'Neale's death in November 1936, therefore, did not result in the crushing of the ideas he had advocated for the establishment of a workers' movement. Wickham had also noted that Adams had become increasingly concerned with defending and extending workers' rights by constitutional reform, and welcomed him as a critic and opposer of planter chauvinism and oligarchy. The Democratic League did not survive O'Neale, and with Wickham's political exile, Adams was well positioned at the Parliamentary level to subordinate what was in fact a socialist workers' movement under the wider umbrella of a radical civilrights movement. Wickham had long recognised and argued that the representation of workers, and the general pursuit of civil-rights, were two distinct processes, but realised that with the presence of Adams a 'marriage of convenience' was perhaps necessary.

The disintegration of the Democratic League did not result in the disappearance of grass root political organisations and debates. In fact, once again, workers returned to placing greater emphasis upon the role of friendly societies and lodges as places of community politicisation. The UNIA branches continued to be active and political meetings became a feature of village life during the 1930s. While Adams was consolidating his position within the Assembly, radical workers, some of who remained sceptical and hostile to his liberal political style and ideas, saw the need for autonomous organisations to further the process of agitation. It was this development which threw up the radical Clement Payne, and constitutes an important part of the background to the 1937 workers' revolution.[7]

NOTES

1   See, the *Times [Barbados]* Jan. 2, 1895; The Royal Commission on the Depression in the West India Sugar Industry, 1897–98.

2   The *Times [Barbados]* Jan 2, 1895.

3   All references to the Report in this Chapter can be found between p. 151–231.

4   See Bonham Richardson, 'Panama Money and Social Change in Barbados, 1900–1920', History Seminar, UWI, Barbados, 1981; see also by Richardson, Panama Money in Barbados, 1900–1920. Knoxville: Tennessee Univ. Press, 1985.

5   Richardson, 'Panama Money and Social Change in Barbados, 1900–1920'.

6   See George Belle, 'The Struggle for Political Democracy: 1937 Riots', Public Lecture, March 17, 1987 Bridgetown, Barbados.

7   Hilary McD Beckles, *A History of Barbados: From Amerindian Settlement to Nation-State.* (Cambridge: Cambridge Univ. Press, 1990), 151–170.

Bibliography

BOOKS

Alleyne, Warren, *Historic Bridgetown*. Bridgetown : Barbados National Trust 1978.

Anderson, Benedict, *Imagined Communities: Reflections on the Origins and Spread of Nationalism*. 1983. Reprint. London and New York: Verso, (1983) 1991.

Anon. *Addresses to His Excellency Edward John Eyre, Esq., 1865, 1866*. Kingston: DeCordova & Co., 1866.

Anon. *Jamaica: Its State and Prospects*. London, 1867.

Anon. *Memoirs of the First Settlement of the island of Barbados*. Bridgetown: 1741.

Aptheker, Herbert. *American Negro Slave Revolts*. 50th Anniversary Edition New York: Monthly Review Press, (1943) 1993.

Augier, Fitzroy, et. al . *The Making of the West Indies* London: Longmans 1960.

———. & S. Gordon, Sources of West Indian History. London: Longmans, 1962.

Bakan, Abigail B., *Ideology and Class Conflict in Jamaica: The Politics of Rebellion*. Montreal and Kingston: McGill-Queen's University Press, 1990.

Banbury, Rev. T. *Jamaica Superstitions; Or, the Obeah Book: A Complete Treatise on the Absurdities Believed in By the People of the Island* . Kingston: Mortimer De Souza, 1895.

Barton, G. T. *The Prehistory of Barbados*. Barbados: Advocate News, 1953.

Bayley, Frederick. *Four Years Residence in the West Indies*. London: n.p., 1830.

Beachy, R. W. *The British West Indian Sugar Industry in the Late Nineteenth Century* 1978 edit. Westport: Negro University Press, 1978.

Beckles, Hilary. Black Rebellion in Barbados: the Struggle Against Slavery, 1627–1838. Bridgetown: Antilles, 1984.

———. and Verene Shepherd, eds. *Caribbean Freedom Economy and Slavery from Emancipation to the Present*, Kingston, Jamaica: Ian Randle Publishers, 1993.

Beckles, W. A. *The Barbados Disturbances: 1937*. Bridgetown: Advocate News, 1973.

Bell, Howard H., ed. *Black Separatism and the Caribbean, 1860*. Ann Arbor: University of Michigan, 1970.

Bennett, J. Harry. *Bondsmen and Bishops: Slavery and Apprenticeship on the Codrington Plantations of Barbados, 1710–1838*. Berkeley: University of California Press, 1958.

Blackburn, Robin, *The Overthrow of Colonial Slavery, 1776–1848*. London: Verso, 1988.

Blackett, R.J.M., *Building an Antislavery Wall: Black Americans in the Atlantic Abolitionist Movement, 1830–1860*. Baton Rouge and London: Louisiana State University Press, 1983.

Blackman, Francis, *Dame Nita: Caribbean Woman, World Citizen*. Ian Randle Publishers: Kingston, 1995.

Bridenbaugh, Carl & Roberta, *No Peace Beyond the Line: the English in the Caribbean, 1624–1690*. Oxford: Oxford University Press, 1972.

Bryan, Patrick, *The Haitian Revolution and its Effects*. Kingston and Exeter, NH: Heinemann, 1984.

Burton, Richard D.E., *Afro-Creole: Power, Opposition and Play in the Caribbean*, Ithaca and London: Connell University Press, 1997.

Campbell, Peter, *The Church in Barbados in the Seventeenth Century*. Bridgetown: Barbados Museum, 1982.

Chevannes, Barry, *Rastafari: Roots and Ideology. Syracuse,* NY: Syracuse University Press, 1994.

Clarke, Charles, *The Constitutional Crisis of 1876 in Barbados*. Bridgetown: N.p. 1896.

Cooper, Carolyn, *Noises in the Blood: Orality, Gender, and the 'Vulgar' Body of Jamaican Popular Culture*. Durham: Duke University Press, 1995.

Craton, Michael, *Testing the Chains: Resistance to Slavery in the British West Indies*, Ithaca: Cornell University Press, 1982.

————. *Sinews of Empire: A Short History of British Slavery*. London: Doubleday, 1974.

Curtin, Philip, *The Atlantic Slave Trade: A Census Madison*. University of Wisconsin Press: N.p., 1969.

————. (1955) *Two Jamaicas: The Role of Ideas in a Tropical Colony, 1830–1865*. Cambridge, MA: Harvard University Press, 1955.

————. *The Rise and Fall of the Plantation Complex: Essays in Atlantic History,* Cambridge: Cambridge University Press, 1990.

Davis, Darnell, *Cavaliers and Roundheads of Barbados, 1650–1652*. Georgetown: N.p., 1887.

Davis, Kortright, *Cross and Crown in Barbados* . Frankfurt: N.p., 1983.

Dickson, William, *Letters on Slavery* . London: N.p., 1789. *Mitigation of Slavery*. London: N.p., 1814 .

Drescher, Seymour, *Econocide: British Slavery in the Era of Abolition*. Pittsburgh: Pittsburgh University Press, 1977.

Du Bois, W.E.B., (1935) 1992. *Black Reconstruction in America, 1860–1880*. Reprint. New York: Atheneum.

Dunn, Richard, *Sugar and Slaves: The Rise of the Planter Class in the English West Indies, 1624–1713*. Chapel Hill: University of North Carolina Press, 1972.

Dupuy, Alex, *Haiti in the World Economy: class, race and underdevelopment since 1700*. Boulder, CO: Westview Press, 1989.

Edghill,. J.Y., *About Barbados* London: N.p., 1890.

Eltis, David, *Economic Growth and the Ending of the Transatlantic Slave Trade*. New York: Oxford University Press, 1987.

Fick, Carolyn E., *The Making of Haiti: The Saint Domingue Revolution from Below*. Knoxville: University of Tennessee Press, 1990.

Foner, Eric, *Nothing But Freedom: Emancipation and Its Legacy*. Baton Rouge: Louisiana State University Press, 1983.

Frere, George, *A Short History of Barbados*. London: N.p., 1768.

Galenson, David, *Traders, Planters, and Slaves Cambridge*. N.p., Cambridge University Press, 1986.

Gaspar, David B. and David P. Geggus, 1997. *A Turbulent Time:The French Revolution and the Greater Caribbean*. Bloomington and Indianapolis: Indiana University Press.

Geggus, David P., *Slavery,War and Revolution:The British Occupation of Saint Domingue, 1793–1798*. Oxford: Clarendon Press,1982a.

Genovese, Eugene,. *From Rebellion Revolution:Afro-American Slave Revolts in the Making of the New World*, NewYork:Vintage, (1979) 1981.

Gilroy, Paul, *There Ain't No Black in the Union Jack: the Cultural Politics of Race and Nation*, Chicago: University of Chicago Press, 1991.

————. (1993) 1995.The Black Atlantic: Modernity and Double Consciousness. Cambridge: Harvard University Press.

Goodridge, Sehon, *Facing the Challenge of Emancipation:A Study of the Ministry ofWilliam Hart Coleridge, First Bishop of Barbados, 1824–1842*. Bridgetown: Antilles, 1981.

Goveia, Elsa, Slave Society in the British Leeward Islands. New Haven:Yale University Press, 1965.

————. *TheWest Indian Slave Laws of the Eighteenth Century* Barbados: Caribbean University Press, 1970.

Greenfield, Sidney, *English Rustics in Black Slain*, New Haven:Yale University Press,1966.

Habermas, Jurgen, (1989) 1992. *The Structural Transformation of the Public Sphere*, Cambridge, MA: MIT Press.

Hall, Catherine, *White, Male and Middle Class: Explorations in Feminism and History*, Cambridge: Policy Press, 1992.

Hall, Douglas, *Free Jamaica, 1838–1865:An Economic History*. New Haven:Yale University Press, 1959.

Hamilton, Bruce, *Barbados and the Confederation Question, 1871–1885*. London:William Kidd, 1956.

Handler, Jerome & Lange, Frederick, *Plantation Slavery in Barbados:An Archaeological and Historical Investigation* . London: Harvard University Press, 1978.

Handler, Jerome, *The Unappropriated People: Freedmen in the Slave Society of Barbados*. Baltimore: Johns Hopkins University Press, 1974.

Harlow,Vincent, *A History of Barbados, 1625–1685*. Oxford: Oxford University Press, 1926.

Helg, Aline, *Our Rightful Share:TheAfro-Cuban Struggle for Equality, 1886–1912*, Chapel Hill and London: University of North Caroline Press,1995.

Heuman, Gad J. 1981. *Between Black andWhite: Race, Politics and the Free Coloreds in Jamaica, 1792–1865*, Westport, CT: Greenwood.

————. *'The KillingTime':The Morant Bay Rebellion in Jamaica*. London: Macmillan, 1994.

Hewitt, J.M., *TenYears of Constitutional Development in Barbados*. Bridgetown: Advocate News, 1954.

Higman, Barry, *Slave Populations of the British Caribbean, 1807–1834*. Baltimore: Johns Hopkins University Press, 1984.

Hoyos, F.A., Barbados .A *History from theAmerindians to Independence* . London: N.p., 1978.

Hoyos, F.A, *Grantley Adams and the Social Revolution* . London: MacMillan, 1974.

Hughes, Griffith, *The Natural History of Barbados*. London: N.p., 1750.

Jamaica Baptist Edward John Eyr. . . In Reference to the Letter Addressed by Dr. Underhill to the Rt. Hon'ble Mr. Cardwell, Secretary of State for the Colonies'. Montego Bay: *County Union* Office, 5 June 1865.

Jamaica Committee, *Facts and documents re alleged rebellion in Jamaica and the Measure of Repression*: *including Notes of the trial of Mr. Gordon,* Jamaica Papers, no. 1. London: The Jamaica Committee, 1866.

James, Winston, 1998. *Holding Aloft the Banner of Ethopia: Caribbean Radicalism in Early Twentieth-Century* America. London and New York: Verso.

Kelley, Robin D.G., *Race Rebels: Culture, Politics and the Black Working Class* . New York: The Free Press, 1996.

Knight, Franklin, *The Caribbean: The Genesis of a Fragmented Nationalism*. N.Y: Oxford University Press, 1978.

Lamming, George, *In the Castle of my Skin* . London, N.p., 1953.

Levy, Claude, *Emancipation, Sugar, and Federalism: Barbados and the West Indies, 1833–1876*. Gainesville: University of Florida Press, 1980.

Lewis, Arthur, *Labour in the West Indies* . London: Fabian Society, 1938.

————. *The Agony of the Eight* . Bridgetown: Fabian Society, 1965.

Lewis, Gordon, *The Growth of the Modern West Indies*. London: Mac Gibbon and Kee, 1968.

Ligon, Richard, *A True and Exact History of the Island of Barbados*. London: N.p., 1657.

Lowenthal, David, *West Indian Societies* . N.Y. : Oxford University Press, 1972.

Mack, Raymond, *Race, Class and Power in Barbados*, Cambridge: Mass., 1967.

Mallon, Florencia, 1983. *The Defense of Community in Peru's Central Highlands: Peasant Struggle and Capitalist Transition, 1860–1940*. Princeton: Princeton University Press.

————. *Peasant and Nation: The Making of Postcolonial Mexico and Peru*. Berkeley and Los Angeles: University of California Press, 1995.

Mark, Francis, *The History of the Barbados Workers' Union*, Barbados: Barbados Workers Union, 1966.

Marshall, Woodville, (ed.) *The Colthurst Journal* . N.Y. : KTO Press, 1977.

Martin, Tony, *Race First: The Ideological and Organizational Struggles of Marcus Garvey and the Universal Negro Improvement Association* . Westport, CT and London: Greenwood Press, 1976.

McCusker, John & Menard, Russell, *The Economy of British America; 1607–1789*. Chapel Hill: University of North Carolina Press, 1985.

McGlynn, Frank and Seymour Drescher, eds. *The Meaning of Freedom: Economics, Politics and Culture after Slavery*. Pittsburgh & London: University of Pittsburgh Press, 1992.

Metraux, Alfred, *Black Peasants and Their Religion*. Trans. Peter Lengyel. London: George Harrap & Co., 1990.

Mintz, Sidney and Douglas Hall, *The Origins of the Jamaica Internal Marketing System*. New Haven: Yale University Publications in Anthropology, 1960. no. 57, pp. 3–26.

Mintz, Sidney and Sally Price, eds. *Caribbean Contours*. Baltimore: Johns Hopkins University Press, 1985.

Morris, Aldon D. *The Origins of the Civil Rights Movement,* New York: Free Press, 1984.

Morrissey, Marietta, *SlaveWomen in the NewWorld: Gender Stratification in the Caribbean*. Lawrence K.S.: University of Kansas Press, 1989.

Newton, Velma, *The Silver Men:West Indian Labour Migration to Panama, 1850–1914*. Kingston: ISER, UWI, 1984.

Nicholl, David, *From Desalines to Duvalier: Race, Colour and National Independence in Haiti*, 3d ed. London: Macmillan Caribbean, 1996.

Orderson, J.W., *Creoleana: Or Social and Domestic Scenes and Incidents in Barbados in days ofYore*. London: N.p., 1842.

————. Directions toYoung Planters for their Care and Management of a Sugar Plantation in Barbados London: N.p., 1800.

Parry, J. & Sherlock, P., *A Short History of theWest Indies*. London: MacMillan, 1956.

Pinckard, Dr. George, Notes *on theWest Indies*, London, 1806. 3 Vols.

Pitman, Frank, *The Development of the BritishWest Indies, 1700–1763*. Newhaven:Yale University Press, 1917.

Poyer, John, *The History of Barbados*. London: N.p., 1808.

Puckrein, Gary, Little England, Plantation Society and AngloBarbadian Politics, 1627–1700. NY: University Press, 1984.

Richardson, Bonham, *Panama Money in Barbados, 1900–1920*, Knoxville: N.p., 1985.

Robotham, Don, *The Notorious Riot.:The Socio-Economic and Political Bases of Paul Bogle's Revolt*. Working Paper 28. Kingston: Institute of Social and Economic Research, University of the West Indies, 1981.

Rodney,Walter, *A History of the GuyaneseWorking People, 1881–1905*. Baltimore: Johns Hopkins University Press,1981.

Saville, Julie, *TheWork of Reconstruction: From Slave toWage Laborer in South Carolina, 1860–1970*. Cambridge: Cambridge University Press, 1994.

Schomburgk, Robert, *The History of Barbados* . London: Longman, 1848.

Schuler, Monica, '*Alas,Alas, Kongo':A Social History of Indentured African Immigration into Jamaica, 1841-1865*. Baltimore: Johns Hopkins Univ. Press,1980.

Scott, James, *The Moral Economy of the Peasant*. New Haven:Yale University Press, 1976.

————. *Weapons of theWeak: Everyday Forms of Peasant Resistance*. New Haven:Yale University Press, 1985.

Scott, Rebecca, *Slave Emancipation in Cuba:TheTransition to Free Labor, 1860–1899*. Princeton: Princeton University Press,1985.

Semmel, Bernard, *The Governor Eyre Controversy*. London: Macgibbon & Kee,1968.

Sheppard, Jill,The *Redlegs of Barbados: Their Origins and History*. N.Y.: K.T.O. Press, 1977.

Shepherd, Verene, *Transients to Settlers:The experience of Indians in Jamaica, 1845–1950*. Leeds, England: PeepalTree,1994.

————, and Bridget Brereton and Barbara Bailey, *Engendering History: CaribbeanWomen In Historical Perspective*. Kingston: Ian Randle Publishers; London: James Currey,1995.

Sheridan, Richard, Sugar and Slavery:An Economic History of the BritishWest Indies, 1623–1775 .Barbados: N.p., 1974.

————. *The Development of the Plantation to 1750* . Kingston: Caribbean Universities Press, 1970.

Skeete, C.C., *The Condition of Peasant Agriculture in Barbados* . Bridgetown, N.p., 1930.

Spurdle, Frederick, *Early West Indian* Government . Christ Church, N.p.,n.d.

Starkey, Otis, *The Economic Geography of Barbados*, N.Y.: Columbia University Press, 1939.

Stern, Steve, ed. *Resistance, Rebellion and Consciousness in the Andean Peasant World: Eighteenth to Twentieth Centuries*. Madison: University of Wisconsin Press, 1987.

Stewart, John , *A View of the Past and Present State of the Island of Jamaica*. Edinburgh: n.p., 1823.

Stewart, Robert J., *Religion and Society in Post-Emancipation Jamaica.* Knoxville,TN: University of Tennessee Press, 1992.

Stuckey, Sterling, *Slave Culture: Nationalist Theory and the Foundations of Black America.* New York: Oxford University Press,1987.

Sturge, Joseph & Harvey,Thomas, *The West Indies in 1837*. London: Hamilton and Adams, 1968 edit).

Tinker, Hugh, A New System of Slavery:The Export of Indian Labour Overseas, 1830–1920, 2d ed. London: Hansib Publishing, 1993.

Trouillot, Michel-Rolph, *Haiti: State Against Nation:The Origins and Legacy of Duvalierism*, New York: Monthly Review Press,1990.

Turner, Mary S., 1982. Slaves and Missionaries:The Disintegration of Jamaican Slave Society, 1787–1834. Urbana: University of Illinois Press.

Turner, Mary ed., *From Chattel Slaves to Wage Slaves: The Dynamics of Labour Bargaining in the Americas.* London: James Currey; Kingston: Ian Randle Publishers; Bloomington: Indiana University Press, 1995.

Underhill, Edward Bean, *The Tragedy at Morant Bay:A Narrative of the Disturbance in the Island of Jamaica in 1865* . London: Alexander & Shepheard, 1895.

Waddell, Rev. Hope Masterton, *Twenty-Nine Years in the West Indies and Central Africa:A Review of Missionary Work and Adventure, 1829–1858*. Reprint. London: Frank Cass, [1863] 1970.

Ward, Samuel, (Ringold). Reflections Upon the Gordon Rebellion , Pamphlet,N.p.n.p, 1866.

Watson, Karl, *The Civilised Island, Barbados: A Social History, 1750–1816*, Barbados: N.p., 1979.

Watts, David, *The West Indies: Patterns Of Development, Culture and Environment Change Since 1492* Cambridge: Cambridge University Press, 1987.

Williams, Eric, *Capitalism and Slavery*. London: Andre Deutch, 1964.

———. From Columbus to Castro:The History of the Caribbean,1492–1969.London:Andre Deutch,1970.

———. *Documents of West Indian History* .Port of Spain: Andre Deutch, 1963.

Worrell, Delisle, (ed) *The Economy of Barbados, 1946–1980*. Bridgetown: Barbados Central Bank, 1982.

Wrong, Hume, Government of the West Indies. Oxford: Oxford University Press, 1923.

ARTICLES

Barrow, Christine,'Ownership and Control of Resources in Barbados: 1834 to the Present', *Social and Economic Studies*,Vol. 32, No.3, (1983) p.83–120.

Beckles, Hilary, 'The Slave Drivers' War: Bussa and the 1816 Barbados Slave Rebellion', in *Boletin de Estudios Latinoamericanos y de Caribe,* (Dec. 1985), No. 39, p.85–109.

————, 'Black People in the Colonial Historiography of Barbados', in W.K. Marshall, ed. *Emancipation II*. Barbados, 1987) p.131–143.

Belle, George, 'The Abortive Revolution of 1876 in Barbados', *Journal of Caribbean History*, Vol.18, 1984, p.1–3.

————. 'The Initial Political Implications of Emancipation: Barbados'. Paper presented at the 14th Annual Conference of Caribbean Historians Puerto Rico, April 16–21, 1982.

————. 'The Struggle for Political Democracy: 1937 Riots', Public Lecture, Bridgetown, March 17, 1987.

Bellegarde-Smith, Patrick. 'Haitian Social Thought in the Nineteenth Century: Class Formation and Westernization'. *Caribbean Studies* 20.1 (1980): 5-33.

Besson, Jean, 'Symbolic Aspects of Land Tenure in the Caribbean'. In *Peasants, Plantations and Rural Communities in the Caribbean*, ed. Malcolm Cross and A. Marks, 86–116. Guildford, England: University of Surrey, 1979.

————. 'Reputation and respectability reconsidered: a new perspective on Afro-Caribbean peasant women'. In *Women and Change in the Caribbean: a Pan-Caribbean Perspective*, ed. James Momsen, 15–37. London: James Currey,1993.

————. 'Land, Kinship and Community in the Post-Emancipation Caribbean: A Regional View of the Leewards'. *In Small Islands, Large Questions: Society, Culture and Resistance in the Post-Emancipation Caribbean*, ed. Karen F. Olwig, 73–99. London: Frank Cass, 1995.

Bigelow, John, *Jamaica in 1850 Or The effects of Sixteen Years of Freedom on a Slave Colony*, Reprint.Including Appendix A: 'A visit to the Emperor of Haiti'. Westport, CT: Negro Universities Press, [1851] 1970.

Bird, Mark B., 'Has Freedom Proved a Failure in Hayti'. *Methodist Quarterly Review*, 46 (1862):561–579.

————. *The Black Man; Or Haytian Independence*. New York: n.p., 1869.

Bennett, J.H., 'The Problem of Slave Labour Supply at the Codrington Plantations,' *Journal of Negro History*, Vol.36, (1958) p.406–439.

Boomert, Arie, 'Notes on Barbados Prehistory', *Journal of the Barbados Museum and Historical Society* (J.B.M.H.S.) Vol.38, No. 1, (1987). p. 8–44.

Brown, Elsa B., ' Negotiating and Transforming the Public Sphere: African American Political Life in the Transition from Slavery to Freedom'. In *The Black Public Sphere: A Public Culture Book*, ed. Black Public Sphere Collective, 111–151. Chicago and London: University of Chicago Press, 1995.

Bullen, A.K. & R.P., 'Barbados: A Carib Centre', in *The Bajan and South Magazine*, (1966), No.155, 6–12.

Bullen, R.P., 'Barbados and the Archaeology of the Caribbean', in *J.B.M.H.S.,* 32, (1966) p.16–19.

Carter, Richard, 'Public Amenities after Emancipation', in Marshall, ed, *The Colthurst Journal* p.46–70.

Carrington, Selwyn, 'West Indian opposition to British Policy: Barbadian Politics, 1774–1782', in *Journal of Caribbean History*, Vol.17, (1982), p.26–50.

Cooksey, C., 'The First Barbadians', *Timehri*, 3:2, 1912, p.142–144.

Drescher, Seymour, 'Public Opinion and the Destruction of British Colonial Slavery'. In *Slavery and British Society, 1776–1846*, ed. James Walvin, Baton Rouge: Louisiana State University Press, 1982. 22–48.

Drewett, Peter, 'Archaeological Survey of Barbados', in *J.B.M.H.S.* Vol. 38, No. 1, (1987), p. 44–81, Vol. 38 No. 2, (1988), p. 196–205 [This was published in two parts].

Dunn, Richard, 'The Barbados Census of 1680: Profile of the Richest Colony in English America', *William and Mary Quarterly*, Vol. 26, (1969), p. 3–30.

Geggus, David P., 'British Opinion and Emergence of Haiti, 1791–1805'. In *Slavery and British Society, 1776–1846*, ed. James Walvin. Baton Rouge: Louisiana State University Press, 1982b.

Gibbs, Bentley, 'The Establishment of the Tenantry System in Barbados', in Marshall, ed., *The Colthurst Journal* p. 23–46.

Hall, Neville, 'Law and Society in Barbados at the Turn of the Nineteenth Century,' *Journal of Caribbean History*, Vol. 5, 1972, p. 20–45.

Handler, Jerome, 'An Archaeological Investigation of the Domestic Life of Plantation Slaves in Barbados', *J.B.M.H.S.*, Vol. 34, No. 2, (1972), p. 64–72.

———. 'The Amerindian Slave Population of Barbados in the Seventeenth and Early Eighteenth Centuries', *Caribbean Studies*, Vol. 8, No. 4, 1969, p. 38–64.

———. 'Aspects of Amerindian Ethnography in Seventeenth Century Barbados', *Caribbean Studies*, Vol. 9, No. 4, (1970), p. 50–72.

Heuman, Gad J., "Runaway Slaves in Nineteenth Century Barbados.' In *Out of the House of Bondage: Runaways, Resistance and Marronage in Africa and the New World* edited by Gad Heuman, 95–112, London: Frank Cass, 1986.

Hughes, Ronnie. 'The Origins of Barbados Sugar Plantations and the Role of the White Population in Sugar Plantation Society.' In *Emancipation I*, edited by A. Thompson, Bridgetown: Department of History, University of the West Indies, 1984. 26–33.

Hunte, Keith. 'Church and society in Barbados in the Eighteenth Century'. In *Social Groups and Institutions in the History of the Caribbean*, edited by Blanca Silvestrini, San Juan: University of Puerto Rico Press, 1975. 13–26.

———. 'The Democratic League and Charles Duncan O'Neal', Public Lecture, Bridgetown, March 3, 1987.

Innis, F.C. 'The Presugar Era of European Settlement in Barbados', *Journal of Caribbean History*, Vol. 1, (1970), p. 1–22.

Johnson, Howard, 'Barbadian Immigrants in Trinidad, 1870–1897', *Caribbean Studies*, Vol. 13, (1973), p. 5–30.

Karch, Cecelia. 'The Growth of the Corporate Economy in Barbados: Class/Race Factors, 1890–1977'. In *Contemporary Caribbean: A Sociological Reader*, Vol. 1 edited by Susan Craig. Port of Spain: The College Press, 1997.

Lewis, Gordon, 'The Struggle for Freedom', *New World Quarterly*, Vol. 111, Nos. 1–2, Barbados Independence Issue (1966) p. 14–29.

Lowenthal, David, 'The Population of Barbados', *Social and Economic Studies*, Vol. 6, (1957), p. 445–501.

Marshall, Trevor, 'The White's in Perspective.' *The New Bajan* (July 1990).

———. 'The Riots of 1937' *The New Bajan*. (October 1989).

————. 'The Termination of Apprenticeship in Barbados and the Windward Islands: An Essay in Colonial Administration and Politics.' *Journal of Caribbean History*, Vol. 2 (1971): 1–45.

————. 'Post-Emancipation Adjustments in Barbados, 1838–1876.' In *Emancipation I* edited by A. Thompson, Bridgetown: Department of History, 1984. 88–108.

————. 'Nineteenth Century Crisis in the Barbadian Sugar Industry'. In *Emancipation II* edited by W.K. Marshall, Bridgetown: Department of History, 1987. 85–102.

Marshall, Woodville. 'Amelioration and Emancipation (with Special Reference to Barbados)'. In *Emancipation I*, edited by A. Thompson, Bridgetown: Department of History, 1984. 72–88.

————. et.al. 'The Establishment of a Peasantry in Barbados.' In *Social Groups and Institutions in the History of the Caribbean,* edited by Blanca Silvestrini, San Juan: University of Puerto Rico Press, 1975.

Molen, Patricia, 'Population and Social Patterns in Barbados in the Early Eighteenth Century', *William and Mary Quarterly*, Vol. 28, 1971, p. 287–300.

Morris, Robert, 'Slave Society in Barbados', in Thompson, ed., In *Emancipation I.* p. 33–45.

————. 'Slave Society in Barbados.' In *Emancipation I,* edited by A. Thompson, 33–45, Bridgetown: Department of History, 1984.

Nicholls, David, 1974, 'A Work of Combat: Mulatto Historians and the Haitian Past, 1847–1867', *Journal of Interamerican Studies and World Affairs.* 16: 1: 15–38.

Patterson, Orlando, The Unholy Trinity: Freedom, Slavery and the American Constitution. *Social Research.* (1987): 54: 3: 543–578,

————. *Freedom in the Making of Western Culture.* Vol. 1. Cambridge, MA: Harvard University Press, 1991.

Phillips, Anthony, 'The Confederation Question', In *Emancipation II edited* by W.K. Marshall, 70–85. Bridgetown: Department of History, 1987.

————. 'The Confederation Question', in Marshall, ed., *The Colthrust Journal* p. 7085

————. 'The Racial Factor in Politics in Barbados, 1880-1914', History Department Seminar Paper, UWI, Cave Hill, 1973

————. 'The Political Elite in Barbados, 1880–1914: Aristocracy, Plantocracy, or Bureaucracy', History Department Seminar Paper, UWI, Cave Hill, 1976 '

————. The Origins of the Bushe Experiment: A Governor's Eye View', History Department Seminar Paper, UWI, Cave Hill, 1983;

————. 'An Assessment of the Ideological Position of Grantley Adams in 1937–38, 1948–49', paper presented at the 16th Annual Conference of Caribbean Historians, Barbados, 1984.

Ramsaram, Ramesh, 'The PostWar Decline of the Sugar Economy in the commonwealth Caribbean', University of Hull, Conference Paper, Wilberforce Anniversary, July, 1983.

Reddock, Rhoda, 'Women and Slavery in the Caribbean: A Feminist Perspective', *Latin American Perspectives*, Issue 44, 12: 1 (Winter): 63–80, N.p. 1985.

Roberts, G.W., 'Emigration from the Island of Barbados', *Social and Economic Studies*, Vol. 4, (1955), 287.

Rodney, Walter, 'Barbadian Immigration into British Guiana, 1863–1924', Paper presented at the 9th Annual Conference of Caribbean Historians, Barbados, 1977.

Scott, Rebecca, 'Exploring the Meaning of Freedom: Postemancipation Societies in Comparative
   Perspective'. *Hispanic American Historical Review*. (1988). 68: 407–28.
Sheller, Mimi, 'Sword-Bearing Citizens: Militarism and Manhood in Nineteenth Century
   Haiti'. *Plantation Society in the Americas*, (1997) 4: 2/3: 233–78.
————. 'Quasheba, Mother, Queen: Black Women's Public Leadership and Political Protest
   in Post-emancipation Jamaica, 1834-65'. *Slavery and Abolition*, (1998)19: 3: 90–117.
————. 'The Haytian Fear': Racial Projects and Competing Reaction to the First Black
   Republic', in Research in Politics and Society. Vol. 6, The *Global Perspective*, ed. Pinar
   Batur-Vanderlippe and Joe Feagan Greenwich, CT: JAI Press, (1999) 285–303.
Sheridan, Richard, 'The Crisis of Slave Subsistence in the British West Indies during arid after
   the American Revolution', *William and Mary Quarterly*, Vol. 33, No.4, 1976, pp. 615–641.
Sleeman, Michael, 'The AgroBusiness Bourgeoisie of Barbados and Martinique', in P.I. Gomes
   ed. *Rural Development in the Caribbean*. Kingston: n.p., 1985.
————. 'The Agri-Business Bourgeoisie of Barbados and Martinique.' In *Rural Development in
   the Caribbean*, edited by P.I. Gomes. Kingston: Heinneman, 1985.
Smith, Raymond T. 'Race and Class in Post Emancipation Caribbean.' In *Racism and Colonialism*,
   edited by Robert Ross. Leiden: University Press, The Hague, 1987.
Stoddart, Brian, 'Cricket and Colonisation in the English Speaking Caribbean to 1914: Steps
   Towards a Cultural Analysis', Seminar Paper, UWI, History Department, Cave Hill,
   Barbados, 1985
Vaughan, H.A., 'The Shaping of the New Order: Barbados, 1834–46', History Department
   Seminar Paper, No.9, 1981–82, UWI CaveHill.
Ward, J.R., 'The Profitability of Sugar Planting in the British West Indies, 1650–1834',
   Economic History Review, Vol. 31, No. 2, (1978), p. 197–212.
Wilmot, Swithin 'Political Development in Jamaica in the Post-Emancipation Period, 1838–
   1854'. D Phil. Thesis, Oxford University, (1977) 1984.
————. 'Emancipation in Action: Workers and Wage Conflict in Jamaica , 1838–1840',
   Jamaica Journal, (1986)19: 55–62.
————. 1994. 'The Growth of Political Activity in Post-Emancipation Jamaica'. In *Garvey:
   His Work and Impact,* ed. Rupert Lewis and Patrick Bryan, 39–36. (Trenton, NJ: Africa
   World Press).
————. 1995. ' "Females of Abandoned Character"? Women and Protest in Jamaica. 1838–
   65.' In *Engendering History: Caribbean Women in Historical Perspective,* ed. Shepherd et al.,
   London : James Currey, 1995 p. 279–295.

OFFICIAL DOCUMENTS AND REPORTS

A Report from the Select Committee of the House of Assembly appointed to inquire into the
   origins, Cause, and Progress of the late Insurrection (Barbados, 1818).
A Report of a Committee of the Council of Barbadoes, appointed to inquire into the Actual
   Condition of the Slaves in this Island, (Barbados, 1822).
Report of Select Committee of the House of Commons on West India Colonies, 1842.
Report on Census of Barbados, 1881–1891 (Bridgetown, 1899).

Report and Evidence of West India Royal Commission, 1897.

Report on the Elementary Education for the year 1899 (Bridgetown, 1899).

Henry Lofty, Report on the Census of Barbados, 1911–1921.

Proceedings of West Indian Sugar Commission, (Bridgetown, 1929).

Report of the West India Royal Commission (Moyne Report), 1945.

UNPUBLISHED THESES

Belle, George, The Politics of Development: A Study in the Political Economy of Barbados, PhD. diss., Manchester University, 1977.

Davis, Karen, The Position of Poor Whites in a Colour-class hierarchy: A Diachronic Study of the Ethnic Boundaries in Barbados. PhD. diss., Wayne State University, Detroit, Michigan, 1978, p. 365.

Karch, Cecilia, The Transformation and Consolidation of the Corporate Plantation Economy in Barbados, 18601877, PhD. diss., Rutgers University, New Brunswick, 1979, p.482

Innes, Franck, Plantations and Peasant Forms – Barbados, 1627-1960. PhD diss., McGill University, Montreal, 1967, p. 291.

Manyoni, Joseph, Social Stratification in Barbados: A Study in Social Change, PhD diss., University of Oxford, 1973, p.269 .

Will, Wilber, Political Development in the Mini-State Caribbean: A Focus on Barbados, PhD diss., University of Missouri, 1973.

Index

Abolition movement: British parliament and the, 29–31

Adams, Grantley: and O'Neale, 189–192

Afro-Barbadian culture: Revivalist churches and, 184

Agricultural Aids Act (1887), 112, 160

Agricultural Society: and the Norman Commission, 160

Alleyne, C.W.: submission to the Norman Commission, 172

Anglican Church: control by the, 126; and education, 59; and racism, 58, 67–68

Anti-slavery movement: free-Blacks and the, 23

Apprentices: scale of allowances, 31

Apprenticeship System: abolition of the, 37; children under the, 36–37; institution of the, 33; operation of the, 40; provisions of the, 34–40

Arson: and labour resistance, 76–77

Assembly: planter elite domination of the, 113–120

Austin, John Gardiner: and the 1876 labour revolution, 148; profile, 122–123; submission to the Norman Commission, 161, 162

Austin, Rev.: and racism, 67

Baeza, E.I., 123

Baird, 'Colonel' Smith: and the 1876 labour revolution, 136

Barbados Challenge Cup Competition, 130

Barbados Chamber of Commerce: and free-Blacks, 5

Barbados Defence Association (BDA), 130; and Crown rule, 142–143, 156

Barbados Herald: and Black political mobilisation, 185–186, 190

Barbados Labour Union, 185

Barbados Mutual Life Assurance Society (BMLAS), 121, 132

Barbados Produce Exporters Association (BPEA), 133

Barbados Shipping and Trading, 132

Barbados Sugar Industry Agricultural Bank: establishment of the, 125

Barbados Workers' Union Cooperative Company, 188

Barbados Workingmen's Association: establishment of the, 188–189

Barbadian, 43–44; and the debate on freedom, 74

Beet sugar: and the WI sugar industry, 128

Black-on-Black slavery: ambiguities of, 15–26

Black enterprises: restrictive legislation and, 14–16

Black entrepreneurs: Bridgetown free Coloured and free, 16

Black merchants: in Bridgetown, 16

Black middle class: emergence of a, 131

Black slave-holders: in Barbados, 2

Blacks: and cricket, 131; and the debate on freedom, 42–44; the 1863 famine and land ownership by, 82–83; and friendly societies, 180–182; killed in the 1876 labour revolution, 152–154; and landless freedom, 44–50; and landships, 182–183; resistance to ideology of white supremacy, 68; and revivalist churches, 183–184; and the tenantry system, 48–58

Blacks in business. *See* Black entrepreneurs

Boscobel Plantation: potato riots at, 159

Bourne, London: business of, 17; status of, 5

Bourne, William: and the manumission of London, 8; status of, 5

Brathwaite, Chrissie: entry into Parliament, 187, 188

Brathwaite, Rev. John: slave-owner, 67

Bree Commission Report (1896): and working class education, 126

Bridgetown: free-Blacks in, 12–14; merchant elite, 121

Bridgetown constituency: formation of the, 90

British aid: to the Barbados sugar industry, 124– 123

British Guiana: and Barbados immigrants, 78, 79–80

Bryden, Arthur Sydney: profile, 123

Buck, Henry: and the *Contract Law*, 73–74

Business: free-Blacks in, 16–17

Bussa, 'General': and the 1816 labour revolution, 137–139, 140

Cameron, A.: submission to the Norman Commission, 161, 162

Canada: sugar exports to, 128

Capital market: development of a local, 121

Carrington, George: and the tenantry system, 50

Central Negro Emancipation Committee: and the *Contract Law*, 86

Challenor, George, 130

Chamberlain, Joseph: and the beet sugar industry, 128

Chancery Court System: implementation of the, 121

Chattel houses: symbolism of the, 58–59

Child abandonment: under apprenticeship, 37

Children: apprenticeship and enslaved, 36–37

Cholera: outbreak, 61–62

Cipriani: Captain Arthur: O'Neale and the influence of, 186

Civil rights: attempts to reduce black workers', 86–87; free Blacks and the struggle for, 23; Prescod and the struggle for, 90

Clarke, C.P.: submission to the Norman Commission, 161, 168, 169

Clarke, Frederick James: profile, 117, 120; submission to the Norman Commission, 169

Clarke, Robert Boucher: and the Apprenticeship System, 35–36; and the Franchise Bill, 90

Clarke, Solicitor-general: and the Apprenticeship System, 38, 43; and post-emancipation labour legislation, 57

Cleaver, Betsy: ejection of labourer, 88–89

Clergy: and the Norman Commission, 162

Codrington College: and racism, 58

Colbrook, Governor: and the post-Emancipation labour market, 72

Coleridge, Bishop: and the abolition of the Apprenticeship System, 38; and Blacks in post-emancipation Barbados, 63

Collective bargaining: Apprenticeship and, 69–70

Colonial Union of Coloured Classes: and resistance to post-Emancipation labour conditions, 75

Commission Merchants Association, 132

Combermere College, 131

Compensation: paid to planter elite, 31

Compulsory education, 126

Confederation politics, 141–143

Constitutional change (1876), 115

Constitutional reform: crown rule and, 141– 143

Contract Law (1838): and the 1876 labour revolution, 137; and post-Emancipation labour control, 86; provisions of the Barbados, 70–72. *See also Masters and Servant Act* (1838)

Corporate power: emergence of, 132–133

Court of Reconciliation: recommendation for a, 73

Cricket: and cultural apartheid, 129–131

Crown rule, 141; Barbadian Assembly and, 142–143, 156; and the Morant Bay Rebellion (Jamaica), 141

Cultural domination: cricket and, 129–131

Daniel, George: submission to the Norman Commission, 165, 171

Democratic League: formation of the, 187–188; G. Adams and the, 190–192

Dickson, William: and Barbadian slavery, 21

Dottin Brothers: and the 1876 labour revolution, 135–137

Dorwidge, Fitzgerald: submission to the Norman Commission, 164–167, 172, 174

Easter labour revolutions, 137–138

Economic crisis: planter-merchant elite and the, 128–129; post-1876, 158–164; and the sugar industry, 108–113

Education: for Blacks, 59, 119; Norman Commission and workers, 175–176; and political control, 118–120; for Whites, 60; working class, 125–126

Education Act (1878), 60, 126

Ejectment: and post-Emancipation labour control, 88–89

Emancipation: and landlessness, 44–50

Emancipation Act (1834): amendment to the, 35; provisions of the, 30

Emancipation Act (1838), 38

Emancipation Bill: introduction of the, 29–30

Emancipation Day (Barbados): 1834, 33–34; 1838, 39

Emigration: recommendations for policy on, 173, 176–180

Emigration law: and labour control, 78, 89–90

Emigration movement: 1863 famine and the, 96, 107–108; to Guiana (1863–1870), 109; post-1838, 77–80;

Employment: of Bridgetown free Black and free Coloured population, 14

Encumbered Estates Act (1854), 121

Enslaved females: sexual exploitation of, 19

Enslavers: free Blacks and free Coloured, 16–17, 18

Executive Council: structure of the, 118

Exports: 113; Barbados (1848–1858), 110; Barbados sugar (1883–1897), to the USA, 111

Famine (1863): impact of the, 95–108

Financing: for sugar planters, 112

Food rebellion: in St Phillip, 100–102

Forde, Phoebe: self-purchase and entrepreneurship of, 17

Franchise: limited Black, 187; white domination of the, 117–118

Franchise Bill: Prescod and the, 90

Free Blacks: anti-slavery attitudes of, 17–18; in Barbados, 1–5; in Bridgetown, 12–14

Free Coloured: manumissions by, 12; plantation owners, 18

Free Trade Act (1846), 110

Freedom: Blacks fear of loss of, 42–44; demand by apprentices for full, 36; and the 1876 labour revolution, 148–149; and gender, 6–12; landless, 44–50; myth, 58–63; Prescod and the debate on, 87–89; workers and the meaning of, 73–77

Friendly societies: emergence of, 180–182

Garvey, Marcus: influence of, 185, 186–187

Gender: and freedom, 6–12

Glenelg, Lord: and the Barbadian Apprenticeship, 35

Goodman, G.A., 130

Goodridge, F.B.: and the Popular Party, 90

Government structure, 115, 118

Graham, Patience: status of, 5

Green, 'General' J.P.: and the 1876 labour revolution, 135–137, 139–141

Haitian revolution: influence on Barbadian Blacks, 24

Harrison's College, 131; and racism, 58

Haynes, A. Percy: property of, 116

Haynes, Richard: property, 116

Hennessey, Governor John Pope: and Crown rule, 141–143, 156

Holetown: free-Black entrepreneurs in, 17

Huckstering: legislation against, 15

Imperial government: and Emancipation, 69

Infant mortality: rates of working class, 136; under the apprenticeship, 37

Innis, Clement, 185

Intellectual elite: Black and White, 119–120

Jamaica: development of the peasantry in, 96–98

Labour control: ejectment as a strategy of post-Emancipation, 88–89; emigration law and,

78, 89–90 post-emancipation legislation and, 56–57

Labour market: conflicts in the post-Emancipation, 69, 75

Labour relations: post-Emancipation, 50–51, 52, 54–57

Labour revolutions (1816 and 1876), 1876, 139–141, 144, 146–150; failure of the, 114; military suppression of the, 150–156

Land: 1876 revolution and the issue of, 147, 148; Jamaica and the access to, 96–98; and power, 44–46

Land ownership: and labour control, 125; the Norman Commission and the issue of, 168–171, 173; and post-Emancipation control of labour, 80–83

Land reform: Norman Commission and, 174–175

Land values: BWI (1840s), 80; and Panama money, 178, 179

Landless freedom: for Blacks, 44–50

Landships: role of, 182–183

Latrobe report: an the church and education of Blacks, 68

Lawrence, Inspector C.J.: submission to the Norman Commission, 162

Leeward Islands: and confederation politics, 141

Legislation: against emigration, 78; anti-Black, 62–63; Black enterprises and restrictive, 14–16; post-emancipation labour, 56–57, 70–73

Legislative Council: reform, 115; structure, 118

Liberal: and the Black working class, 41; and the debate on freedom, 75; and Apprenticeship, 74

Liberal Party. *See* Popular Party

Lynch, James A., 120; profile, 122

MacGregor, Governor: and the *Contract Law* (1838), 71–72; and the Court of Reconciliation, 73, 75: and the emigration scheme, 79

Manual work: Black resistance to, 18

Manumission: of apprentices, 36; by free Black, 19, 21; rates among free Black slave-holders, 2, 11–12; of Phoebe Ford, 17; by whites, 6–7, 10, 12; costs, 8

Masters and Servants Act (1838): provisions of the Barbados, 70–73. *See also Contract Law* (1838)

McGregor, Governor: and the abolishment of Apprenticeship System, 38–39

Medical practitioners: submission to the Norman Commission, 162–163

Merchant elite: development of a, 121–123

Mitchinson, Bishop: and crown rule, 142; and the 1876 working conditions, 145

Money remittances: from Panama, 178, 179

Morant Bay rebellion (Jamaica): and Crown rule, 141

Mortality: among working class, 127–128: rates among the working class, 162–163, 164

Mount Hillaby Estate: and the St.Thomas wage riots, 103

Myth of freedom, 58–63

Neale's Plantation: victimisation of Betsy Cleaver by, 88–89

Norman Commission: investigation into the WI sugar industry, 123–127, 158, 159–174; recommendations, 174–176

O'Neal, Charles Duncan: and Black political mobilisation, 186–193

Panama Canal: and the Barbados emigration movement, 176–180

Panama money: and friendly societies, 180–182; and land values, 179–180

Parkinson, Rawle: and the development of political Black consciousness, 185

Payne, Clement, 193

Peasant movement: limits placed on the, 80–83

Peasantry: development of the Jamaican, 47–48, 96–98; Norman Commission recommendation re the development of the Barbados, 124, 125, 127, 172–175

Pickwick Cricket Club, 130

Phil: *Contract Law* and the case of, 73-74

Phillips, Anthony: and white supremacy in Barbados' post-Emancipation government, 114–120

Pile, G.Laurie: profile, 115–116, 120

Pile, Hon. A.J.: submission to the Norman Commission, 159–161, 168, 169

Plantation Aid Acts, 125

Plantation system: recommendations for the reform of the, 172

Plantations Company Limited: establishment of the, 132

Planter elite: and the Apprenticeship System, 36; control of Black labour, 42; free-Coloured, 18; and cricket, 129–131; and Crown rule, 142–143, 156; and the 1876 labour revolution, 148; and the Norman Commission, 159–162 political control, 120–121, 122; and the representative system, 113–120; Samuel Prescod, 85–87; and the St. Thomas wage riots, 102–108

Police magistrates: powers of, 62

Political control: and the challenge of the merchant elite, 122–123; by the planter elite, 120–121, 122

Political mobilisation: Black, 184–193

Poor relief: 1844 report and, 60–61

Poore, Betty-Burk: and manumission of her children, 8

Popular Party: Prescod and the, 90

Population statistics: of free Blacks in Barbados, 6

Potato riots (1895), 158–159, 180

Poverty: in Bridgetown slave society, 14; in 18th century Barbados, 18; and landlessness, 45–47; Norman Commission and, 162–164; post-emancipation, 51–52; rural, 127

Poyer, John: racist ideology of, 64–65

Prescod, Samuel Jackson: challenge to planters, 119; and education for Blacks, 60; and *Emigration Laws*, 89–90; and labour provisions of Apprenticeship, 74; rise of, 41–44; and the struggle for freedom, 85–89

Property-ownership: 1803 petition and limitations to Black, 20; in 1838 Barbados, 58

Prostitution: of enslaved women, 19

Public health: Norman Commission and issues of, 162; post-emancipation, 61

Public Health Act (1851), 61–62

Rachell, Joseph: Black Bridgetown merchant, 16; Bridgetown business of, 16–17

Racism: and the 1876 labour revolution, 148–149; and labour control, 58–59; and oppression of Blacks, 63–69; and oppression of workers, 87

Rebellion (1816): free-Blacks and the, 24–25

Reece, H. Walter, 120

Reece, J.E.: report on Black education (1899), 125–126

Reeves, Sir Conrad, 114, 119, 130

Representation of the People Act (1901), 187

Representative system: planter domination of the, 113–120

Resistance: to post-Emancipation labour conditions, 75–77

Revivalist Churches: emergence of, 183–184

Riots: St. Thomas (1863) wage, 102–108

Sealy, Elliot: property of, 116; submission to the Norman Commission, 169, 170

Self-purchase: by apprentices, 36; by Blacks, 10–11; by Phoebe Ford, 17

Sexual exploitation: of enslaved females, 19

Sierra Leone: exile of rebellious slaves (1816) to, 91–95

Skilled slaves: and self-purchase, 11

Slave rebellion (1816): exile of participants in the, 91–95

Slave system: and free-Black enslavers, 21–23

Slave trade: impact of the abolition of the, 22

Slave-holding: by free-Blacks, 2

Slave-owners: resistance to the Emancipation movement by WI, 30–31, 33

Slavery: conditions under Apprenticeship, 73–74; racism and, 64

Smith, Sir Lionel: and the abolition movement, 29, 33

Social welfare: White opposition to government policy on, 60–62

Spartan Cricket Club, 130

Speightstown: free Black and Coloured entrepreneurs, 16

St. James: and the 1863 famine, 98, 99

St. Lucy: and the 1863 famine, 99

St. Mary's Church: and racism, 67

St Michael's Cathedral: and racism, 67

St. Peter: and the 1863 famine, 99

St. Philip: and the 1863 famine, 99–102

St. Thomas: wage riots in, 102–108

Stanley, E.G. (Lord Derby): and the Emancipation Bill, 29–30

Status mobility: of free Blacks, 1–2, 10, 14

Stipendary magistrates: report on Apprenticeship, 36

Sugar Duties Act (1846), 109

Sugar Industry: aid to the Barbados, 124–127; enquiry into the WI, 123–127; Norman Commission enquiry into the, 158–176

Sugar Industry Agricultural Bank: establishment of the, 112

Sugar prices: Barbados, 110, 111

Sugar production: Barbados (1830s), 53; BWI (1830s), 54; 1840s–1890, 110

Technical education: recommendations regarding, 173

Tenantry System: description of the, 48–49; and the peasantry, 81–82; as a strategy of controlling Black labour, 50–61; and workers, 127

The Lodge, 131

Thomas, Archdeacon Grant E.: on poverty (1876), 145

Thorne, Rev. E.S.: submission to the Norman Commission, 170

Unemployment (1876), 144

United States of America (USA): sugar exports to the, 111–112, 128

Universal Negro Improvement Association (UNIA), 187, 192

Vagrancy law, 62

Voters (1876), 118

Wage riots: in St. Thomas (1863), 102–108

Wages: Blacks and, 50–51; BWI (1840–1850), 78; BWI (1846–1850), 111; inadequacy of, 127; post-Emancipation, 71–73

Walker, Governor: and the St. Thomas wage riots, 102–108

Waller, John: on slavery in Barbados, 65

War of General Bussa, 137–139

War of General Green. *See* Labour revolution (1876)

Wealth accumulation: free Blacks and, 1–2, 10; Whites and, 10

West India Committee: resistance to Emancipation, 31

White children: and slavery, 65

White slave-holders: and slave-holdings by free-Blacks, 2

White supremacy: ideology of, 63–69; and political power, 113–120; and post-Emancipation Barbados, 44–50, 57; Prescod's challenge to, 85–89. *See also* Planter elite

Whiteness: definition of, 66

Whites: poor, 14

Wickam, Clennell: and the development of Black political consciousness, 185, 191, 192

Will, Jack: and post-Emancipation labour resistance, 77

Women: Bridgetown free Black and free Coloured, 6, 10–11

Workers: freedom debate and post-Emancipation, 73–77; status of post-emancipation Blacks, 53–57; submission to the Norman Commission, 164–167, 171–174

Working class: education, 125–126; mortality, 127–128

Working conditions, 144–145, 146, 147, 163–167

Workingmen's Loan and Friendly Investment Society, 188

Wright, J.O., 123

Yard, William: and the 1816 rebellion, 24